# More Praise for *The Art of the Strategist*

"A comprehensive treatise on the subject of strategy—clear, well organized, simply put, and straight talking. Dr. Cohen has linked leadership and strategy into a helpful guide for businesspeople, politicians, and trailblazers. His numerous well-written examples make it an enjoyable read, as well as a profitable one."—**J. B. Hilmes, Lieutenant General, U.S. Army (retired), Group Executive VP, Computer Science Corporation**

"Outstanding! An indispensable guide for strategists and decision makers. General Cohen has successfully identified the ten essential elements of strategy and strategic leadership. Master the ten principles in this book and you will master your competition."—**Michael A. Mische, CEO, Synergy Industries, former Principal, KPMG Peat Marwick and author of *Strategic Renewal: Becoming a High-Performance Organization***

"In this clear and well-written book, Dr. Cohen has thoroughly and intelligently distilled from history the basic strategic principles that successful businesses must use. Of great interest at this time is his prescription that these principles of strategy do not involve lying, cheating, or dishonesty. Every corporate officer who wants to develop and follow a strategy that will win should read this book."—**Herbert Y. Schandler, PhD, George C. Marshall Professor of Grand Strategy, and former Chairman of the Strategy Department, Industrial College of the Armed Forces**

"Scores of anecdotes and examples show how these ten principles are essential to every successful business strategy, but also to sports, politics, and even romance! *The Art of the Strategist* deserves to be a Best Business Book of the Year!"—**Reginald Rhein, former *Business Week* magazine writer and current Washington editor of *Scrip World Pharmaceutical News***

"*The Art of the Strategist* makes new contributions to the knowledge of strategy. Everyone who reads this book will wish that they had done what it recommends a long time ago."—**Ambassador Ronald F. Lehman II, PhD, former Director of the U.S. Arms Control and Disarmament Agency and Assistant Secretary of Defense for International Security Policy**

"From the simplest tactics to the most complex strategies—in war, as in business, as in science, as in love, throughout history—William Cohen shows that human nature and basic truths lie at the heart of real victories and achievements. Here he offers a guidebook to solid success by means of the art of leadership, of commonsense, and of courage and focused faith."—**Lt. General (Res.) Amnon Lipkin-Shahak, former Chief of Staff, Israel Defense Forces**

# _The Art_ OF THE STRATEGIST

## 10 Essential Principles
## for Leading Your Company to Victory

### William A. Cohen, PhD
MAJOR GENERAL, USAFR, RETIRED

**⊿AMACOM**

**American Management Association**

New York ▮ Atlanta ▮ Brussels ▮ Chicago ▮ Mexico City
San Francisco ▮ Shanghai ▮ Tokyo ▮ Toronto ▮ Washington, D.C.

*This publication is designed to provide accurate and authoritative information in regard to the subject matter covered. It is sold with the understanding that the publisher is not engaged in rendering legal, accounting, or other professional service. If legal advice or other expert assistance is required, the services of a competent professional person should be sought.*

*Library of Congress Cataloging-in-Publication Data*

Cohen, William A., 1937–
      The art of the strategist : 10 essential principles for leading your company to victory / William A. Cohen.
            p.   cm.
      Includes index.
      ISBN 0-8144-0782-X
      1. Leadership.   2. Strategic planning.   3. Success in business.   I. Title.

HD57.7.C6425   2004
658.4'012—dc22

                                                                                      2004003414

Printing number

10   9   8   7   6   5   4   3   2   1

# Contents

# Foreword

**B**ill Cohen has never been afraid to tackle seemingly complex subjects that some feel defy analysis or proscription. In *The Art of the Strategist* he has taken on the important subject of strategy and put it in a framework of principles that are easily understood and ready for the practitioner.

There are several aspects of this book that I found especially useful. First, it is not simply a book about strategy development, but rather a book that flows from determination of an objective through the phases of execution that lead to success. Second, it has interspersed real-world examples to illustrate the principles and the subsets of factors to consider in applying the principles. Finally, it makes clear that sensitivity to environmental factors and a willingness to change strategy, but not objectives, are an integral part of the process.

It is also clear that application of these principles depends on the judgment and leadership qualities of the individual responsible for the success of the undertaking. The need for such leadership is no more apparent than in a crisis situation.

Having been involved with strategy development and execution for three decades in government and over a decade in industry, I recommend this book to all who want to develop the strategic skills that lead to success.

General James E. Dalton, USAF, Retired
Former chief of staff, Supreme Hqs Allied Powers Europe (NATO);
President, Logicon RDA

# Preface

In writing this book, I have taken on a number of "sacred cows" and celebrated writers of business strategy, including even the classic *Competitive Strategy* by Harvard's Michael Porter. I do this with great reluctance, since I have the utmost respect for both Professor Porter, as a strategist and researcher, and Harvard, as one of our nation's leading institutions of higher learning. But he is not the only strategy researcher who has, I believe, led us astray.

Years ago, another academic strategist, writing about marketing strategy, claimed that good tactical implementation can overcome a bad strategy. That notion is ridiculous. If the strategy is bad or wrong, the only thing good tactical implementation will do is make a bad strategy result in something worse. The bad strategy may succeed, but it would be better if it failed.

For example, assume that your strategy involved developing a certain technology instead of an alternative. It was the wrong choice, but you did not know it at the time. Tactically, you did everything right. You convinced investors and got the money. You recruited and motivated an outstanding scientific team. You spent millions of dollars, months of time, and in the end, you developed the technology. But it was the wrong one! You should have developed the alternative technology. Your strategy was wrong even though your tactics were flawless.

Tactical implementation should be directed toward implementing the right thing—a good strategy. Good tactical implementation of a bad strategy is doing the wrong thing in the right way. It is optimizing the kind of approach that will eventually lead to defeat, not to triumph.

I have had the good fortune to call renowned management expert Peter F. Drucker my friend, as well as my professor. One of his most famous quotes is: "What everyone knows is usually wrong." On many key points, much of the advice that business strategists have been giving us for years is quite simply wrong. To be intellectually honest in writing this book, I have had to go against much of "what everyone knows." Consider for a minute those strategists who claim that business is war.

In more than forty years of experience in the three worlds of the military, academia, and commerce, I've read, analyzed, visually scanned, and examined numerous books purporting to explain business strategy in terms of its military antecedents. Some of these books had some good ideas. However, in many cases, authors who had never been in the military attempted to explain something that was not within their area of expertise; many had only the vaguest notion of what military strategy was all about. A number tried to sell the generic idea that "business is war." Others promoted a single military strategist, Carl von Clausewitz (*On War*) being the most popular, as having all the answers. Still others confused tactical military maneuvering and its associated terms with strategy; they spoke of "envelopments" and "flank attacks" and inappropriately applied them to business operations. One might just as well do the same with the technical terms used in medicine or ballet. Few of these authors noted the crucial link between leadership and strategy. In fact, one best-selling book even proclaimed, "Forget leadership, strategy is all that matters."

Ignoring the link between leadership and strategy is absurd. Good plans are made and implemented under the guidance and direction of good leaders at all levels. Successful leaders do not look at their planners and say, "Tell me what to do." Successful leaders look at their planners and say, "Here's what I want to do. Now, tell me my options." Once the planners develop options, and the leader makes a decision and selects one, the leader may turn to the planners and say, "Now work out the details."

We know that good planners make good leaders and top executives. Dwight Eisenhower was an unknown Army lieutenant colonel who had made a name for himself through his planning abilities. In 1940, General George C. Marshall, then U.S. Army chief of staff, plucked Eisenhower from nowhere and made him a brigadier general. (Eisenhower never did hold the rank of colonel, the rank between lieutenant colonel and brigadier general.) Eisenhower was a truly gifted leader. As Supreme Allied Commander during World War II, he led the largest seaborne invasion in the history of the world (D-Day) and formulated the overall strategy that was triumphant in Europe. He was a leader, a planner, and a superb strategist.

I am not a proponent of "business is war." However, I do not think it is smart to ignore 7,000 years of genius-level thinking on strategy simply because its focus was on warfare. If we ignore important things mankind has learned only because they originated from lessons learned from war, we would still be dying from diseases such as yellow fever or from a lack of simple preventive measures such as a surgeon washing his hands. The number of people starving around the world would be double or triple what it is because of our inability to preserve and ship food grown locally to more distant locations. While we would still be flying in aircraft, jet engines would be unknown, and so would the rockets that will eventually take us more routinely into space. I am certainly not advocating warfare as a means of advancing technology or human benefit, but I do advocate using important lessons learned regardless of their source.

This book is a labor of love. It is one that I have wanted to write for a long time, and the research that's gone into it has stretched over more than two decades. I have tried to synthesize the work of the great thinkers on strategy over the millennia, both military and civilian, into ten essential principles. These are principles all of us must follow for success, whether we work on the battlefield or in the boardroom. I have described and given examples of these principles, not as much for specialists who are the planners, but for leaders at every level who must themselves think through the strategies for their organizations.

William A. Cohen, PhD
Major General, USAFR, Retired
Pasadena, California

# Acknowledgments

My sincere thanks to:

Barry Richardson, who went over my labors of years, forced me to rethink what I thought was already perfect, and made sound suggestions that ultimately made this book far better than I ever thought it could be.

Adrienne Hickey, a great editor and friend of long standing who understood and appreciated the value of the concepts I proposed, and convinced me that AMACOM was the right publisher to disseminate these ideas.

General Roger Rothrock, a highly successful strategist in the quest for medical treatment and the betterment of the human condition throughout the world, whose support and encouragement have never faltered.

Finally, to my wonderful wife, Nurit, who though pressed with an incredibly miserable schedule as a practicing psychologist, spent the time and energy to act as a sounding board and to boost my morale when I was tired, frustrated, or just plain confused, kicking my tail when required. She stuck by me through good times and bad, including three wars, two sons, a host of dogs, and management and battle in many countries on five continents over more than three decades.

# The Art OF THE STRATEGIST

# PART 1

# The Roots of Strategy

# For Every Leader, Strategy Is the Key to Success

*"The best of all is not to win every battle by force. The best of all is to make the enemy yield without fighting. So the highest of all military principles is to overcome the enemy by strategy."* —SUN TZU

*"Our ship would come in much sooner if we'd only swim out to meet it."* —ANONYMOUS

I n 216 B.C., the Carthaginian general Hannibal encountered 72,000 Romans at a place called Cannae in Southern Italy. His own army numbered only 20,000. Both armies were equally well armed and trained. Each had a similar cavalry force of about 2,000 horsemen. Besides sheer numbers, the Romans had one other important edge. They were fighting on their own turf while Hannibal's army was hundreds of miles across the Mediterranean Sea from its base of operations.

If you look at the numbers alone, Hannibal should have surrendered or retreated. The Romans expected him to do so. He didn't. He did the unexpected and surprised his opponent. He decided that the only way he could succeed was if he destroyed, not just defeated, the superior Roman army opposing him. He therefore defined this as his clear objective. Moreover, he was fully committed to accomplishing this objective despite the odds against him

## TAKING THE INITIATIVE

Hannibal didn't wait for the Romans to attack and then react. Instead, Hannibal took the initiative and acted first. His plan was not complicated; it was very simple. No one needed to be a military genius to understand it. He divided his army into three main parts. He concentrated the bulk on his left and right flanks. He was stronger than the Romans opposing him at these locations. To concentrate on the two flanks, he economized and stripped his center. He arranged this much-weaker force at his center in advance of his flanks so that his army formed an inverted "V," with the weak point aimed directly at the Romans. As we will see, even the fact that the point was weak was designed to work to his advantage. Of course, the Romans could not see Hannibal's disposition of forces. The apex in the advance of his strong flanks guarded his intentions. All the Romans saw was a solid mass of their enemy. This guarded his intentions.

## ECONOMIZING HIS FORCES

Hannibal posted his cavalry on the left and right flanks of this inverted "V" opposite the Roman cavalry. But there was a difference in how Hannibal placed his cavalry as compared to the Romans. The Romans simply split their cavalry, 1,000 men on each side of their main force. Hannibal concentrated the greater part of his cavalry on the left. The small cavalry detachment he put on the right was told merely to shout and make a lot of noise. The technical, military strategy term for such an action is "a demonstration." They were there to keep the 1,000 Roman cavalrymen opposite them occupied with a demonstration. That way the Roman cavalry was unable to reflect on the fact that it was opposed and held in place by only a small force of horsemen. Hannibal economized the cavalry on his right flank and then concentrated them on his left flank to attain superior numbers there. By the small force of cavalry of the right keeping the larger opposing Roman cavalry occupied, he further maintained security.

## GAINING THE ADVANTAGE

As the battle opened, Hannibal's larger cavalry force on his left, with almost a two-to-one advantage, easily defeated the smaller Roman cavalry detachment. Then, it swept around unopposed, taking the indirect approach, behind the 70,000 Roman foot soldiers. The 1,000 Roman cavalry on the right were now heavily outnumbered and trapped between the two Carthaginian cavalry forces. They were easily overwhelmed and destroyed. The Romans had lost their entire cavalry force in the first few minutes of battle, and the Roman general, Varro, didn't even know it. (This positioning and the action of Hannibal's cavalry in Phase I are shown in Figure A-1.)

The reason for the confusion was that there was so much action going on in the Roman center, where most of their forces were engaged. The 70,000 Roman foot soldiers were marching forward and came up against the weak Carthaginian center. They appeared to be unstoppable. As this massive Roman force advanced, pushing against the much weaker Carthaginian center, the center retreated and passed between the strong Carthaginian forces on the two flanks. The "V" no longer pointed at the Romans, but slowly inverted as the apex retreated while the flanks held fast. Soon, the apex of the "V" pointed away from the Romans. Hannibal had once again taken the indirect approach to trap his enemy, but the Romans did not yet realize it.

*Figure A-1*

THE BATTLE OF CANNAE, PHASE I

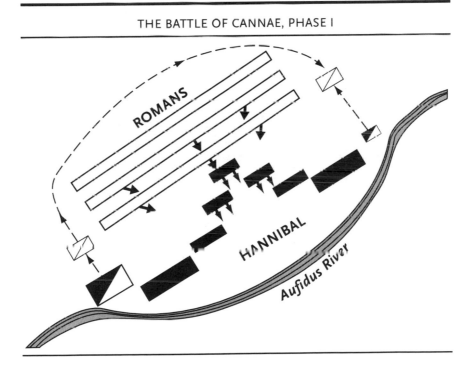

## ▌ MAINTAINING THE INITIATIVE

Varro thought the Carthaginians were crumbling as Hannibal's apex retreated. So he gave the order to increase the speed of advance. The Carthaginians' apex retreated farther and drew the Romans into their giant trap at an even faster pace. As the Romans advanced into the funnel formed by the now-inverted Carthaginian "V," they were forced closer and closer together by the heavy numbers of Carthaginians on either side. As the density of Roman soldiers between the two strong Carthaginian flanks increased, movement became difficult and the Romans could scarcely wield their famous short swords.

It was at this point that Hannibal, again maintaining the initiative, gave the order to go from a defensive posture to full attack. Like two great doors, the two wings of the "V" swung in on the closely packed Romans. The Carthaginian cavalry joined in from the rear. Pressed from all sides and unable to defend themselves, the well-trained Roman infantry faltered and broke. As they attempted to get away, it was every man for himself. Hannibal exploited his success until he completely destroyed the opposing force, as he had intended. Of the original Roman army of 72,000 with which Varro began the fight, only 12,000 survived. (Phase II of the Battle of Cannae is shown in Figure A-2.)

Remember, the battle wasn't a question of training or fighting harder. The Romans had the best-trained armies in the world . . . and both sides were fighting to the death.

What if Varro had taken a different course in this battle? Let us say that instead of attacking right up the middle, he had attacked against either the left or right flank of Hannibal's army. Hannibal was positioned to use multiple alternatives. He had strong forces on both flanks. Had Varro attacked either flank, Hannibal could have enveloped the attacking force with the strong forces he had placed at the opposing flank. Varro didn't know it, but because of Hannibal's positioning for multiple alternatives, the Roman general would probably have been defeated no matter what he did, despite having an almost four-to-one advantage. That is the power of properly employing the principles of strategy.

Hannibal used military strategy to conquer a superior force in a life-and-death battle. However, the art of strategy is used to achieve victory every day in all kinds of situations.

*Figure A-2*

---

THE BATTLE OF CANNAE, PHASE II: THE POWER OF STRATEGY

---

**CARTHAGINIAN CAVALRY**

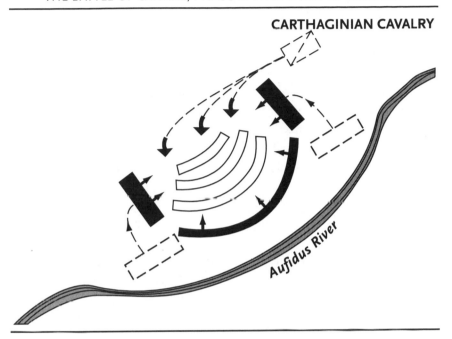

*Aufidus River*

▐ **STRATEGIC LESSONS FROM A TELEVISION SHOW**

In the spring of 2001, more than 36 million viewers watched the final episode of *Survivor* on CBS television. They saw a forty-year-old nurse and mom, Tina Wesson, win the $1 million first prize after forty-two days in the Australian outback with little food while enduring severe environmental conditions. Fifteen other competitors, younger and stronger, of both genders, and with arguably better survival skills, had been eliminated. For every "immunity challenge" won during a physical and mental competition with the others, the rules granted someone immunity against being eliminated from the game for a week. Tina hadn't won a single one of these challenges. Colby Donaldson, the superbly conditioned twenty-seven-year-old rodeo rider, won eleven immunity challenges. Yet, in the overall contest, he came in second against Tina and won $100,000. Both contestants stated that while luck was an important factor, Tina's victory was based primarily on her strategy of being a valuable but inconspicuous underdog. Thus, she was not voted out, and with luck of a single voting in the final round, she managed to win out against a much stronger competitor.

For those unfamiliar with *Survivor,* the first of the successful "reality" television series, contestants are taken to remote locations and divided into two separate "tribes." With little food and under extremely primitive conditions, not only must these individuals survive, they must also compete at "immunity challenge" tasks. At first, this competition is between tribes. The winning tribe is granted immunity for all of its members for that week. The losing tribe must vote to banish one of its members. After everyone casts a vote and collectively declares "the tribe has spoken," the person who has been voted out is sent packing. As the numbers dwindle, the two tribes are integrated into a single tribe. Thereafter, challenges grant immunity for one cycle to an individual, not the entire tribe. When there are only two survivors remaining, the previous six survivors eliminated pick the single survivor, who is awarded $1 million.

Richard Hatch, fifty pounds overweight and the winner of the first *Survivor* contest, emphasized the importance of strategy in his victory. "I won," he said, "by sticking to my strategy." Hatch formed and led a coalition that, voting as a bloc, was strong enough to eliminate candidates they selected. When only the coalition members remained, he again took actions to give himself the advantage. Thus, although the second-place contestant won the last immunity challenge, it was Hatch who won the overall contest. In fact, the second-place contestant, wilderness guide Kelly Wiglesworth, had won four straight individual immunity challenges. She fully expected to win over Hatch, who was unpopular and known to all as "the survivor you love to hate." Still, like Colby Donaldson, Wiglesworth also lost to a superior strategy, as have all *Survivor* winners since these first two. Strategy is clearly what it takes to win.

## ▌ THIS STRATEGY WAS SIMPLE, BUT IT HELPED WIN AN ELECTION

In Bill Clinton's first presidential campaign, he was behind in every poll in his race for president. With allegations of sexual misconduct and philandering swirling around him, leading political analysts and columnists agreed that it was just a matter of days before he would be forced to drop out. Then, employing an amazing strategy based on just four words—"It's the economy, stupid!"—Clinton strategist James Carville turned it all around. Clinton concentrated on this short message to the exclusion of all else. This simple strategy led to defeat for George Bush and two terms for Clinton as president. Though living 2,500 years before the Clinton bid for the presidency, the Greek general Xenophon would have related to Carville's strategy, and the ancient Chinese strategist Sun Tzu would also have understood it perfectly.

## Mastering Strategy Means Success . . . Even in Romance

When I first studied military strategy at West Point, I recall one of my professors stating that the same principles of strategy for war were also true for romance. This motivated an immediate interest among the young cadets in my class, who in those days were all male. Their professional interest might be battle, but their primary interest for the coming weekend inevitably had to do with besting the competition to win the favor of members of the opposite sex. Thus informed, cadets soon learned it was ultimately much more effective to concentrate their efforts on one girl, brought to a dance by another cadet, than to attempt to try to impress many girls in a single evening.

## Strategy and Business

If you examine why some businesses always seem to best their competition, you will again and again find evidence of a thoughtful strategy. These companies seem to be able to take almost any product or service and go up against almost any competitor and win. It doesn't make any difference whether they are a "learning organization." It doesn't matter whether they use "one-to-one marketing." If there is an economic downturn, these companies seem to either get out just in time, or somehow use the downturn to become even more profitable. Technological breakthroughs, which drive others into bankruptcy, always seem to help them. Shortages are turned to their advantage. Moreover, these winners are in every industry from cottage to high tech, and they come in all sizes, from giant corporations to home businesses.

What all these winning companies share is their ability to overcome the competition in nearly every situation that crops up. But they share something else, and that is the reason that they are able to overcome their competition. What these companies also share are identical principles that their leaders employ again and again. Early on, I suspected that principles for business strategy success existed that were probably identical to principles of military strategy.

If common strategy principles could be codified, they would certainly be invaluable to business, because once revealed they could be used by others to repeat a success again and again. Strategy analysts have tried to find such principles in the past, especially those with a military bent. This is because the study of strategy started with warfare, and the concept that there are military principles for success in strategy has been accepted for several thousand years. It is perhaps for this reason that the very word "strategy" comes from the Greek word "strategos," which means "the art of the general."

## ∎ WHY STRATEGY THAT "APES" WARFARE USUALLY FAILS

However, attempts to copy warfare as a model for business strategy have generally failed. Except in the sense of commitment to win, there is no such thing as "marketing warfare," for business is not war. War necessitates the taking of human life, whereas the practice of business does not. Furthermore, there are other basic reasons why war and business do not equate.

First, war is not a continuous activity. A war is fought, and then it is over. It may start up again later, but for the time, it is done. Successful and unsuccessful forces are disbanded, nations frequently disarm, and citizens look for a "peace dividend." A successful business goes on and on, nonstop. In the United States, there are businesses that are more than a hundred years old. In Europe and Asia, there are businesses that are several centuries old. Some of these businesses haven't missed a day. In battle, even the Hundred Years' War came to an end.

Second, speed is crucial to war strategy. Colonel John Boyd, a brilliant Air Force strategist of the 1980s, developed what he called the OODA loop. OODA stands for observation, orientation, decision, and action. From personal observations as a fighter pilot during the Korean War, he theorized that anyone who could "get inside" a competitor's OODA loop (by doing one of the four parts faster than his opponent) would invariably emerge victorious. His theories provided considerable insight into modern land combat to the extent that it is said that at one time the U.S. Marine Corps completely altered its concept of land battle based on those theories.

After Boyd's death, some business strategists adopted his concepts of the OODA loop and ancillary theories. Even the editors of *Harvard Business Review* were impressed, and they published an article about Boyd's theories some years ago. But alas, while the OODA concept may have universal concept in warfare, it has much less application to business. As Peter Drucker has noted, astute business competitors actually can succeed by electing *not* to be first in the market, but in allowing someone else to do the groundwork and make mistakes first. So speed, at least when it comes to being first to market, may not always be all that important. Despite the success of Apple Computer in creating the computer market, which in itself was a masterful application of basic strategic principles, it is IBM, makers of IBM clones, and Microsoft that are currently the market leaders in this field.

This does not mean that theories such as Boyd's have no application to business. What it means, however, is that such theories do not represent a universal principle with general applicability. It also means that attempts to model business strategy based mainly on military strategy principles or military maneuvers (the latter seems to me to be particularly absurd, but some very prominent business researchers have attempted to do precisely that) are no more likely to succeed than formulating strategy based on, say, legal or medical strategy. What this sort of approach essentially amounts to is simply tacking on military terminology—"encirclement" or "guerrilla warfare," for example—to business actions.

So while a book intended to unearth the essence of strategy for business should, of necessity, include an analysis of military strategy, it must be far broader. It must also include a thorough examination of strategy in many different disciplines, including business itself.

---

**STRATEGIST'S LOG** ▏ LAYING THE GROUNDWORK

As we delve more deeply into the principles of strategy, it is important to keep five key points in mind:

1. Strategy is critical in everything we do, including not only war and business, but also games, politics, and even romance.

2. With the right strategy, we can overcome adversaries with much greater resources.

3. The essential principles of strategy are universal.

4. Battle strategy can be analyzed for lessons that are useful to business strategy.

5. However, business is *not* war, and we must be careful not to apply these lessons without thought or analysis. ▪

# Determining the 10 Essential Principles of Strategy

*"A wise man can sometimes learn from a fool—as soon as it can be determined which is which."* —ANONYMOUS

*"The object in war is not to die for your country, but to get other men to die for their country."*
—GENERAL GEORGE S. PATTON

**A**s I noted in the previous chapter, strategy analysts have long sought the essential secrets to winning. In the past, some have claimed their principles of strategy to be "universal," but they are usually talking about one set of principles from a single source. In the United States, this is usually the strategic principles of the U.S. Army. However, even in war, different strategists and different countries have developed many different principles of strategy—some of which have been wildly successful, some of which have failed miserably, and most of which have fallen somewhere in between. (Figure B-1 compares some various principles developed from different sources.)

## UNEARTHING THE CRUCIAL PRINCIPLES OF STRATEGY

If we want to really understand strategy, we've got to go much deeper. To determine the essential principles of strategy, I researched the greatest strategists and strategic thinkers of the millennia. These included strategists from both East and West over a period spanning more than 7,000 years of recorded history, in almost every country on earth, and representing a wide variety of fields.

*Figure B-1*

| Principles and Alternate Titles | U.S. Army | U.S. Air Force | U.K. | USSR | Sun Tzu | Mao | Clause-witz | Fuller |
|---|---|---|---|---|---|---|---|---|
| SAMPLES OF PRINCIPLES OF STRATEGY FROM VARIOUS SOURCES* | | | | | | | | |
| Aim Purpose Objective Direction | X | X | X | | X | X | X | X |
| Initiative Offensive | X | X | X | | X | X | X | X |
| Concentration Mass | X | X | X | | X | X | X | X |
| Economy of Force | X | X | X | | | | X | |
| Maneuver Mobility Movement | X | X | | | X | X | X | X |
| Unity of Command | X | X | | | | X | | |
| Cooperation Coordination | X | | | | X | | | |
| Security | X | X | X | | | | | X |
| Surprise | X | X | X | | X | X | X | X |
| Simplicity | X | X | | | | | | |
| Flexibility Freedom of Action Autonomy | | | X | | | | X | |
| Administration | | | X | | | | | |
| Morale Spirit | | | X | X | | X | X | |
| Exploitation Pursuit | | | | | | | X | |
| Quantity/ Quality of Divisions | | | | X | | | | |
| Armament | | | | X | | | | |
| Ability of Commanders | | | | X | | | | |
| Stability of the Rear | | | | X | | | | |
| Timing/Tempo | | X | | | | | | |
| Logistics | | X | | | | | | |
| Cohesion | | X | | | | | | |
| Continuous Action | | | | | | X | | |

*Adapted from John M. Collins, *Grand Strategy*, U.S. Naval Institute, Annapolis, 1973, p. 23.

I studied the writings of ancient Chinese strategists like Sun Tzu, T'ai Kung Chiang Shang, and Sun Pin. But I also studied Epaminondas of Thebes, who at Leuctra in 371 B.C. defeated the "unbeatable" Spartans, although they outnumbered his forces, two to one. My research included the well-known German Carl von Clausewitz, but also his contemporary, and some say the superior strategist, the Swiss Henri de Jomini. Then there were more modern strategists such as the Englishman B. H. Liddell Hart and the Italian economist-strategist Vilfredo Pareto. In 1897, Pareto found he could prove the value of economizing to concentrate statistically. He developed the 80/20 principle: Eighty percent of results are derived from only 20 percent of the effort—a crucial comment on the proper allocation of always-limited resources. Most strategy from history is military or political. I tried to relate what resulted in these successes to what might prove successful in modern business.

From this research, I developed several hundred principles of strategy. I identified fourteen principles as being nonrepetitive and of potential universal application. I extended the results of my research to other endeavors. This confirmed that the principles of strategy I had identified did, in fact, lead to success in all kinds of competitive life situations— most important for our purposes, business.

However, further analysis showed that my initial fourteen principles needed some additional refinement. Some of them had to be employed together to be effective. Others needed to be separated out of a single principle for clarity and emphasis. After considerable experimentation and trial and error, I refined my original list to ten essential principles (or lessons) of strategy. They are distilled from the thinking of the greatest strategists who have ever lived in many areas of human activity. These ten essential principles of strategy are:

1. Commit fully to a definite objective.

2. Seize the initiative, and keep it.

3. Economize to mass your resources.

4. Use strategic positioning.

5. Do the unexpected.

6. Keep things simple.

7. Prepare multiple, simultaneous alternatives.

8. Take the indirect route to your objective.

9. Practice timing and sequencing.

10. Exploit your success.

## ▌ PUTTING THE STRATEGY PRINCIPLES INTO ACTION

From a study of historical cases, it is clear that overwhelming, or even superior resources, are not decisive factors in winning. (Think of Hannibal and his outnumbered army achieving their great victory at Cannae.) Some organizations have abundant resources. Some do not. Some actually have very limited means. Companies that have somehow learned these essential strategy principles and applied them generally seem to prevail, whatever their circumstances. Through common principles of strategy, many of these companies have grown into great corporations.

If successful businesses have applied common principles of strategy and great strategy thinkers have explored these universal truths since the dawn of recorded history, why, then, don't others emulate their lead and copy their success? I believe there are several reasons for this. Among those reasons, these principles frequently do not follow conventional wisdom, and some may even seem contrary to logic. Many companies simply do not recognize the principles of strategy that are creating the success of other companies. Sadly, some do not even realize what has produced their own success.

Even the great companies are headed for defeat if they abandon the principles of strategy that made them great. However, this does not mean that they should continue to employ the same strategies that helped them to prevail in the past. Peter Drucker has repeatedly warned that any company that continues to do what made it successful in the past will eventually fail. This is because the environment, which includes technologies, competition, laws, politics, buyer behavior, and the economy, is in a constant state of flux. Such changes ensure that blindly sticking to what was once a very successful strategy must lead only to failure, because the former success was based on an environmental condition that no longer exists.

I also came to understand that the principles of strategy do not involve lying, cheating, or dishonesty of any kind. Many companies employing these essential principles are among the most ethical in their industry and in the marketplace in which they compete. Successful strategists may sometimes deceive the competition by bluffing or misleading adversaries regarding their intentions, but they do not deceive customers or employees or intentionally break the law. There is no reason for companies to develop strategies that are illegal, or unethical, in their desire to win. Companies that do this, as a number of prominent companies have learned in recent years, sooner or later run into serious problems.

## WHY PREVIOUS STRATEGY-DEVELOPING SYSTEMS FAILED

In some ways, the ten principles of strategy are the antitheses of much that business has been taught about strategy development over the last forty years. In 1960, Bruce Henderson of the Boston Consulting Group developed a four-celled matrix that attempted to quantify strategy through measurement of market growth rate and market share of "strategic business units" that shared certain critical commonalities in their products or services. This approach came to be known as "portfolio management" and was really a grand strategy for managing a portfolio of businesses, or products.

In later years, General Electric, working with the consulting firm of McKinsey and Company, introduced a nine-celled matrix. With this method, different entry arguments allowed different and multiple factors to be considered simultaneously and then weighted by relevance and situational importance. Later, the emphasis shifted to an attempt to model successful strategies statistically. All of the current methodologies for developing strategy for business are some variation of these approaches.

Unfortunately, business situations are far too complex to achieve replicable, successful strategy in this fashion. The results of an election, a slight change in the economy, a new CEO with a different style, or even the weather can cause any quantitative model attempting to formulate strategy in this way to produce differing results, and in the face of intelligent competition, probably to fail. This is true, even though powerful, cutting-edge computer software may be employed. In contrast, the ten essential principles of strategy, eternally true when applied properly, can always be relied upon.

Several years ago when others fought it out for market share using four-celled or nine-celled matrixes to quantify strategy, some businesses didn't follow this course. Most of these companies avoided the losses (in certain cases, the bankruptcies) caused by this wrongheaded strategic prescription that argued for acquisition and market domination at any cost. Yet the portfolio method of strategy development was recommended by almost all strategic gurus of the time. Others determined strategy using complex competitive analyses and statistical advice based on the percentage of times an action has worked, or not worked, in the past. They were likewise surprised to find that while statistically they should have succeeded, it didn't always work out that way. Keep in mind that even if a certain action produces success 99 percent of the time, if you are in that 1 percent when it doesn't, you personally have achieved 100 percent failure.

## ▌ Beware the Number-Crunching Strategist

Strategies based totally on numbers should always be suspect. Again, this is because the strategic environment is so complex that accurate and relevant quantification of all factors simply isn't possible. During Robert McNamara's tenure as secretary of defense, all U.S. military strategies were based to some significant extent on economic analysis. There is nothing wrong with economic analysis. In fact, to exclude it when making decisions regarding allocation of resources, especially the billions involved in defense, would be irresponsible. However, it is foolish to look at economic analysis to the exclusion of all else, which is pretty much what went on at the time. While it would be an oversimplification (and wrong) to claim that this is why the United States failed in its war in Vietnam, strategies based solely on numbers were certainly a contributing factor.

In the late 1960s, I was just beginning to attain a level in the military where it was important for me to understand the approach required by civilian analysts in the Department of Defense (DOD). Consequently, the Air Force sent me to a graduate MBA program in the School of Business at the University of Chicago. I vividly recall one visiting DOD expert professing this new philosophy of economic analysis in weapons procurement and acquisition. He told us that until this era the Air Force simply tried to develop and build the best-performing aircraft. Period. This civilian analyst said this was wrong. What the Air Force should be doing, he declared, was to develop and build an aircraft that in production would yield a desired overall combat power for the lowest cost. He gave us an example.

Let's say a new fighter with the best performance attainable will cost

$5 million per aircraft. This would provide the Air Force with a certain combat power. "Combat power" could be defined any way we wanted—say, the ability to down an enemy aircraft of current or anticipated enemy capabilities. But we could build a lesser-performing aircraft for only $1 million each. To get the same "combat power" as the $5 million aircraft, we might need to only build, say, three of the $1 million planes. Since we would not spend the $5 million for the single aircraft, we would save $2 million for every unit of combat power we bought. Sounds good in theory, right? Then one of the students pointed out that the mere fact that the $5 million, high-performing plane existed in our inventory would give a certain level of self-confidence to the American pilot, and it would be correspondingly depressing to an enemy pilot who would face him in battle. Moreover, the same psychological concept probably applied in reverse to the U.S. Air Force versus potential enemy air forces. This was, therefore, an important factor in the psychology, as opposed to the economics, of the situation.

As an example, this student cited German technical superiority in aerial weaponry as a major factor in Hitler's "bloodless" conquests, such as the annexation of Austria, or the dismemberment of Czechoslovakia, prior to World War II. These psychological factors were difficult or even impossible to quantify. Moreover, they affected grand strategy as much or more than the tactics of air warfare as quantified by "combat power." The civilian expert from the DOD had no answer to this except to mumble something about everything being quantifiable; he just needed time to think about it. Again, I am not saying that we should throw out quantified analyses as inputs to developing strategy. Only that numbers should be *guidelines* for strategy, not governing principles.

## ARE THE REAL LESSONS OF HISTORY TOO SIMPLE?

After World War II, then General (later President) Eisenhower said in his book *Crusade in Europe* that the basic principles of strategy for war are so simple that even a child could understand them. Eisenhower stated that the problem comes in understanding these principles to the degree that they can be applied in a coherent fashion to work in a specific instance and on a consistent basis.

While the essential principles of strategy are often overlooked because they seem so simple, successful businesses do follow common threads of strategy, even if they don't realize it. Their actions, taken either consciously or subconsciously, confirm the universal applicability of these strategic principles. The lessons of the great thinkers and practitioners from history are as applicable today as they have been throughout time. The basic strategy principles used by all successful organizations are so powerful that their varied interpretations by those who have sought, discovered, and rediscovered them over the millennia are conspicuous not so much for their differences as for their similarities.

## ▌ APPLYING THE ESSENTIAL PRINCIPLES TO BUSINESS

Apple Computer in its birth and initial growth has to be one of the greatest success stories of modern times. Sure, Apple has had serious problems with strategy since its founding. But there is no denying that in a few short years after he began, Steven Jobs not only built a billion-dollar business, but an entire industry.

Let's take a closer look at Apple and see what the ten essential principles of strategy had to do with this success. Many think they know the story. Steve Jobs and Steve Wozniak, two college dropouts, worked in their garage and developed the personal computer. The rest, as they say, is history. In reality, it wasn't that simple. Here's the whole story.

Before Apple came on the scene, IBM's 5100, Wang's 2200, Hewlett-Packard's 9830 series, and Datapoint's 2200 dominated the professional/business sector of the computer market. These companies' products sold for $5,000 to $20,000; that's even more in today's dollars. Large companies with lots of resources manufactured these products. Not surprisingly, IBM had 70 percent of the computer market. IBM not only had the resources and marketing clout, but the undisputed, best research and development team around. There was also a home market for computers, but this was mostly for video games. Commodore, Radio Shack, and National Semiconductor all sold products priced from $500 to $1,000 through computer stores, electronic shops, and department stores. These were not, however, programmable personal computers.

Jobs didn't have money, didn't have the technical know-how about computers, didn't have the marketing background or experience, didn't have a development team, didn't have production facilities to build anything, and didn't have distribution for anything he might build. He had no track record, and he didn't have a college education. However, Jobs recognized the need for personal computers that were priced lower and easier to use, computers that could be used by anyone at home or in a business. Filling this need became his clearly defined objective. This is the first, and most fundamental, of the ten principles of strategy.

Passionately committed to his vision, he seized the initiative by recruiting and forming a partnership with Steve Wozniak, a Hewlett-Packard design engineer and a former high-school friend. Jobs's plan was simple. First build and sell small circuit boards. That way the company would prove itself. Then get backing from a major computer company to develop a computer that would fill the niche in the market he had identified. Note that he did not plan on designing a personal computer and entering the computer market directly, or immediately. Jobs clearly took an indirect, but much more doable approach, and he demonstrated an innate knowledge of the importance of timing.

By the spring of 1976, the two Steves were building and selling computer circuit boards successfully. One, named Apple I, was sold in small numbers through retailers. They now approached Atari and Hewlett-Packard about financial backing to build a personal computer. Both companies turned them down. But Jobs had mastered the principle of simultaneous approaches. He realized that just building and selling circuit boards hadn't made them sufficiently attractive to corporations.

Jobs had planned multiple alternatives and now he sought to implement one of his alternate approaches. He raised $1,300 by selling his Volkswagen Bus and Wozniak's Hewlett-Packard calculator. In addition, concentrating their efforts on the critical point at the time, they cut back on their technical work to focus on nothing but raising money. As a result, they were successful in getting $10,000 more in parts and credit. Instead of using this for developing a computer, the "dynamic duo" went back into the circuit board business. Only after circuit boards provided the additional financial resources they needed did the two strategists again economize to concentrate elsewhere and build the computer Jobs had envisioned and believed in.

They named the computer Apple II. By once again concentrating where the major payoff was—this time on selling the computer—sales reached $200,000.

Jobs proceeded to exploit this success. He placed an article in a leading technical journal, which got lots of attention and built Apple's credibility. Using the article as a tool, Jobs was able to sign distribution agreements with several retailers.

Apple was on a growth curve, and Jobs could have borrowed a modest amount from a bank for a continued, but gradual increase based on limited production of the Apple II. Instead, Jobs and Wozniak exercised the principle of surprise. They recruited Mike Markkula, marketing manager of Intel Corporation, to join the partnership. Markkula made a $250,000 personal investment and helped arrange a credit line with Bank of America. With one stroke, Apple acquired high-powered marketing talent and more than doubled its financial resources. Suddenly, Apple was a force to be reckoned with by its potential competitors, and the company was very attractive to venture capitalists.

Again, Jobs took the initiative and continued to exploit his success by concentrating his efforts at the new critical point in the corporation's development. In just a few months, Apple received over $3 million in investment capital, more than enough to begin major production. The company moved out of the garage and into a plant in March 1977. Markkula became chairman and began to build a bigger distribution system. Jobs served as vice chairman but was still the company strategist. By 1979, Apple had 500 retailers selling its computers in the United States. It was still far outnumbered by Tandy, which had 8,000 Radio Shack outlets selling its computer. Moreover, as a result of Apple's success, more than thirty companies were planning on entering the personal computer field. Many analysts thought that Apple would limit itself to the relatively small niche it had carved out.

Instead, this relatively small company again surprised the competition by adding 100,000 square feet of manufacturing capacity to the 22,000 square feet it already had. It expanded its distribution through five independent distributors to reach a greatly increased number of retail outlets. What was Apple planning? When Apple entered the business market shortly thereafter, the competition realized what was happening, but it was too late for them to do much about it.

In 1980, the year Apple Computer went public, sales hit $200 million with $12 million net profit. A year after that, it became number one in its primary market and simply drove most of its direct competitors out of business. Not bad for a college dropout with no technical know-how and only a garage to work in. Jobs's achievement, along with that of his early partners Wozniak and Markkula, once again demonstrates the power of the ten essential principles of strategy. However, remember what I said earlier: If you keep the same strategy that made you successful in the past and ignore the ten principles, you are, as Peter Drucker said, certain to eventually fail.

## MASTER THE ESSENTIAL PRINCIPLES INDIVIDUALLY AND IN COMBINATION

The following chapters of this book look at the ten essential principles of strategy in depth. You cannot gain anything by simply knowing that surprise is a principle, or that timing is important. There is much more to it than that. Knowing when and how to apply these principles and when and how they must be ignored (yes, there are times when the lessons work against one another and you must ignore one to better emphasize another) in order to win out over the competition are equally important. Moreover, even the personal instincts of individual corporate leaders and the culture of the organizations they lead must be considered. What may be a brilliant strategy for one company could be a disaster for another, even though their resources and expertise are the same.

| STRATEGIST'S LOG | DETERMINING THE TEN ESSENTIAL PRINCIPLES |
|---|---|

Many systems for developing strategy have been introduced into business over the last fifty years. These include portfolio management, statistical analysis of results, and seeking of insights through application of the names of military maneuvers. None of them have worked consistently.

Great thinkers through the ages and different military and other experts from many countries have recommended numerous "principles of strategy" that lead to success. However, these principles frequently differ, and attempted adaptation of any single set, while providing insight, would not be universal to all organizations or situations, much less to business.

Through in-depth analysis and comparison among different sets of principles, analysis of strategic situations through the ages, and confirmation and refinement through empirical research, I have determined ten essential principles that are the basis of all successful strategy. These ten principles, which are detailed in Part 2, must be the basis for the development of all successful business strategies. ■

# *The 10 Essential Principles*

## CHAPTER 1

# The Fundamental Principle: Commit Fully to a Definite Objective

*"Pursue one great decisive aim with force and determination. . . ."*　—CARL VON CLAUSEWITZ

*"It is not enough to be busy . . . the question is: What are we busy about?"*　—HENRY DAVID THOREAU

Amilya Antonetti started a multimillion-dollar company because she wanted to find some relief for her suffering child. Like all successful strategists, she had a clear objective—helping her son—to which she was passionately committed.

According to Ms. Antonetti, "Soapworks was born out of my baby's frantic cries for help. My infant son David's first years of life were mysteriously filled with nonstop screaming, breathing difficulties, and rashes. After countless hospital visits, I turned to homeopathic and alternative doctors for help. They suggested I become my own detective, and study David's environment and symptoms to see what was causing his severe reactions. I kept a detailed, daily journal of David's life, including when and where he reacted, and eventually discovered David's screams and difficulties were an allergic reaction to the chemicals in everyday cleaning products. The household cleaners from the grocery store shelves were loaded with toxic chemicals! When I tried natural cleaners, David did not react adversely to them, but they were expensive, hard to find, and did not clean very well.

"So I started making my own natural soap products. I spent endless hours speaking with moms, dads, and people all over, especially those with sensitivities, asking them what kinds of cleaning products they would make for their own home, if they could have anything. When I shared my cleaners with friends and neighbors, word spread like wildfire. That was when I decided to start my own company."

Amilya became determined to tackle an even greater objective—she was going to break into the $4.7 billion U.S. laundry-detergent market. Everyone knew this was impossible. Large corporations like Procter & Gamble dominate that business. Amilya consulted industry experts. According to her own account, they laughed hysterically. Undaunted by the negative response, Amilya decided to commit fully to a definite objective.

"I hired a team of top formulators and worked with them to design a line of natural, soap-based household cleaners for those who suffer from allergies, asthma, and chemical sensitivities—and for those who want the safest products and the cleanest clean for their families at the best price.

"We liquidated everything we had to put into this business idea," says Amilya. "My husband gave up his career. Talk about commitment."

Indeed, commitment is what it was. And the bigger the task, the better. Today, Soapworks has shelf space in 3,000 stores, and annual revenues in excess of $10 million.[1,2]

## ▌ START WITH DEFINING THE OBJECTIVE

Everywhere you look, you see people who, logically, should not even attempt what they are trying to do. But they are so committed to a definite objective that more often than anyone can believe possible, their strategies are successful, and they win. Jesse "The Body" Ventura, a former professional wrestler, became governor of Minnesota after professional politicians told him, "There is no way you can accomplish this—no former professional wrestler has ever been elected to public office." Neither of the major political parties would support him. But Ventura persisted against the odds with his clear and definite goal always before him, and he won anyway, despite what the experts said. How does this happen? The basis for this type of success lies in a fundamental principle of strategy: commitment to a definite objective.

Some years ago, a young man was determined to make a living as an actor. During World War I, the young man had been a sailor, and his lip was injured when a German submarine torpedoed his ship. This gave him an unusual, tight-lipped expression and a slight lisp. On stage in

New York, his disfigurement and speech impediment limited him to small roles. He went to Hollywood and appeared in eight films, again, in bit parts. Most thought that his deformity would forever keep him from larger roles. Although he was from a wealthy family, he had gone through his entire inheritance. He returned to New York and read for the part of a gangster in a major play on Broadway. Here, his war wound worked for him—he sounded like a gangster. He got the part, and when Warner Bros. bought the rights and produced the movie, he played the part. The producers were so impressed with his performance that he went on to the major roles that had eluded him. With his clear and definite goal always before him, Humphrey Bogart persisted to become the great actor he envisioned, despite the odds against him.[3]

I don't know of any strategist who does not begin with a clear definition of a definite objective. You can't develop an effective way to get "there" until you know exactly where it is. The U.S. Armed Forces Commanders Estimation of the Situation outline begins with these words: "Mission. State the assigned or deduced task and its purpose." Peter Drucker says that top management must first answer the question, "What is our business, and what should it be?"[4] Benjamin B. Tregoe, developer of an early systematic approach to planning, says that you must first ask, "What should the scope of our products and markets be?"[5] All of these sources are talking about essentially the same thing—commitment to a definite objective.

## THE MAGIC OF COMMITMENT TO AN OBJECTIVE

Several years ago, I did the research that resulted in the book *The Stuff of Heroes: The Eight Universal Laws of Leadership* (Longstreet Press, 1998). I surveyed and interviewed more than 200 combat leaders from all military services and from all ranks (private through four-star general and admiral). I asked these battle veterans, all of whom had gone on to extraordinary positions of leadership in civilian life, this question: What, if anything, had they learned about leadership from combat that they could use successfully in their civilian careers? I asked for three specific answers from each of them.

I expected to get hundreds of ideas and thoughts from my interviews. I would write a book filled with leadership ideas that was the size of a small encyclopedia. Instead, I was amazed to discover that 95 percent of the responses fell into only eight categories. (That's how I got the title of the book.) One of these eight laws of leadership was to show uncommon commitment. What's so special about showing uncommon commitment? Why do others follow a leader who demonstrates this quality both on and off the battlefield? Psychologists have identified two main reasons why showing uncommon commitment yields such dramatic results:

1. It proves that the goal is worthwhile and really important.

2. It proves that the leader isn't going to quit.

## We Go All Out Only for Important Goals

People don't generally exert themselves very much for small, unimportant goals. We work hard, take great risks, and let nothing stop us only for big, important goals. That's why leaders who try to play down the difficulty of a task or strategists who think too small make a big mistake. It is far better to be honest with yourself and others. Tell things exactly as they are, no matter how serious the situation is, or how much effort will be required.

## Others Follow if They Know the Leader Won't Quit

People won't follow you if they think that your commitment is temporary, or that you may quit the goal short of attainment. Why should they? Why should they invest their time, money, lives, or fortune in something if the leader isn't going to lead them there? Others will only follow when they are convinced that you won't quit, no matter how difficult the task looks, or no matter what obstacles you encounter along the way.

## ▌ THE THREE FORCES ON WHICH COMMITMENT IS BUILT

British major general J.F.C. Fuller wrote many books on strategy, based on his personal observations and analysis beginning with his first-hand participation during World War I. He first articulated the concept of a foundation consisting of the three aspects of physical, mental, and moral forces on which all strategy is based. The physical force he described has to do with actual physical strength or resources, the mental force with knowledge or intelligence, and the moral force with attitudinal or spiritual values. According to Fuller, "Mental force does not win a war; moral force does not win a war; physical force does not win a war; but what *does* win a war is the highest combination of these three forces acting as *one* force."[6]

When we analyze any successful strategy after a competition, business or otherwise, we will invariably find that at the foundation of the victory is the commitment of the strategist, based on these three forces. Jesse Ventura won his election, even though it appeared that he had no chance. He had a commitment to the definite objective of gaining the governorship of Minnesota, based on the physical, mental, and moral forces that he was able to bring together synergistically.

## APPLYING COMMITMENT TO STRATEGY

Any strategist can apply the principle of commitment to both the planning and implementation of strategy, while keeping Fuller's three forces in mind. Here are five proven techniques that will help you incorporate your commitment into your strategy:

1. Think your goals through until they are clear and definite.

2. Make a public commitment.

3. Promote your goals and objectives.

4. Expect (and deal with) the dragons.

5. Adjust your strategy, but not your objectives.

### *Think Your Goals Through Until They Are Clear and Definite*

Your commitment must start with defining your goals clearly. Only in this way can you proceed to strengthen your dedication, publicly committing to your goals, then promoting them to others. You can't make a public commitment to go somewhere until you know where this "somewhere" is yourself. Once you know this, you can publicly commit to reaching your goals.

On May 25, 1961, President John F. Kennedy made a bold challenge to a joint session of Congress: "I believe that this nation should commit itself to achieving a goal, before this decade is out, of landing a man on the moon and returning him safely to earth."

Embarrassed by the Bay of Pigs fiasco in Cuba, and sick of watching the United States fall behind the Soviet Union in the space race, Kennedy wanted to publicly commit himself and the country to a definite objective. He consulted with Vice President Lyndon Johnson and his science advisers in order to formulate a plan. Together, they determined that although safely landing a man on the moon would be a difficult undertaking, it was a goal that the United States could achieve before the Russians.

Despite the view of skeptics, Kennedy's vision became a reality on July 20, 1969, when Apollo 11 Commander Neil Armstrong took a small step off the ladder of the lunar module *Eagle* and set foot on the moon's surface.

## Make a Public Commitment

Many people are afraid to make a public commitment to the objective or goal they select. They are afraid that they will appear foolish or incompetent if they don't reach the objective. Let me tell you about a man who made a public commitment, although he had failed repeatedly throughout his career.

Before attaining the presidency, the career of our sixteenth commander in chief, Abraham Lincoln, can only be termed "unique." By 1854, Lincoln had encountered failure in just about everything he had tried, including working as a lawyer and independent businessman, working as a government employee, and campaigning as a political candidate for office. Yet Lincoln was known to be honest, smart, upright, and courageous. That's why those who knew him continued to back him, despite his incredibly poor track record. But the truth was he had approached all of these previous challenges in a halfhearted way, and his public commitment to attaining these goals was wishy-washy at best. How do we know? Because Lincoln himself told us this.

In 1854, Senator Stephen A. Douglas from Lincoln's home state of Illinois, who was chairman of the Senate Committee on Territories, agreed to a repeal of the Missouri Compromise of 1820. The repeal would permit slavery to be introduced in the new states forming in the western territories. Lincoln was incensed. According to Lincoln's own writings, the repeal of the Missouri Compromise stirred him as never before. He expressed his ideas to everyone who would listen, and he told them that he was totally committed to ending slavery in the United

States. For the first time, he made a truly public commitment to attaining a definite goal he had set.

Just before Douglas's actions, Lincoln had decided to give up politics. He had been a lifelong member of the Whig party. With Lincoln's newfound "arousal" to a clear and definite purpose, and a public commitment to his goal, he resigned from the Whig party and joined the new, small, but growing, Republican party.

In 1858, Douglas's senate term came to an end, and he ran what was thought to be an easy campaign for reelection. By common consent, the impassioned and committed Lincoln represented the Republican party and opposed him. He challenged Douglas at every turn. Finally, Douglas agreed to a series of seven debates. Lincoln was eloquent and he did very well, but in the end, Douglas still won his reelection. For the first time, however, the fully committed Lincoln had reached a national forum. The debates received national attention, and they were carried by every newspaper in the country, not just in Illinois. Moreover, Lincoln's arguments for the abolishment of slavery not only gained national attention, but also convinced tens of thousands that the time had come to move toward this goal.

In the election of 1860, the Republican party held its convention in Chicago. It was expected that William H. Seward of New York would be nominated. He was the party's leader. But if his nomination failed, Salmon P. Chase of Ohio was thought to be the delegates' overwhelming choice. On the convention floor, however, it was clear that both of these men, who had spent years in public life, had acquired too many enemies. Neither one could gain the nomination.

After two inconclusive ballots, the delegates remembered the 1858 debates. They recalled that Lincoln came from a pivotal state, had won national recognition, was a frontiersman, and had fought as a captain in the Black Hawk Indian War. Moreover, he lacked the baggage of all the other leading candidates. Lincoln won the Republication nomination on the third ballot. Meanwhile, the Democratic party had split in two. As a result, Lincoln's election as president was assured.

For years, many have tried to discover just how Lincoln had pulled off this amazing coup. What was his incredible strategy that turned him from the on-again, off-again loser he had been previously to become president of the United States? (The best-selling book *Winning Through Intimidation* even claimed that Lincoln won through intimidating others. There is no historical evidence for this.) But, the one principle of strategy that he applied was certain. He knew that to stop the expansion of slavery he needed to have political power. His strategy, whatever it was, was no longer halfway. He was totally committed to gaining the power he needed to accomplish his clear, precise objective, and this commitment was public, with no turning back. It took several years and a devastating Civil War that culminated in his own assassination, but Lincoln did succeed. His commitment to a clear, precise, objective resulted in the abolishment of slavery, and it changed this country forever.

## Promote Your Goals and Objectives

One of the key reasons that we won the Gulf War with minimum casualties was the unique strategy carried out by General Norman Schwarzkopf, the overall commander. Yet that strategy was initially opposed by just about everyone. It violated the strategic doctrine of at least two military services, and it even violated the methodology by which strategy was supposed to evolve in the military. On top of that, Air Force Colonel John A. Warden III (the strategy's creator) did not have the political clout, high rank, or salesman's personality to persuade others of the value of his concepts. But thanks to his expertise and commitment, he achieved his goal anyway.

Colonel Warden was known as a very bright, innovative thinker in the Air Force. He became convinced that the way in which airpower had been employed in the past (in World War II, Korea, and Vietnam) was completely wrong, or at least obsolete. Never mind that leaders from the U.S. Army, Navy, and Marine Corps didn't understand how to employ modern airpower. According to Warden, even Air Force generals didn't have it right. Still, this wasn't necessarily heresy. General Henry H. "Hap" Arnold, who commanded the U.S. Army Air Force during World War II, and who was the only Air Force general ever promoted to five-star rank, had said, "Any air force which does not keep its doctrine ahead of its equipment, and its vision far into the future, can only delude the nation into a false sense of security."

Warden was committed to his ideas and his goal of getting them accepted as doctrine in the Air Force. He began promoting these ideas with the publication of his book *The Air Campaign: Planning for Combat* (Washington, D.C.: NDU Press, 1988). Many considered this book a breakthrough. Though brilliant, Warden could be outspoken, tactless, and abrasive and would sometimes move faster than those commanders he wished to move. As a result, he could get himself into trouble.

Eventually, the Air Force thought they had found a great job for him. They assigned Warden as Air Force deputy director of war-fighting concepts in the Pentagon, heading up a contingency planning group known as "Checkmate." Those who ran the Air Force thought that in this way Warden would be able to give free rein to his advanced thinking about strategy. They would gain the benefits of his ideas, but he would be out of the way and wouldn't irritate too many senior leaders in the Air Force and other services who were senior organizational commanders.

When Saddam Hussein invaded Kuwait, precipitating the Gulf War in August 1990, Colonel Warden was on vacation with his wife in the Caribbean. As soon as the ship docked midway, he caught the first flight to Washington and returned to the Pentagon. He was determined to put together a proposal for ousting Iraq from Kuwait based on his concepts, and to develop and implement a strategy to sell it to his civilian and military superiors. That an officer of this rank, in his position, would commit to such a goal is in itself almost unbelievable to those who understand how the military works.

The overall commander's air component commander normally develops the air strategy plan for a war. In 1990, this was Lieutenant General Chuck Horner, who reported to General Schwarzkopf, CENTCOM commander. Even Schwarzkopf could only implement the strategy after approval by General Colin Powell, then chairman of the Joint Chiefs of Staff, and of Secretary of Defense Richard Cheney. In addition, such a strategy would never come from an advanced or contingency planning group. It would probably be developed within Tactical Air Command (TAC), which owned most of the Air Force aircraft assets, and which would be shifted to General Horner's command for the war. Colonel Warden shouldn't have had any role, except perhaps as a consultant regarding contingency plans his group had developed, and then only if asked. Moreover, we're talking about only the air strategy plan, not the whole strategic concept for the employment of all the military services: U.S. Army, Navy, Air Force, and Marines Corps for the war. But Warden's concept impacted directly on any overall plan.

Warden had some other things working against him. The Army's concept for a regional war of this type was called the Air Land Battle. This concept envisioned a joint attack by an overwhelming force of ground and air forces operating together to defeat an enemy. Both General Schwarzkopf and General Powell were Army generals. If that weren't enough, General Horner, the air component commander, had seen the terrible results and waste of men and air power during the Vietnam War, when strategy was planned thousands of miles from the battle in Washington. Horner was certain that planning had to be decentralized and done by the force that would be implementing it. The idea of a "think tank" for contingency air-war fighting in the Pentagon that would develop his part of the war plan was contrary to everything he had learned, knew, and understood. He would fight the process, if not the concept, in every way he could. And, he did.

Despite all of these serious obstacles, Warden successfully directed his group in developing his concept of an air campaign (initiated separately and prior to the ground campaign) that was eventually adopted and implemented for the Gulf War. He succeeded by promoting his objective unceasingly. For the first time in history, a ground campaign was preceded by an extensive air campaign developed on Warden's new model. The campaign, implemented by Horner's handpicked chief planner, then Brigadier General Buster Glossom, resulted in a decisive defeat for Hussein, and without a doubt, saved thousands of allied casualties.

Upon Warden's retirement from the Air Force several years later, General Schwarzkopf sent him a personal letter acknowledging his contribution to the victory. Since then, Warden's ideas have influenced a new generation of U.S. Air Force leaders. In fact, it would not be out of place to credit his concepts with another victory in which few allied casualties were suffered—in Bosnia, several years later.

## Expect (and Deal with) the Dragons

Once you've committed to a clearly defined objective, you can focus on what you want to accomplish—your mission. But getting there is often not so easy. There will invariably be obstacles—dragons—that will appear along the way. You must deal with them, while keeping your eye on your ultimate goal.

In 1996, Lance Armstrong was among the world's top cycling racers. He had set a lifelong, extremely difficult (but not impossible) goal for himself. Armstrong wanted to win the Tour de France. The Tour de France is arguably the most difficult trek for cycling racers in the world. It is 2,286 grueling miles long, much of it in mountainous areas. Previously, only one American had ever won this tough race. Lance Armstrong set out to be the second. Then he ran into a dragon, and it was a big one.

Armstrong was diagnosed with advanced, stage three, testicular cancer. Doctors gave him, at most, a 50 percent chance of survival; some estimated his chances were as low as 30 percent.

He had surgery. Afterward, it was discovered that the cancer had spread to his lymph nodes, abdomen, and lungs. He had twelve tumors in his abdomen, some as large as golf balls, and more than twice that number in his lungs. It was questionable whether Armstrong would survive. After more surgery; twelve weeks of chemotherapy; and a forced, yearlong hiatus from racing, Armstrong was told he was cancer free. But his body was damaged and broken from battling the disease. He was hardly in the top physical condition he had been in prior to its onset. He still wanted to race, but his friends told him he should consider himself lucky to be alive, and let it go at that.

When Armstrong announced that he was going to compete in the Tour de France, everyone was stunned. Doctors advised against it. No one gave him even the slightest chance of winning. Many thought that he would not even be able to finish, and that he may not even survive. But that is not how Armstrong thought. He expected dragons along the way. Maybe he did not expect a dragon as cruel and tough as the one he encountered. But when he started out, he had committed to a clear and definite objective. He knew he would encounter obstacles, and he defined his cancer challenge as just another obstacle that he needed to overcome to reach his goal. He began training to win the Tour de France, although no one gave him any odds at all of succeeding.

Much to every expert's shock and surprise, Armstrong did win the Tour de France in 1999. And then, as if to prove the whole thing wasn't a fluke, he won it again in 2000, 2001, 2002, and 2003. Armstrong won because, despite all else, he committed to a clear and precise vision of what he wanted to accomplish, despite any dragon he might encounter along the way. I cannot say that Armstrong will go on to win this incredibly tough event indefinitely. However, there is no question that his commitment to a clear and definite purpose, despite the worst he might encounter on the way to his goal, was an important part of his strategy. It enabled him to be successful and to do what others considered impossible.

**Dealing with Dragons.** In my studies of strategy, I've found that there are two actions you can take that will help you to maintain your resolve when the going gets rough and dragons appear, as they invariably will, to thwart you on your way toward your goals.

First, during your planning, anticipate what obstacles, problems, or threats are likely to appear. Anticipating obstacles ahead of time allows you to think through and come up with potential solutions. Moreover, the more difficulties you can anticipate, the less they will crop up unexpectedly, catching you unprepared, and forcing you to come up with ad hoc solutions under the pressures of time or competition.

Napoleon, one of history's great strategists, wrote, "If I always appear prepared, it is because before entering an undertaking, I have meditated for long and have foreseen what may occur. It is not genius, which reveals to me suddenly and secretly what I should do in circumstances unexpected by others. It is thought and meditation."

The second action you can take is also during the planning stage, when you are defining your objective. Write down every benefit you will achieve when you attain your objective. Review these benefits frequently, especially when obstacles appear. Keeping the benefits of your goal before you—especially when you must deal with difficult problems—will help you to persist during these periods of stress, when you may ask yourself, "Is it really worth the effort?"

## Adjust Your Strategy, but Not Your Objectives

There is no greater example of commitment to purpose than that of Irwin Jacobs, chairman of Qualcomm, Inc. Yet Jacobs was forced to adjust his strategy on several significant occasions. Because his goals remained basically unchanged until he achieved them, Jacobs's story captures the essence of sticking to a defined objective, no matter what has to be done along the way.

Jacobs, a former engineering professor, cofounded Qualcomm to develop digital wireless technology in 1985. The U.S. wireless industry had previously adopted a system known as time-division multiple access (TDMA) as its digital standard. TDMA had greater reliability than other systems, and this was considered the most important factor in its adoption.

Jacobs stubbornly developed his products using a far less popular system called code-division multiple access (CDMA), based on compression technology. Jacobs was convinced his system had far greater potential because of its increased access capacity. He continued to base his products on CDMA, regardless of development setbacks or criticism. His commitment to his cause was legendary, even though many outsiders said that he was nuts.

It took Jacobs four long years before he got compression technology working reliably. At that point, he approached the Cellular Telephone Industries Association (CTIA) to present his concepts. However, his timing could hardly have been worse. (In Chapter 9, we discuss using timing wisely.) As it happened, the CTIA had just completed its own internal fight over standards and technologies. The main competitor to TDMA was the general standard for mobile communications (GSM), the European standard. The fight had been bitter, but TDMA had finally prevailed. That's when Jacobs wandered in, proposing that they now consider CDMA again. According to Jacobs, "They threw us out on our ears."[7]

But Jacobs stayed focused on his definite objective. He didn't quit. He knew his compression technology would increase networks' capacity many times over that of competing systems. He didn't abandon his definite objective, but he realized he had to change his strategy to reach it. Instead of trying to directly convince the CTIA, he decided he needed to persuade a single corporation to try his system. He reasoned that if he could prove the advantages he claimed in actual practice, he would influence the CTIA indirectly to adopt CDMA as a standard. (We'll look at the indirect approach, another important principle of strategy, in Chapter 8).

After two more years of struggle, Jacobs convinced the wireless division of Pacific Telesis to put up $2 million to build a trial network in San Diego. The results of the trial convinced the CTIA to do something it had once hoped to avoid—reopen the standards debate. Two years later, CTIA approved Jacobs's proposed CDMA as a second standard.

Just when it appeared that Jacobs was on the verge of achieving his objective, another obstacle appeared. Jacobs thought that when CDMA was adopted as a secondary standard, it would help Qualcomm's image, and make things easier. However, the exact opposite occurred. Reopening the standards debate caused even greater problems. Several corporations had already sunk millions into TDMA. Fearing change, they viciously attacked CDMA as too expensive, too complicated, and susceptible to jamming. If that weren't enough, Jacobs was personally branded as a fraud.

Up to now, Jacobs had sought primary status for CDMA from a potential adopter of his system. Now, Jacobs once again adjusted his strategy. He sought any adoption, even a weak secondary adoption. Two large companies, Northern Telecom Ltd. and Motorola, agreed to license Qualcomm's CDMA technology. Actually, their licensing didn't amount to much risk. They were simply covering their bets on the off chance that Jacobs was right about CDMA. Still, this was a success (of sorts) for Qualcomm. To build upon this small success, Jacobs went to Asia looking for more business.

Although his detractors tried everything to prevent additional sales (including sending letters to likely prospects warning of CDMA's problems, suggesting that CDMA be subjected to the closest scrutiny, and stating that Jacobs was not to be believed), objective testing began to support Jacobs's claims.

Then came a huge sales breakthrough. Major carriers of digital wireless, including PrimeCo and Sprint PCS, signed on to use CDMA technology. Unfortunately, no one made CDMA handsets, and Sprint and PrimeCo needed tens of thousands. Yet another dragon had reared its head.

Jacobs didn't falter in his commitment to his definite objective. Although he had decided earlier not to consider making ancillary equipment such as phones, now he adjusted his strategy again. He convinced Sony to put up 49 percent of the money needed in a joint phone-making venture. Qualcomm was now in the cellular phone-making business with a hefty multimillion order for its phones, a product Jacobs hadn't even previously considered.

This led to the next obstacle. A Qualcomm shipment of thousands of phones was halfway across the country at high speed as Jacobs tried desperately to meet a delivery deadline for Sprint. Suddenly, it was discovered that each and every phone had a defective menu screen. Fortunately, Qualcomm managed to catch the delivery truck and get it turned around. It rushed the phones back to Qualcomm's plant in San Diego for speedy reprogramming. Think Qualcomm's problems were at last over? Think again.

Ten days before PrimeCo's national rollout of the phones, someone tried one of the buttons on a Qualcomm phone. An ear-piercing screech nearly deafened him. A second phone was tried with the same result. And then a third was tried. Testing uncovered the problem—it was in the software, so every single phone was affected. They all had deafening screeches. With 40,000 phones already shipped, it was too late to send them back to San Diego. Engineers flew out to PrimeCo's Florida warehouse with a just-in-time fix. Over four days, all 40,000 phones were reprogrammed with help from every set of hands they could find to turn screws, open up the phones, and make changes. Again, Qualcomm managed to barely make the deadline.

How many times along the way did Jacobs have to change his strategy in order to continue pursuing his objective? Who cares! Irwin Jacobs's commitment to a definite objective had its rewards. Today, most of the new generation of wireless systems built use his CDMA technology. Qualcomm revenues increased 30.6 percent last year, to reach $3.9 billion.[8] And, it licenses CDMA semiconductor technology and system software to more than 100 equipment and cell phone manufacturers.[9] Moreover, *Industry Week* named Qualcomm one of the 100 Best Managed Companies, and *Fortune* magazine called it one of the 100 Best Companies in America to work for. Not a bad testimonial for a strategy based on commitment to a fully defined objective, in which the strategy was adjusted, but never the objective.

| STRATEGIST'S LOG | COMMITING TO A DEFINITE OBJECTIVE |
|---|---|

Before you can develop a strategy, you must know where you want to go. That's why the fundamental principle of strategy is commitment to a definite objective. People will willingly follow a leader who shows uncommon commitment to a specific goal. This commitment rests on a foundation based on three forces: physical, mental, and moral. To win out over our competition, we must define our objectives in such a way as to combine all three so they act as one.

There are five separate tactics involved in applying our commitment to strategy:

1. Think through your goals until you can clearly define them to both yourself and those who must help you reach them.

2. Make a public commitment to the objectives or goals you have selected.

3. Hold fast to your commitment while promoting your goals and objectives at every opportunity.

4. Obstacles will inevitably appear along the way. Expect them and deal with them, while never losing sight of your objective.

5. Once you are committed to a fully defined objective, be ready to adjust your strategy as necessary, but not your objective. ▪

## CHAPTER 2

# Seize the Initiative and Keep It

*"If there is no wind, row!"* —ROMAN PROVERB

*"Have you got a problem? Do what you can where you are with what you've got."* —THEODORE ROOSEVELT

In 1977, a young night school student in San Francisco saw a full-page advertisement in a magazine for a solid-state chronograph watch for ninety dollars. The price caught his eye because Seiko had only introduced the chronograph watch the previous year, and it sold for almost $300. The young man was a jogger. At ninety dollars, this young man thought the shock-resistant watch would make a terrific product for runners.

Several hundred thousand people saw that same advertisement, and at least a thousand of them must have been joggers. No doubt many of these people actually bought the watch. Some of these buyers probably had the same idea as this young man but failed to act on it. Richard Thalheimer was the only one who actually took the initiative, cut a deal with the importer, and started selling the "Jogger's Watch." Thalheimer did so by advertising in a different magazine called *Runners World*.

Thalheimer had just finished his law degree at the time and had planned on becoming a lawyer. But his one advertisement in *Runners World* brought in $90,000 in sales. So he started a company selling unusual, hard-to-find, high-technology products through catalogs. Within three years, his annual sales reached $100 million. Today, his Sharper Image stores are well known throughout the country, and the total sales from his stores, catalogs, and Web site exceed $400 million a year.

How many times have you had a great idea and failed to seize the initiative? Later, you saw that someone else took the same idea, acted upon it, and was highly successful. Did you regret your lack of initiative? You can bet the others who saw the initial watch advertisement and had the same idea as Thalheimer, but did nothing, felt the same way as you did.

## TAKING THE INITIATIVE IS CRUCIAL

Nothing happens until you make it happen, until you take action. Putting things off until you can get around to it, or until conditions are perfect, almost always results in failure. W. Clement Stone, who rose from poverty to build an international insurance company, Combined International Corporation, which eventually merged with another company to become the Aon Corporation, a Fortune 500 company, believed that to overcome procrastination, you need only say these three words to yourself, and then act on them: "Do it now!"

Is it any wonder that the rewards in industry, in any organization, go to those who show initiative? Those who sit around waiting for something to happen, or for someone else to tell them what to do, are rarely successful. The same is true for the strategist who looks to the competition to dictate his own actions. General George S. Patton said, "I don't care what the enemy intends to do. I only care about what I intend to do." Patton knew that taking the initiative is always critical for any strategy.

Failing to seize the initiative is a crucial mistake, especially in competitive situations. No matter how well developed your ability to counter the actions of rivals, there is no way that you can win by simply defending against a competitor's actions. This concept can be clearly seen in face-to-face sporting competitions such as boxing, karate, or tennis. A competitor initiates an attack, which must be avoided or deflected. But, as soon as a defensive maneuver is completed, the defender must seek an opening through which to start a counterattack.

Of course, the initiative need not be a physical one. The principle of seizing it places a premium on intellectual ideas, as well as physical action. In fact, an intellectual initiative can sometimes obviate the need for direct physical confrontations. By maintaining the lead, you are able to dominate the situation and to control the time and place of necessary actions, which will lead to attaining your goals and succeeding in your strategy.

## GAIN THE ADVANTAGE BY TAKING ACTION

Henri de Jomini was a great Swiss military strategist during the Napoleonic era. He started his career as a banker, but ultimately became a general, first in the French Army, and later in the Russian Army.

Jomini wrote one of the classic books on strategy, *The Art of War.* Today, when one thinks of the foremost Western war strategist, the name Carl von Clausewitz probably comes to mind. However, this was not always so. In the nineteenth century, Jomini was far more influential than his German contemporary. During our own Civil War, it was said that the generals of both the North and South rode into battle with two books in their saddlebags: the Bible and Jomini's *The Art of War.*

Jomini pointed out that the competitor who takes the initiative has the great advantage because he can strike a blow at a point of his selection, whereas the competitor who acts on the defensive must defend everywhere, is often taken unawares, and must always regulate his movements according to the actions of his adversary.[1]

Keep in mind, however, that there are two parts to this second essential principle, which must be mastered. First, you must gain the initiative; second, you must keep the initiative until you attain your objective. Neither is easy. Sometimes you slip up and allow a competitor to take the initiative. This puts you in a reactive mode. Think of the boxer who must defend himself after being struck first. When this initial blow is unexpected, it can be devastating, and it can put you at an extreme disadvantage. You must take action to regain the initiative or, like the boxer, you'll find yourself down for the count.

## THE ATTACK ON PEARL HARBOR

There is probably no better example to demonstrate the overall concepts involved in the principle of seizing the initiative than the Japanese attack on Pearl Harbor, and its aftermath. Much has been written about the events of December 7, 1941. Let's look at the attack from a strategy viewpoint.

The Japanese felt that their future was in controlling the Pacific Rim and in dominating Asia. To reach these objectives, Japan needed resources and the acquiescence of the United States. It was clear that the

United States would neither help to provide these resources nor agree to Japanese domination of Asia.

In 1941, the United States was unprepared for war, and our armed forces ranked eighteenth in size in the world. The American economy was basically still on a peacetime footing, and the country had just begun to recover from a devastating depression. Still, the Japanese knew that the United States was potentially far more powerful and possessed a strong Pacific fleet that could be a threat to their plans.

The Japanese did not think America could be beaten in a fight to the finish. Admiral Isoroku Yamamoto, commander in chief of Japan's Combined Fleet, had studied at Harvard University and later served as naval attaché in the United States. As a result, he was well acquainted with America and Americans. He knew that the United States could not be defeated in any conventional sense, nor by any conventional strategy. He felt the only hope for success was to keep America from acting until the Japanese actually controlled the resources they needed, and conquered the territories they coveted. Yamamoto said, "If we can destroy the American fleet, for six months I will run wild, and the Americans cannot stop me. However, if we fail to succeed to either destroy the American fleet or in our offensive once the war has started, all we will have succeeded in doing is to awaken a sleeping giant."

So the Japanese concept was to cripple the U.S. fleet and to simultaneously launch offensives all over Asia. Japan would gain immediate access to oil, rubber, and other assets it needed to further supply its war machine. By the time the United States had recovered six months or more later, the Japanese would be in total control, and they would have fortified their conquests. Meanwhile, America would be facing problems from Japan's Axis partners, Germany and Italy. Japan would propose peace in the Pacific on terms that the United States could not refuse. That was the plan.

## A Strategy Based on Initiative and a Surprise Attack

To achieve its objective, Japan formulated a strategy based on seizing the initiative. The Japanese would strike first. To maintain the element of surprise, the attack fleet was to gain its position to strike the main U.S. naval base at Pearl Harbor in secret. Moreover, it would launch the first wave of aircraft making up the strike force even before war was declared, although the strike was timed so that a declaration of war was to be delivered in Washington before the first bomb fell. However, due to problems with decoding the message at the Japanese embassy in Washington, this didn't happen, and the attack came first.

The Japanese attack was devastating. Most of the U.S. Pacific Fleet was sunk, and several thousand sailors, soldiers, marines, and airmen were killed. At the same time, the Japanese launched surprise offenses in the Philippines, Malaya, Singapore, and all over the Pacific. Japan had clearly seized the initiative, and the United States was at an extreme disadvantage. However, as strange as it may seem to say, the U.S. Navy got very lucky on that infamous day. The Pacific Fleet's three aircraft carriers were not in port. Therefore, they remained unscathed.

## Regaining the Initiative

When a disaster as significant as the Pearl Harbor attack gives "a competitor" such a tremendous advantage, regaining the initiative is both extremely important and extremely difficult. The United States was able to do this by a rare combination of tremendous effort; courage; luck; and, of course, a good strategy.

The United States was not an easy enemy, despite its weakened state and the courage and determination of Japan. Certain key factors were going against the Japanese and their hopes for maintaining the initiative gained with the attack on Pearl Harbor.

First, while ultimately successful for the Japanese, the Philippine campaign took more than twice as long as anticipated, and it required far more resources than planned.

Second, as mentioned above, the U.S. aircraft carriers had survived the assault at Pearl Harbor. The loss of battleships forced the U.S. Navy to fight in a new way: with aircraft carriers. Only four months after the attack, a joint U.S. Navy–Army task force got close enough to the Japanese mainland to successfully launch U.S. Army (the U.S. Air Force did not exist yet) B-25 bombers. The planes, commanded by Lieutenant Colonel (later General) Jimmy Doolittle, attacked Tokyo and several other major Japanese cities. These raids did little real damage. However, the fact that the United States was able to successfully carry out such an attack at all forced the Japanese to withdraw forces for homeland defense. Also, this was a major blow to Japanese morale, at the same time that it boosted U.S. morale.

Third, and most significant, U.S. intelligence experts had broken the Japanese naval code. The Americans knew what the Japanese were doing and planning, but the reverse was not true.

## The United States Recaptures the Initiative

The Japanese still had the initiative seven months after Pearl Harbor, in June 1942. Rear Admiral Chester W. Nimitz had been given command of the U.S. Pacific Fleet. His adversary vastly outnumbered him. Admiral Yamamoto had 160 war vessels available. Nimitz had only about twenty. In this situation, few could blame him for some sort of a hit-and-run campaign. However, Chester Nimitz was a fighter, and he knew that he must regain the initiative from the Japanese. This required that he draw the Japanese fleet into battle, and defeat it. He decided to capitalize on his knowledge of Japanese intentions, provided by the ability to read their secret orders.

Meanwhile, Admiral Yamamoto had decided to launch a major attack to capture Midway Island. The conquest of Midway had not been in the original Japanese war plan. However, despite the setbacks noted earlier, overall the Japanese offenses had met their objectives. Capturing Midway would allow the Japanese to harass (and perhaps even capture) Hawaii. Yamamoto thought that luring the American fleet to a major battle at Midway could provide the knockout punch to finish it off completely.

Yamamoto knew he had a tremendous numerical superiority, as compared to his American adversary. He also was told that American carriers were in no position to participate in the battle.

On the other side, Nimitz knew what the Japanese were up to, plus he knew things his adversary did not know. Due to his foreknowledge, not only would he be able to get his three carriers into the battle, but he also determined that they carried about the same number of planes as the four Japanese carriers that Yamamoto had. Moreover, Nimitz would have an additional 109 Army, Navy, and Marine land-based aircraft on Midway Island to commit to the battle.

Nimitz threw everything he had into the fight in a concentrated fashion. Yamamoto, convinced of his overwhelming strength, dispersed his fleet into several forces that were too far away from each other to lend support. In turn, Nimitz concentrated against each of these enemy forces. The result was that despite tactical skill, gallantry, and determination on both sides, the United States regained the initiative. America lost one aircraft carrier, the USS *Yorktown*, and one destroyer. The Japanese lost all four carriers, its total carrier fleet, plus one heavy cruiser. Midway was one of the most decisive battles in history, and it is considered the turning point in the war with Japan.

## HOW TO GAIN AND KEEP THE INITIATIVE

The advantages of seizing the initiative are well documented throughout military history, as well as in countless business success stories. But how can you ensure that your organization gains, and keeps, the initiative? In my research, I have discovered five key effective ways to do this:

1. Analyze the situation carefully.

2. Seek hidden opportunities and new solutions.

3. Act now!

4. Act boldly.

5. Keep the pressure on.

### *Analyze the Situation Carefully*

It's amazing what happens when you stop to scan your environment and analyze the situation before you act. You will find opportunities you previously missed. You will also see threats to be avoided and problems that must be solved before you can go ahead. It's always surprising to me that so many companies that should know better blunder into situations without first making a careful analysis. Yet, a careful analysis can be the basis of great success, even as you seize the initiative and act.

Stratton Sclavos founded a company called VeriSign, Inc. If there has been a problem with your Web site, or you've had a hacker, Sclavos probably knew it before you did. If you've bought anything on the Net, it was Sclavos who protected your credit card number. And it was Sclavos who moved payments around to and from the right banks. Since the year 2000, every time you surfed the Web, you ran into one of VeriSign's servers. If you had a domain name, Sclavos probably sold it to you. Sclavos had the world's biggest Internet "tollbooth," and he got (and continues to get) money from everyone. But, for all his initial success, Sclavos provides us with a valuable insight regarding the importance of doing a thorough analysis of your situation in order to maintain the initiative.

In 1995, Sclavos first seized the initiative by setting a clear objective: to build what he called cyberspace's first "utility company." By his definition, such a company would handle all the boring, but necessary, complex and comprehensive support activities regarding e-commerce. No one else had done this before, but Sclavos had a plan, and by taking the initiative, he began to implement it. No one else would take on this burden, but Sclavos was ready, willing, and able to do it. As a result, while everyone else in e-commerce took a bath during the dot-com collapse, VeriSign's revenues went up 8 percent over the previous year, and its operating profits rose by 14 percent. Amazon.com and Yahoo! may have set out to change the world, but *Fortune* magazine said that their impact was going to be marginal, compared with VeriSign's.

For the first five years, like Admiral Yamamoto in the first seven months of World War II, Sclavos was successful everywhere in building his e-commerce security business. By the end of the decade, VeriSign's stock was in the stratosphere at $200 a share.

Network Solutions was a company with a government-sanctioned monopoly to manage *.com, .net,* and *.org* domain names. It was looking for a merger partner. There were a number of large, well-known companies interested in bidding for the opportunity. But Sclavos, flushed with his prior success, jumped in and bid preemptively to acquire what he saw as an effective way for VeriSign to absolutely maintain the initiative. Sclavos bid a stunning $19.6 billion in stock. Of course, the competition disappeared, and VeriSign became the proud owner of Network Solutions.

Wall Street experts knew Sclavos had overbid, but apparently, he did not. At first, VeriSign looked good. It had no competition. Moreover, the banks, which were previously some of VeriSign's biggest competitors in the e-commerce security business, were now some of his best customers. Why? Sclavos gave them business, including not only payment-processing volume, but also new account leads. After all, the electronic directions to every Web site in the world with an electronic address ending in *.com, .net,* or *.org* sat on VeriSign computers. This amounted to 30 million–plus names. To the banks, this access to information was a lot more important than the Web-security business. They were happy to give it all to VeriSign. VeriSign's shares rose 20 percent in three days, after it acquired Network Solutions.

Unfortunately for VeriSign, 2002 was the year of reckoning. As e-commerce lost some of its luster, the demand for domain names was bound to slow dramatically. But Sclavos had failed to allow for this. VeriSign's sales plummeted. Its stock shares lost 70 percent of their value in 2002, wiping out about $6 billion in shareholder wealth. It was one of Silicon Valley's worst-performing stocks. Timothy Leehealey of

Wedbush Morgan Securities summed up VeriSign's downfall this way, "This is a good business run by some smart people, but they didn't do a very good job analyzing the data they had in front of them to anticipate this slowdown."[2]

Sclavos is a good strategist, and he is fighting hard to turn the situation around. Yet VeriSign's stumble provides a valuable lesson for all of us. While the initiative must be maintained, this must be based on good intelligence, and analysis of the situation.

## Seek Hidden Opportunities and New Solutions

You may have heard that a company either grows, or it fails. I've seen organizations or businesses that are successful in their initial strategy eventually fail. I wondered if there might be a connection. There is. Here's what I discovered: The organization, company, or business that fails never deviates from its initial successful strategy. Yet the environment changes, competitors come up with new and better ideas, technology advances, and so on.

But just changing for change's sake is silly. Instead, to keep the initiative, keep looking for new opportunities, new ways to satisfy your customers, new ways to help your employees, and new ways to be more efficient and to provide better products and services. There is an old saying that within each problem in business lies the seed for an equal, or even greater, benefit. Seeking hidden opportunities and new solutions when problems arise can help you regain the initiative.

### Hidden Opportunities Help Regain the Initiative

There are many situations in business where the strategist is faced with a situation where initiative must be regained. That's when the strategist really has to keep her eyes open for opportunities.

With no forewarning, a newly formed company union called a strike. The company had never had difficulties with its workers in the past. But the union was inexperienced and "feeling its oats," and the workers were seduced by the union's misrepresentations. To demonstrate its power, the union called a strike. The strike was cleverly timed to occur when the president was scheduled to be in Europe with his wife on his annual vacation. The union set very limited objectives and expected to achieve them with little trouble, settling the strike in its favor very quickly. The union suspected that the company actually would have agreed to what it wanted without a strike, if it had been asked. It wasn't even sure that the president would return from vacation to do this. But he did.

On learning of the strike, the president returned immediately. As the union's demands were hardly of much significance, he was tempted to simply give in at once, since as the union had surmised, he would have acceded to what the workers wanted without the necessity of a strike. The president's advisers were baffled and angry. One vice president couldn't understand what was going on and recommended that the president quickly agree to the union's terms, since what it demanded was so easy to provide. Another vice president understood exactly what was going on. He was furious and recommended not acceding to the union's demands under any circumstances, so as to demonstrate the company's resolve. "If we give in on this, we will continue to have strikes over anything the union wants in the future," he said.

The president considered the advice from both vice presidents but looked into the situation for the opportunities, which are always there, but sometimes hidden. He found such an opportunity and decided on a strategy that would take the initiative from the union.

Before the two sides could even meet to negotiate, the company's president ordered hot meals to be provided to striking workers on the picket line. Before the union could decide how to respond to this gesture, he ordered that baseball equipment be provided and an area reserved for the workers to play during the time that they weren't actually picketing. This was soon followed by a day care center where the strikers' spouses could work to replace wages lost during the strike, if it were extended.

The message was clear: The company may not agree with the striking workers, but it was a company "team," and the company would do everything it could to help out all members of the team until matters were settled. Of course, the union's only response was that the company was trying to seduce the workers into accepting less than the objectives set and to which they were entitled. But again, the president maintained the initiative. At negotiations, he announced that not only was the company acceding to what the union wanted, but it was going a step further and was going to provide a good deal more. He maintained the initiative until he reached his objective, and the strike was settled on the company's terms. What was the union going to do? Continue the strike because the company's proposals were too favorable?

The result of this company president's search and discovery of the hidden opportunities in the situation (and his adherence to the strategy principle of seizing the initiative) was that the whole thing ended well, with greatly enhanced respect for the company. By seizing the initiative, the president stayed well ahead of actions by the union. ▪

## *Act Now!*

Unfortunately, there is a trap that lies in wait for even the most brilliant strategist. In fact, sometimes it is the most brilliant strategist who is most susceptible. The trap is delay, usually caused by the desire to overanalyze the situation and make it perfect before proceeding. Too many strategists want the perfect situation, all the information, everything "just so" before proceeding.

General George S. Patton, with a record during World War II that clearly demonstrates his mastery of the principle of seizing the initiative, had a definite opinion regarding delay in implementation. Said Patton, "A good plan violently executed now is better than a perfect plan next week."

Of course, Patton was referring to warfare, so we don't need to take him literally regarding executing the plan "violently" for strategy in business. Rather, we should translate his meaning as this: A good plan energetically executed now is better than a perfect plan next week.

Most of us are familiar with the phrase "analysis paralysis." Analysis paralysis is not a careful analysis of the situation to unearth new opportunities and to avoid falling into obvious traps to avoid, as described earlier. Rather it is an overanalysis, seeking perfect results in order to develop the perfect plan. Neither a perfect analysis nor a perfect plan is possible. This is because we never gain perfect information, never get all the information we need, and never get it in a timely fashion. As a result, the delay (while seeking this perfection) is almost always deadly, and acting *now* is an important part of seizing the initiative.

**Analysis Paralysis at a Major University.** I was once appointed to the image committee of a major university. This university had a lot going for it including good scholarship, a great faculty, and an industrious student body. It had recently won a major national award in engineering by which a group of mostly undergraduate students had vanquished every major graduate engineering school in the entire country! Despite this proven track record, the image of this school among potential students was very low. The image committee was supposed to find out what was wrong with the university's image, and to come up with a plan to correct it. However, after several years in operation, the committee had been unsuccessful. In fact, they hadn't come up with a plan at all. What was wrong? The university president contacted me and asked if I would join the committee and find out what was holding things up.

I discovered the answer to this question in the first thirty minutes of the very first committee meeting I attended. The members of the committee asked for my input in designing a student survey, which would be distributed to both the university's 23,000 students and thousands of other prospective students throughout the state.

Since the committee had been in existence for several years, I was surprised that they were just getting around to doing a survey. "Oh, this isn't the first survey we've done," I was told. "But every year the demographics change, and we learn additional questions we should ask, or we discover that we didn't ask some of the previous questions in the right way, so we have to do the survey again. After all, we don't want to waste money. We want the plan we develop to be perfect."

These very smart individuals had not only failed to accomplish the task set out for them, but they had cost the university much in wasted effort and lost revenues from potential students, who never applied to the university due to its poor image.

## Act Boldly

Showing initiative implies taking a risk, because there is the possibility that you can fail. Still, the opportunities for major success lie in assessing the risk by thoroughly analyzing the situation you face, finding the hidden opportunities, and then acting boldly to implement the strategy and initiate the action that will lead your company to success.

### Sam Walton Succeeded by Acting Boldly

Sam Walton was a bold actor on the business scene. The watchwords for retail stores had always been the same as for real estate: location, location, location. Yet, after Walton analyzed the situation and found new opportunities, his strategy seemed pretty bizarre to many observers. He decided to go as far as twenty miles outside town to build his stores. Critics said that he was going where his potential customers weren't, and he would soon fail. However, Walton had concluded that if he offered quality merchandise at a good price, his customers would be less concerned about convenience. He took the initiative and implemented his strategy, which allowed him to acquire land for his stores at far less cost than the competition was paying for prime locations.

Today, Wal-Mart is one of the world's top retailers, with more than a million employees in the United States alone and another 300,000 internationally. In some instances, even during downtimes for retailers—and challenging times for Wal-Mart itself—its sales actually climbed to record highs. ■

## Boldness Was Costco's Strategy, Too

An analysis of the strategy and the initiative and risk taking demonstrated by the founders of the membership club wholesaler Costco reveals a story similar to that of Wal-Mart.

James Sinegal and Jeffrey Brotman founded Costco in 1983. Convenience was hardly emphasized. The first store, built in Seattle, Washington, was a cinderblock building with concrete floors. There wasn't anyone on the floor to assist customers, and the store didn't take credit cards. It looked like the owners had designed their strategy (and their store) to keep customers away. But, whereas the typical retailer operated on a gross margin of 25 percent, Costco's gross margin varied between 9 percent and 11 percent. The company passed this cost advantage on to customers with low prices for quality merchandise. Very little has changed since the corporation's founding . . . at least in terms of ignoring convenience and emphasizing value. What were the results?

Today Costco operates 400 wholesale warehouses with 38 million members in the United States and abroad. It is the largest American membership club wholesaler. Despite the lack of frills at Costco, the company has won J. D. Power's Consumer Satisfaction Award. And like Wal-Mart, Costco also increased sales during down years. ■

## *Keep the Pressure On*

When I was in high school, we wore uniforms that included military caps. Six of my classmates hit upon a unique way of tormenting their peers, including me. During the exercise period outside, they lined up in a single column. The leader looked for someone who was blissfully unaware, and looking in another direction. When he spotted a target, he would remove his cap and run directly at the unsuspecting victim. The other five classmates would remove their caps and follow, single file, directly behind the leader.

As soon as the leader was at arm's length, he would swerve so as not to run into his target, reach out, and whack the victim in the back of his head with his cap. Before the individual could recover, a second attacker was on him, giving him another blow, and so on. I was amazed at just how effective this method of attack was. It didn't make any difference how big the victim was, how athletic, or what he did to try to ward off successive blows. In every case I witnessed, including my own, the target of the attack wasn't able to mount any kind of defense. In several cases, the defender was knocked to the ground, even though the weapon was made of cloth and couldn't possibly cause serious damage. Still, and I speak from experience here, the cumulative effect of the blows, one instantly following another, was stunning.

In business, we see a similar scenario when a company introduces a new technology or product into the marketplace. Seeing a successful introduction, competitors usually rush in with copycat products, or similar technologies of their own. If the initiating company is practicing good strategy, it will stay ahead of its competition by maintaining the initiative and having important improvements (or new products) always in the pipeline, ready to go. That way, no matter what competitors do, they always end playing catch-up.

## Building Southwest Airlines

Although Herb Kelleher helped found Southwest Airlines in 1972, and became chairman in 1978, he didn't take the reins as CEO until 1982. At that point, the airline had only twenty-seven planes, $270 million in revenues, and 2,100 employees. It flew to fourteen cities. When Kelleher retired in 2001, Southwest was a $5.7 billion business with 30,000 employees flying to fifty-seven cities.

Kelleher took the initiative and kept the pressure on. When 12,000 air traffic controllers went on strike during his first year as CEO, and all airlines were strictly regulated by a preference system as to which could fly and in what order of preference, he analyzed the rules. He saw that preference was given to new airlines. Taking advantage of the government's own rules, he immediately started a new subsidiary called Midwest Southwest Airlines. It only owned one small Lear jet. The government knew exactly what he was up to, and so did other airlines. They may have wanted to do the same thing, but Southwest beat them to it. As soon as Midwest Southwest Airline passengers got booked, and the airline had secured the preferred slots for flight scheduling, they transferred passengers over to the mother company. The U.S. government didn't like it. But Kelleher was Southwest's attorney before he became CEO, and he knew what he was doing. Southwest got its preferred flight slots before his competitors could repeat his strategy.

When fuel prices were low, other airlines coasted. Not Southwest. Kelleher started a major campaign to reduce nonfuel costs. He bought fuel and hoarded it while the price was low. In 1991, fuel costs shot up as a result of the Gulf War, and the airline industry went into a recession. But Southwest was ready, and while others were operating in the red, Southwest remained profitable.

During the airline recession of 1999, Kelleher did the same thing. He bought fuel at $22 a barrel and weathered the storm as the price rose much higher. Then, Kelleher kept the pressure on competitors by reducing costs for in-flight food. While other airlines provided elaborate meals, you got nuts, and nuts alone (well, maybe a soft drink, too), if you flew Southwest. Today, most domestic flights have been forced to emulate Kelleher's in-flight feeding strategy.

Kelleher wasn't shy in the promotional area either. Once he had the unmitigated nerve to appear in an advertisement and offer customers who were ashamed to fly on a cheap airline a paper bag to put over their heads to conceal their identities.[3] Bookings on Southwest only increased.

Kelleher well knew the principle of keeping the pressure on. Through his customer-friendly attitude on service and his innovative strategies for cutting costs, he tried to stay one step ahead of his competitors—and he usually succeeded. █

---

| STRATEGIST'S LOG | SEIZING AND KEEPING THE INITIATIVE |

Military and business strategists alike have long recognized the principle of seizing the initiative in order to gain a significant advantage over the competition. It is an equally powerful strategic principle in any field of endeavor. You choose when and where to take action, putting your competition immediately on the defensive. But, remember that there are two parts to this principle. First, you must gain the initiative; second, you must maintain it.

To seize and maintain the initiative, follow these five steps:

1. Thoroughly analyze the situation before taking action. A careful analysis can lay the groundwork for great success.

2. Maintain the initiative by looking for hidden opportunities, and new solutions. Don't just rest on your laurels.

3. Act now! You cannot afford to wait for conditions to be perfect in order to implement your strategy.

4. Once your strategy is set, take bold action to gain the advantage. There is always some risk involved in taking the initiative, but if you have studied the situation carefully, you should be well aware of the potential risks.

5. After you've gained the advantage, keep the pressure on. That way, your competition will always be playing catch-up. ▮

## CHAPTER 3

# Economize to Mass Your Resources

*"If you would be pope, you must think of nothing else."*
—SPANISH PROVERB

*"Beware of dissipating your powers; strive constantly to concentrate them."*   —JOHANN WOLFGANG VON GOETHE

Once I watched a friend play a board game called Risk® with some other acquaintances. To his utter frustration, my friend just could not win at this game of strategy. The object of the game is to occupy every territory on a board on which a map of the world is represented, and in so doing to eliminate all other players. You accomplish this by contesting with other players whose pieces, each representing one army, are placed on this map. Six continents are subdivided into territories. The smaller continents have fewer territories, the larger ones have more. At the start of the game, the territories are divided up among the players by chance, so that one army occupies every territory. This determines the initial placement of armies.

Business has rules that we must play by. So does the game of Risk. When it's your turn, you accumulate additional armies, depending on the number of territories you occupy at that time. If you own an entire continent, you are awarded additional armies more for the larger continents, less for the smaller ones. You can place these additional armies wherever you want in one or more of your territories.

To challenge an opponent, your territory must be adjacent to his, and you must have at least two armies in the territory from which you are launching your attack. Attacking is done by rolling dice, so there is an element of chance involved. If you win the throw, your opponent must remove one army. The more armies you have, and the less your opponent has, the better. Even though you're rolling dice, your superior force will usually whittle down a weaker force. You can more easily afford to lose some of your armies along the way. If you defeat all the armies an opponent has in a territory, the territory is yours and you move in at least one of your armies.

My friend complained bitterly about his luck. Eventually, he lost all of his armies, and he lost the game. In fact, out of six people playing, he was the first one eliminated. After observing his playing style and watching how the others played, I took him aside and pointed out to him that luck had very little to do with his inability to win. He just didn't economize to mass his armies anywhere. He fought all over the board with no apparent goal other than to contest with his adversaries to capture territories. He was relying on luck, not strategy, and so he lost. I explained the third essential principle of strategy: Concentrate superior resources at a point or position that would enable him to overwhelm an opponent.

I reminded my friend that every continent he controlled meant additional armies he would get to use when it was his turn to roll the dice. To win, he first had to decide on the continent he wanted (and was in a position to contend for), and then identify the decisive place on the map that he must control to win this continent. He also needed to think ahead as to where he would concentrate after winning one continent. Thereafter, rather than spreading his armies around the board at random, he would concentrate as many armies as he could to go after another continent, and so on. In addition, he would benefit from economizing his resources—allowing those of his territories that were less important to his plan to be weaker.

After I explained this basic strategic principle to him, he applied it the next time he played Risk. Not surprisingly, he won. He concentrated his armies at decisive points. Because he had massed his armies, when he attacked, he attacked with superior numbers against weaker numbers of armies held by his opponents. He would gain control of one continent, and then move on to the next in the same fashion. With just average luck, he won repeatedly.

## ▌ MASSING AND CONCENTRATION IS CRITICAL IN BUSINESS

Good business strategists follow the same model that succeeds in Risk. They mass their resources where it counts. Only then do they move on to mass their resources at the next important point. They know that they can't concentrate and be strong everywhere.

Al Ries, author of a number of business books with his partner and coauthor Jack Trout, wrote an entire book on the concept of massing, aptly entitled *Focus* (Harper Business, 1996). In his classic book *Competitive Strategy: Techniques for Analyzing Industries and Competitors* (Free Press, 1980), Michael Porter called focus a "generic strategy." I disagree with Porter on this point. Massing, concentration, or focus (three names for essentially the same thing) can hardly be termed a full-fledged strategy in its own right, when every strategy must incorporate this concept as part of its basic makeup. In fact, many experts consider this principle to be the basis of all strategy.

Microsoft founder Bill Gates is certainly no slouch. He built the most successful technology company in the world virtually from scratch, and along the way he became the richest man in America. In an interview with *Fortune* magazine, Bill Gates said, "You know, the notion that a kid who thought software was cool can end up creating a company with all these smart people whose software gets out to hundreds of millions of people, well, that's an amazing thing. I've had one of the luckiest situations ever. But I've also learned that only through focus can you do world-class things, no matter how capable you are."[1]

In any situation, winning requires us to have more resources at the decisive strategic position than an opponent whose very success requires our failure or demise. The only way we can win is if our resources are greater than those of our opponent. We bring these resources—money, people, time, skill, know-how, influence, or whatever—together by massing them, concentrating them, or focusing them at the right place and at the right time.

## This Woman Started with Nothing

Tanya York immigrated to this country from Jamaica with nothing at age 17. Now in her thirties, she is a multimillionaire and head of her own film production company, York Entertainment. *The Hollywood Reporter* named her one of the 100 most powerful women in the entertainment industry. In an interview with *Entrepreneur Magazine*, she revealed the secret of how she succeeded in the highly competitive movie production business, despite her lack of a business or film school education when so many people with these advantages have failed. She said, "As soon as we have something under control and are doing well, I'll move on to setting up a new part of the business and expanding it."[2]

In other words, Tanya York is saying that after massing her resources at the point she perceives to be important and succeeding there, only then does she move on to the next challenge. She doesn't try to succeed everywhere at once. To do that, she would need to be strong everywhere. She could only do that if she had unlimited resources. ■

## DECIDE ON YOUR OBJECTIVE; THEN MASS RESOURCES TO ACHIEVE IT

Once you know what you want and you understand your goals and objectives clearly, you concentrate your resources to achieve them just like Tanya York. No individual, no business, even no country has unlimited resources. Resources may be natural, such as minerals, water, or oil. But resources may also include money, time, effort, or good looks. Resources are anything that can be used in some way to attain an objective.

Because resources are always limited, you must make constant trade-offs as to where they will be used. Again, you usually cannot be strong everywhere. If you try to do this, you will fail because at any one point, you will be weak, relative to a competitor. Unless you mass your resources against a clearly defined objective, so you are stronger than your competition at that point, you will have little chance of success. I call a potential point where you may concentrate your resources a strategic position. A strategic position can be a target market, a business, an industry, a product, or a geographical location. Strategic positioning is discussed in more depth in Chapter 4.

You probably remember Priceline.com, the online sales giant, the company that allowed customers to set their own prices for airline tickets. Once it became profitable, the company expanded into everything: groceries, insurance, cars, etc. In other words, it tried to be strong everywhere and beat the competition in a wide range of venues. Unfortunately, Priceline couldn't keep pace, and the company got buried in customer complaints. The stock dropped from $160 to just $1.12 a share. The chief financial officer quit and the CEO was booted out. Along came Hong Kong supertycoon Li Ka-shing, who bought 30 percent of the rubble of the failed e-commerce business. Gaining a controlling interest, he dropped the stuff that didn't make sense and concentrated on what did—airlines and hotel rooms. Goldman Sachs upgraded Priceline's earning estimate, and a rapid return to profitability was predicted.

## Case in Point: How "Massing" Is Critical in Business

You can see the importance of massing for business with a simple example. Assume there are two companies. One company, Firm A, is the dominant firm in the widget industry. It has one major competitor, Firm B, about half its size and with half its resources available to spend on advertising. This is represented in Figure 3-1.

Over the next three months, Firm A has $10 million to spend on advertising in each of five different markets of equal size. As Firm A is the dominant firm, it must maintain a strong presence in all five markets. Therefore, it is reasonable that Firm A must spend a certain minimum amount of advertising in each market. We will assume that this minimum amount is $1.5 million, and that the company must spend at least this much in advertising in each and every one of the five markets that constitute this industry. An example of Firm A's choice is represented in Figure 3-2.

Over the same three-month period, Firm B has only $5 million to allocate among the five target markets. That's half as much as Firm A. However, unlike Firm A, it can allocate its $5 million in any way it sees fit. Now, note that the five markets represent strategic positions. That is, they are potential points of concentration for monetary resources for both firms.

Both firms would like to allocate their advertising dollars to maximize their profits. This will require selling more product. Other things being

*Figure 3-1*

FIRM A's ADVERTISING BUDGET VS. FIRM B's BUDGET

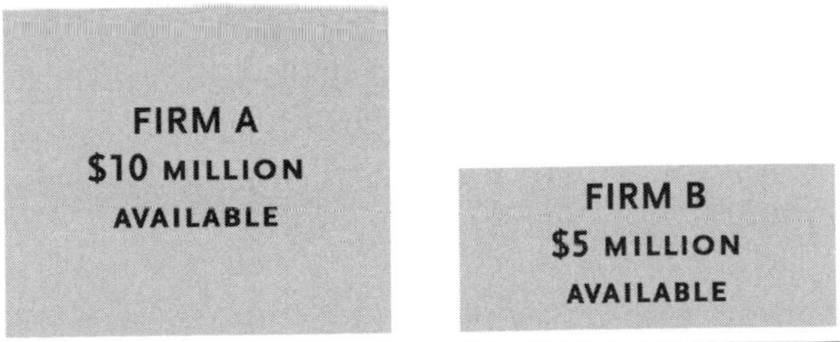

**FIRM A**
**$10 MILLION**
**AVAILABLE**

**FIRM B**
**$5 MILLION**
**AVAILABLE**

*Figure 3-2*

---

FIRM A's BUDGET ALLOCATION

---

*Because Firm A is the dominant firm, it must spend at least $1.5 million in each market. It decides to spend $1.5 million in markets 1 through 4 and $4 million in market 5.*

| MARKET 1 | MARKET 2 | MARKET 3 | MARKET 4 | MARKET 5 |
|---|---|---|---|---|
| Firm A = $1.5 million | Firm A = $1.5 million | Firm A = $1.5 million | Firm A = $1.5 million | Firm A = $4.0 million |

---

equal, to do this will require a greater expenditure of resources in a particular market, or strategic position, than the competition. Since no additional information is provided, there is no basis for selecting one of these markets over another in which to mass. The best way to sell more product is to concentrate resources in as few markets or strategic positions as the firm can, only one if possible, even though intuitively this may not seem to be the correct action to take. Some strategists think that by spreading their resources over several strategic positions, they have a better chance of winning at one of them. Like my friend who played Risk, they are relying on luck, not strategy. This is true for both firms, even though the arbitrary rules we have established for this example do not permit Firm A to mass as much as Firm B because it must spend a minimum of $1.5 million in each market.

If Firm B simply divides its $5 million equally into all five markets, we know that in every market Firm A will win out over Firm B, since it is going to allocate a minimum of $1.5 million for advertising in each market, and Firm B will only have $1 million allocated to each. Firm B will lose everywhere, because Firm A will outspend it by at least $0.5 million in each market. You can see this in Figure 3-3.

However, if Firm B concentrates its resources over the three months in any one market, it can easily defeat Firm A there, even though Firm A is twice its size and has twice the money to spend.

Though considerably larger, Firm A is actually at a disadvantage against Firm B in at least one market because it must spend a minimum amount of its resources ($1.5 million in each of the five markets). Thus, the most resources that it can concentrate in dollars in any single market

*Figure 3-3*

---

### FIRM B's BUDGET ALLOCATION

---

*Firm B can spend its $5 million any way it chooses. If it spends $1 million in each market, it loses to Firm A in every market.*

| MARKET 1 | MARKET 2 | MARKET 3 | MARKET 4 | MARKET 5 |
|---|---|---|---|---|
| Firm A = $1.5 million | Firm A = $1.5 million | Firm A = $1.5 million | Firm A = $1.5 million | Firm A = $4.0 million |
| Firm B = $1.0 million | Firm B = $1.0 million | Firm B = $1.0 million | Firm B = $1.0 million | Firm B = $1.0 million |

---

is $4 million. As long as Firm B concentrates its $5 million in any one of the five markets, it will be superior to the largest firm by at least $1 million in one market. Other things being equal, Firm B's advertising will stand out from the competition (Firm A) in that one market. Again, at worst, its stand-out measure of success in dollars will be $1 million ($5 million to $4 million), but it could be as much as $3.5 million ($5 million to $1.5 million). This can be readily seen in Figure 3-4.

Of course, in the other four markets, Firm A will win, since Firm B will be a no-show. But even this can be recoverable by simply concentrating in another single market over the following three months. So, if the rules remain the same, Firm B can repeatedly defeat its much stronger competitor in one market over any three-month period.

If Firm A were free to allocate resources in whatever way it wants, it would have the flexibility to defeat Firm B in every market—if it is lucky enough to select the same market as where Firm B chose to concentrate. And it would be luck, since with no other information supplied, there is no basis to select one market as being better than another, or one in which Firm B would be more likely to mass its resources. Therefore, even if freed to allocate its money as it wishes, Firm A must allocate its resources by chance, in the hope of overwhelming Firm B, depending on its location and its allocation. However, it still cannot guarantee a win in every market if Firm B masses all $5 million of its resources in any single market. In this situation, it would have to depend on luck.

Naturally, real business is much more complicated than this simpli-

*Figure 3-4*

FIRM B's BUDGET AFTER MASSING ITS RESOURCES

*If Firm B masses all its resources in any one market, it will defeat Firm A in that market, even if it happens to choose its competitor's strongest market concentration (market 5).*

| MARKET 1 | MARKET 2 | MARKET 3 | MARKET 4 | MARKET 5 |
|---|---|---|---|---|
| Firm A = $1.5 million | Firm A = $1.5 million | Firm A = $1.5 million | Firm A = $1.5 million | Firm A = $4.0 million |
| Firm B = $5.0 million or $0 | Firm B = $5.0 million or $0 | Firm B = $5.0 million or $0 | Firm B = $5.0 million or $0 | Firm B = $5.0 million or $0 |

fied example, and there are many other factors to consider, including the quality and theme of the advertising, the vehicles and media selected, frequency and timing of the ads, and much more. Even the intelligence that one firm obtains about each other, other competitors, other environmental factors, business conditions, and the target markets will affect outcome. But this does not diminish the importance of the concept of massing. Concentration, or massing by itself, can be very powerful. For example, it is the whole basis of what has come to be called niche marketing.

## This Little Firm Took on IBM and Won

A small firm, ICS, Inc., with only eighty employees went up against mighty IBM in a field IBM totally dominated—automatic typewriters. ICS, Inc. selected as its strategic position a small market, or niche, in the teaching field, and it concentrated all its resources there. In that niche, ICS, Inc. could specialize and service this market better than IBM could with its more generalized products and services. The result? IBM actually withdrew entirely from the teaching market for automatic typewriters. IBM could have devoted the resources toward the market and defeat little ICS, Inc., if it wished to do so. But it wasn't worth the trouble. IBM had bigger fish to fry. It was easier for IBM to simply cut its losses and withdraw.

Massing or concentrating your resources at a strategic position like ICS, Inc. did may be far from easy in practice. It requires discipline to bring together resources from wherever you can in order to mass them where it counts. This means taking the resources from somewhere else, even stripping some other strategic position. That's known as "economizing." Mass must work together with economization. You economize your resources where their application is of lesser importance, are less needed, or are less needed temporarily, in order to have greater resources at the strategic position you have selected as decisive. ∎

## ECONOMIZING MEANS RISK

Economizing is frequently painful. There is clearly an element of risk, and this risk can be significant. What if you economize and vacate resources from a strategic position selected for concentration by a competitor? Or, what if a competitor sees what you are doing, and goes after the strategic position you uncovered? Both of these scenarios can happen, and they can cause problems.

At that strategic position, whether it is a target market, a business, a geographical location, or a category of product, you will be at a disadvantage to your competitor, even as you have the advantage at the strategic position where you mass. If the strategic position you have selected is of more importance, or you can defeat your competition at that strategic position and redeploy your resources to the other weaker strategic position before he can react to significant impact on your weakened position, then your economization is well worth the risk. The critical issue to keep in mind is that risk is always present. You cannot elude it.

### A Firm Believer in Massing to the Very End

At the beginning of the twentieth century, Germany confronted France and the world knew that a war between these major powers was only a matter of time. Alfred von Schlieffen was head of the German General Staff, and he had a master plan for a quick victory once the war began.

In his plan, von Schlieffen conceived of a massive German force concentrated to create an unstoppable right-wing juggernaut containing 90 percent of the German mobile troops, while only a few troops were placed to defend against the French Army on the German Army's left wing. The huge right wing, heavily outnumbering the French, would swing like a door through neutral Belgium, trapping the bulk of the French Army and ending the war in a matter of weeks, or even days. This "good" end, he felt, outweighed any moral consideration regarding the violation of Belgium neutrality and justified the means. On the Eastern front, von Schlieffen planned to hold the Russians in check using reserve and fortress troops. Aptly, this secret arrangement became known as the Schlieffen Plan of 1905.

So strongly did von Schlieffen believe in the plan that bore his name, and so sure of the importance of massing heavily on the right wing, that on his deathbed, his final words were "Keep the right wing strong." Then he expired.

However, by the time World War I actually began in 1914, more than a year after von Schlieffen's death, various factors were considered sufficiently important to dilute his original strategy and alter the economization that he knew would be required. First, it was decided not to merely defend the area in which the German left wing operated, but to counterattack from this strategic position. Supporting this action required weakening the right wing. Similarly, it was decided to launch an offensive on the Eastern front as well. So the right wing was further weakened to strengthen that strategic position too.

When the German wheel through Belgium was actually launched, the right wing was far weaker than von Schlieffen had ever envisioned. Some measure of this can be seen by the ratio of the right wing to the left wing in numbers. Whereas von Schlieffen had planned for a ratio of seven to one, right-wing to left-wing troops, when the Germans actually attacked in August 1914, the ratio of right to left had fallen to four to one. Moreover, the total number of German soldiers involved was even less due to the troop diversions to the Russian front. In the end, not only did the Germans fail to win and conclude the war in a few weeks, they failed to win at all. The following four years of mostly static trench warfare resulted in hundreds of thousands of casualties on both sides, and a German defeat under the humiliating Treaty of Versailles.

Whenever you are tempted to weaken your mass and not to economize—to try to win by being strong everywhere—remember von Schlieffen's final words, and "keep the right wing strong."

### The Secrets of the World's Greatest Lover

Not surprisingly, the principle of massing your resources applies to everything you do in life. Giovanni Giacomo Casanova is generally regarded, for better or worse, as history's greatest lover. He attributed his success with women to his ability to concentrate so completely on the woman he desired at any one time that he rarely failed to win her over. It is important to emphasize that Casanova massed his resources and did not pursue more than one woman at a time. While he pursued one, he concentrated on that woman alone, and thought of nothing and no one else until his conquest was complete, whether this took days or months.

Casanova carried the strategy concept of massing his resources into everything he did in life. Imprisoned in a dungeon in Venice from which no one had previously escaped, he concentrated on the single goal of escape to an incredible degree. He massed every limited resource he had at his disposal toward that single objective. Finally, although Casanova had no prior experience either with prisons, or the means of escaping from them, he succeeded in breaking out of his cell. Later, the successful lover and prison escapee wrote, "I have always believed that when a man gets into his head to do something, and when he exclusively occupies himself in that design, he must succeed, whatever the difficulties."[3]

---

| *STRATEGIST'S LOG* | ECONOMIZING TO MASS YOUR RESOURCES |
|---|---|

Early on, the successful strategist learns that it is essential to concentrate his resources where they'll count the most. In any situation, winning requires that you have more resources at the decisive strategic position than your opponent. Since you can't be strong everywhere, you must mass your resources against a clearly defined objective where you are stronger than your competition. You bring your resources—money, people, time, skill, know-how, influence, or whatever—together by massing them at the right place, and at the right time. In order to do this, you need to economize your resources elsewhere.

There are three important points to keep in mind:

1. You cannot consistently win unless you mass and concentrate your resources.

2. You mass by economizing your resources elsewhere. That is, you take resources from where they are less important and position them where they are more important.

3. Economizing and concentrating requires risk. This risk is unavoidable. ▪

## CHAPTER 4

# Use Strategic Positioning

*"The essence of strategy is, with a weaker army, always to have more force at a crucial point than the enemy."*

*"War is a business of positions."*
—NAPOLEON BONAPARTE

*"The basic approach of positioning is not to create something new and different, but to manipulate something that's already up there."* —JACK TROUT AND AL RIES

In 1902, Philip Morris introduced one of the earliest women's cigarettes. It featured a red tip to hide lipstick marks. The innovation didn't help much, and women didn't flock to purchase it. After a few years, the brand was withdrawn from the market.

Twenty years later, the cigarette was reintroduced by Phillip Morris with the slogan "Mild as May." It no longer had the red tip. The cigarette specifically targeted "decent, respectable" women. Advertising claimed that the brand now "rode in so many limousines, attended so many bridge parties, and was found in so many handbags." Women were interested. They bought the cigarette, but still, despite extensive advertising, it represented less than one percent of the total market for cigarettes. A woman's cigarette was still too far ahead of its time to be an outstanding success. Considering what we have since learned about the hazards of smoking, this was probably fortunate for the women of those years.

In 1954, the Leo Burnett ad agency in Chicago took over the advertising for the brand. The agency decided to abandon the women's market completely. They repositioned the brand as a macho cigarette, and they created an advertising campaign using male smokers in some of the most male-oriented professions. They didn't even bother to change the name of the cigarette, or the tobacco content of the product. Yet within a short period of time, sales began growing at 10 percent a year. Using its "Marlboro men" in ads, Marlboro, named after a street in England where a Philip Morris London factory was located, became one of the most successful cigarette brands of all time.[1]

---

### Montgomery Ward Is No More, Whereas Sears Goes On

A classic example of successful (and unsuccessful) positioning is illustrated by the differing strategies of Sears and Montgomery Ward immediately after World War II. Before the war, Montgomery Ward was the larger company. However, after the war, Sears took a big risk. It massed its resources. It took all the cash it had (or could get hold of), economized everywhere else, and focused on opening new stores all over the country with the goal of becoming America's biggest retailer and putting stores where there were potential customers before Montgomery Ward could do anything about it.

Montgomery Ward, expecting a cash shortage and recession such as had occurred after World War I, held on to what it had and improved its existing stores. Its strategy was to make each store better than a Sears store. This strategy required much less of an investment. Maybe Montgomery Ward stores were "better," whatever the term means. I don't know, and I'll leave it to someone else to argue that issue. But the fact is, Sears massed its resources at the right strategic position (the opening of new stores) and in this crucial competition, Montgomery Ward never recovered. ▮

---

## POSITIONING IS CRITICAL

Concentration and its corollary economization, important as they are, are still only half the story. The other half is the selection of the strategic position at which to concentrate. The strategic position is the decisive point that will make the difference in attaining your well-defined objective. The process is the principle of strategic positioning.

Some strategic positions should be obvious, but are still ignored in the heat of business and competition. For example, at the height of the e-commerce frenzy, dot-com companies advertised all over the Web. Yet, according to Keith Regan of EcommerceTimes.com, only fourteen Web sites controlled 60 percent of online time during this period. Clearly, if dot-com companies wanted to advertise, advertising on these fourteen Web sites was the way to mass to do it. Although other factors impacted on the decision of where to advertise, these companies generally should have economized elsewhere to concentrate on these fourteen sites. This should be basic stuff. Yet, supposedly sophisticated strategists continue to violate this lesson repeatedly, with predictably poor results.

There was a certain government contractor that was in business for years. During all those years, it kept good records. It won some contracts and lost others. Overall, it was profitable. Yet, the contractor's employees all knew that when competitor A was in the bidding, they usually won, and when bidding against competitor B, they usually lost. Since the contractor knew the types of projects on which both of its rivals competed, its outcome on each competition was almost perfectly predictable. But it continued to compete against B, even at times giving up the opportunity to bid against A. By this company's reasoning, or rather lack thereof, one contract was as good as another. Consistently concentrating resources against the contracts bid by competitor A should have been a no-brainer. Yet, for years the company failed to do this, and it forfeited millions of dollars in lost work and tens of thousands of dollars by focusing on beating competitor B.

## HOW TO RECOGNIZE THE CORRECT STRATEGIC POSITIONS

How do smart strategists recognize the right strategic position? Here are five things to look for:

1. A strategic position that if you succeed there, you will succeed everywhere

2. A strategic position that has significant potential for the future

3. A strategic position that maximizes your advantages

4. A strategic position to use as a stepping-stone for a more important victory later

5. A strategic position that allows you to defeat a competitor and reposition elsewhere rapidly

### If You Succeed There, You Will Succeed Everywhere

A careful examination may reveal a strategic position where, if you can win against your competition at that position, you will win everywhere.

Recall my friend the Risk player from the beginning of Chapter 3. Once he learned to recognize the key strategic position in order to implement his plan, he began to master the game. Carl von Clausewitz called such important points "centers of gravity."

**The Five Concentric Rings.** Colonel John Warden, architect of the successful strategy in the Gulf War of 1991, which we discussed in Chapter 1, defined any such position as "the point where the enemy is most vulnerable and the point where an attack will have the best chance of being decisive."[2]

In his book *The Air Campaign*, Warden noted that Alexander the Great needed to secure the Mediterranean Sea to continue his operations against his enemy, the Persians, but his fleet was too weak to overcome the Persian fleet. Looking at the situation closely, he saw that the center of gravity, or strategic position, for the Persian fleet was its shore bases. So Alexander attacked and seized them. By doing this, he destroyed Persian naval power without fighting a single sea battle.[3]

In developing the air campaign for what became Operation Desert Storm, Warden used a five-ring concept he had developed two years earlier. You can see this represented in Figure 4-1. According to Warden, the modern nation-state consisted of five concentric rings representing five important strategic centers of gravity. Central, and most important, was the nation's leadership. The others in descending order of strategic importance for victory were key production, infrastructure, population, and only lastly, field military forces. The leadership was the most important strategic position. If it could be destroyed, disrupted, or cut off, victory was certain.[4] As proof of this theory, Warden outlined a map of Washington, D.C. and illustrated how snowfall paralyzes the city and its leadership almost every year.[5] Paralyzing the leadership of an adversary, as snowfall paralyzes the leadership in our nation's capital every year, and keeping it paralyzed, and would result in victory. The basic strategy Warden developed was based on this concept. When Schwarzkopf and his air commander, General Chuck Horner and his planner, then Brigadier General (later Lieutenant General) "Buster" Glossom, implemented it, it worked.

**How President Bush Beat His Competition in 2002.** In the 2002 midterm elections, I watched NBC's Tim Russert interview the leaders of both parties the Sunday before the election on his television show, *Meet*

*Figure 4-1*

WARDEN'S FIVE-RING CONCEPT OF CENTERS OF GRAVITY

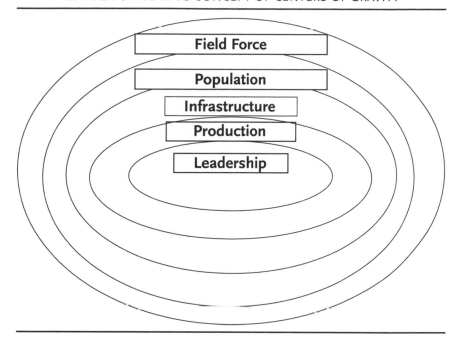

the Press. As one might have expected, both leaders predicted a victory for their side in the upcoming elections. According to the Republican representative, his party would hold the House of Representatives and pick up just enough seats to regain Republican control of the Senate. Of course, the Democratic leader predicted the exact opposite. The Democrats would pick up a bit in the House and would increase control in the Senate . . . slightly. Neither predicted a landslide for his party.

Both leaders had ignored the rather unusual actions of the head of the Republican party, President George W. Bush. Bush wasn't up for reelection, but he hit the campaign trail anyway and he worked for Republicans all over the country. President Bush's extensive campaigning for Republicans was termed "desperation" by his opponents. "If he left the campaigning to others and worked on the nation's business, the country would be in a lot better shape," they said. Even members of his own party spoke off the record that they wished Bush would spend more time on getting key bills, like the formation of an antiterror homeland agency, through Congress.

However, when the smoke cleared, Republicans had recaptured control of the Senate, ending seventeen months of Democratic rule, and giving President Bush dominance over both houses of Congress and their legislative agendas. Republican candidates knocked off two Democratic incumbents, in Georgia and Missouri, and held all but one of their own endangered seats, losing only in Arkansas. Nor was the situation any better for the Democrats in the House elections. The Republicans added half a dozen seats to their previous majority. The results marked a surprising victory, as Bush became the first Republican president since the nineteenth century to help his party expand its ranks in midterm elections. In fact, only two Democrats had done this previously, Franklin Roosevelt in 1934 and Bill Clinton in 1998.

Bush accomplished this victory by spending more time on the campaign trail rallying support for his party's candidates than any president in history. This turned the election into a referendum on the president. His campaign blitz, including his final five-day, seventeen-stop, fifteen-state swing, helped make the difference in Minnesota, Missouri, Georgia, and New Hampshire.[6]

Political analysts said that the effort put Bush in a strong position to get his agenda through Congress over the next two years. In fact, only a few days later, the *Los Angeles Times* ran this headline: "Bush's Security Bill Foes Give Up: Democratic opposition to labor provisions of an anti-terror homeland agency erodes in light of GOP electoral gains. It's a win for the president."[7]

What President Bush and his political strategist, Karl Rove, had done was classical economizing and massing at the correct strategic position (or center of gravity) to win these elections for the Republicans. Bush had intentionally economized, temporarily, on his efforts to get his agenda through Congress, knowing that if he could win a decisive midterm victory, he had a good chance of attaining his agenda over the remaining two years of his term.

## *A Strategic Position That Has Significant Potential for the Future*

Some strategic positions may not offer much competitive advantage right now, but may indeed have great potential for the future. If you can identify this kind of strategic position, and get there before your competition, the rewards can be significant.

## How KFC Beat McDonald's in China

If you've visited China recently, you know that American corporate icons such as Starbucks, McDonald's, and Kentucky Fried Chicken (KFC) are all over the place. But KFC stands out. When I taught in Chengdu, China a while back, I found that there were no less than five KFC outlets in this one Chinese city. A KFC outlet in Shanghai even claimed the highest one-day sales volume ever recorded for any KFC outlet in the world.

It was not always so. Things didn't look all that bright when KFC opened its first outlet in Beijing on November 12, 1987. To give you some perspective, this was almost two years before the infamous events at Tiananmen Square in the same city and a full five years ahead of fast-food competitor McDonald's arrival in China. Did KFC know something that "The Golden Arches," the king of fast food, did not?

Since that first outlet, KFC has pulled out all the stops. Very much like the winning strategy involved in the game of Risk (see Chapter 3), KFC had identified China as a most important strategic position, and it economized elsewhere in the world and hung on against competitors in those areas in order to mass its resources in China and succeed there.

It was a risk that paid off. Today, KFC has more than 500 outlets in China and is still growing, compared with less than 400 outlets for McDonald's. Can McDonald's catch up? Maybe. McDonald's world-wide sales last year were $14,870 million, compared with KFC's $2,300 million. So from a worldview, KFC is still, by far, the underdog. Yet, ACNielsen surveys consistently show a preference for KFC's product over McDonald's in China. This may have to do with a Chinese prefer-ence for chicken over beef, or it could have to do with the fact that KFC got there five years ahead of McDonald's by economizing elsewhere. But in China, with a population of 1.3 billion, KFC rules!

Famed Confederate cavalry leader General Nathan Bedford Forrest said that massing successfully was a matter of "getting thur fustest with the mostest." That's essentially what KFC did. ■

## *A Strategic Position That Maximizes Your Advantages*

Every company, no matter its size or resources in comparison with a competitor, has certain advantages, as well as limitations. Some strategic positions allow you to maximize these advantages so that you can bring to bear their full power. With other positions, it is the opposite. Dell Inc. used its early experiences in dealing directly with the consumer in defining its major strategic position. When it deviated from this idea before it was ready, it had real problems.

## The Day Dell Stumbled and Almost Fell

Dell Inc. is a story of almost unbroken success. Whereas many Web-based retailers and other computer companies have taken a bath, Michael Dell's company has gone on to greater things. Yet, Dell admits that he almost blew it when he committed the major blunder of failing to correctly note his decisive strategic position and his concentration there, which is what made his company successful.

To understand what happened, you have to understand Dell and the secret of its success. Michael Dell started by building and selling add-on upgrade hard-drive systems. Then he hit on the idea of selling directly to the consumer, so the customer could have exactly what he wants. The keywords here are "directly to the consumer." That's been Dell's decisive strategic position. Dell migrated to the Internet to allow a customer to order a computer before the company even builds it. Dell massed at this means of distribution, still part of selling direct. This gives the company a number of important advantages. First, it keeps inventory costs down. The result is a cost advantage, which Dell can pass on to customers in a lower price. Second, Dell gets the latest market intelligence before anyone else, and it gets it directly from the customer. So Dell keeps ahead of its competitors in changing its products and services. Dell has mastered the logistical chain of customer direct as no one else in the computer business.

In the early 1990s business was growing, but the experts advising Michael Dell told him that direct-to-consumer sales was really only a niche business, and it limited the company's growth potential. "If you want to be a major player," they told him, "you've got to expand your systems of distribution." So Dell forgot the essential principle of massing and concentration at his traditional strategic position (selling direct). Moreover, the timing wasn't right. That, too, is important. (We'll look at timing and sequencing in Chapter 9.) Dell decided to go after more conventional means of distribution in order to expand out of his company's supposed niche, as advised by "the experts."

Dell was attracted by the high-volume sales of the new wholesalers such as Sam's Club. He imagined sales of Dell computers with Sam's Club really taking off, as it had with so many other products. It was a big mistake. In this means of distribution, Dell Inc. lost the advantages it had acquired by selling direct. It lost the direct customer relationship. It lost the immediate feedback. It lost the ability to deal at lightning speed with its customers. Not surprisingly, Dell Inc. suffered a severe drubbing at the hands of the competition.

Fortunately for his company, Michael Dell is no fool. Once he realized his mistake, he didn't hesitate to correct it. He cut his losses and returned to massing at the direct channel, dealing directly with his customers. He massed at his traditional means of distribution and economized elsewhere. This massing didn't limit sales, as the so-called experts had warned, and you would hardly say that Dell serves a niche market today. Dell Inc. is so strong that its competitors, Gateway, Compaq, and Hewlett-Packard, are happily fighting for the number-two position. With $31 billion in annual sales and 36,000 employees, Dell Inc. is number one in the U.S. market. ▨

## *A Strategic Position to Use as a Stepping-Stone for a More Important Victory Later*

There are certain strategic positions that you do not intend to retain for very long. You hold them just long enough to do what you have to do to reach the next strategic position, which you really want to attain your objective. The Datsun (later Nissan) Motor Co. provides us with an excellent example.

### Nissan Gains an Advantage

When Datsun introduced the 240Z into the U.S. market, it was underpriced by as much as $10,000, compared to similar sports cars offered by other manufacturers. It quickly dominated the market as a low-cost, but very high-quality vehicle. However, that was not the strategic position that Nissan had in mind for this car. After using this penetration strategy to establish the 270Z in the American market, the price was slowly but steadily raised. Within ten years, it was priced significantly higher than similar sports cars. This high-priced positioning was an entirely new strategic point, which Nissan successfully established and was able to defend—but only after first using its lowball strategic position as a stepping-stone. ▨

## *A Strategic Position That Allows You to Defeat a Competitor and Reposition Elsewhere Rapidly*

This last strategic position concept works well when your competitor has superior resources. For a real master of the successful use of this strategy concept, we need look no further than the U.S. Civil War and one of the Confederacy's most famous generals, Thomas "Stonewall" Jackson.

**Stonewall Jackson's Foot Cavalry.** Unless you are a Civil War buff or studied military strategy, you probably have never heard of a "foot cavalry." That's what they called "Stonewall" Jackson's Corps of Confederate infantry. His corps received this name because of the great rapidity and frequency with which they marched from one strategic position to another.

In Jackson's Valley Campaign of 1862, his mission was to divert as many Union forces as possible and keep them away from General Robert E. Lee's army as he defended Richmond. With fewer than 20,000 troops, Jackson was able to occupy and defeat a Union force of 70,000. He did this by massing at one strategic position after another. At every point where he massed, he was superior in numbers to the Union troops that opposed him. By using interior lines between the strategic positions, which were shorter than the distance his opponents had to travel being on his exterior, and the speed of his marches, he was able to mass and defeat his adversary again and again, preventing them from reaching the Richmond theater of operations.

Later, when the situation required it, Jackson was able to move his corps to the vicinity of Richmond to help Lee defeat the Union army there. Every army in the world studies Jackson's actions, even today, because they represent one of the most successful and outstanding strategic diversions in history.

This concept can be (and is) repeated in business. The most common example is the old "staying ahead of the competition" with a continual stream of new products. By the time a competitor has massed to compete with a product that has been introduced, a new product/strategic position has been selected by the strategist, and he has massed his resources there. This can continue as long as the competitor tries to play catch-up by competing at a strategic position that is no longer decisive. You can see where the same can be applied to a geographic position, which is precisely what Jackson did, a target market, or whatever you choose.

| STRATEGIST'S LOG | USING STRATEGIC POSITIONING |
| --- | --- |

Strategic positioning is the principle of determining exactly where to economize and concentrate your resources. The strategic position is the decisive point that will make the difference in achieving your objective. How do you recognize the right strategic position at which to mass? There are five key scenarios for locating a strategic position. Look for:

1. A point where, if you can win against your competition at that position, you will win everywhere. Such positions have been called "centers of gravity."

2. A point that has significant potential for the future. If you can identify this kind of strategic position, and get there before the competition, you can realize great success down the road.

3. A point that maximizes your advantages. Every company has certain advantages over its competition. Some strategic positions allow you to tap the full power of your advantages.

4. A point to use as a stepping-stone for a more important victory later. There are certain strategic positions that you do not intend to retain for very long. You just use them to reach the next strategic position that you really need to attain your objective.

5. A point that allows you to defeat a competitor and reposition elsewhere rapidly. By the time your competitor has massed to compete with you at the strategic position you have selected, you have moved on to a new strategic position, forcing your competition to play catch-up. ■

## CHAPTER 5

# Do the Unexpected

*"Whatever a thing may be, be it pleasant or terrible, the less it has been foreseen the more it pleases or frightens."*
—XENOPHON

*"Mystify, mislead, and surprise!"*
—LIEUTENANT GENERAL THOMAS "STONEWALL" JACKSON

In 1999 Greg Strakosch cofounded TechTarget, a dot-com company based in Needham, Massachusetts. It was an instant success. In quick order, TechTarget created no less than eighteen industry-specific Web sites. It published the full range of useful material for registered members, including feature articles, expert advice columns, and news bulletins, and it offered other resources. In addition, TechTarget published a magazine, and it hosted technical conferences that it produced.

Like most other dot-com companies, TechTarget wasn't making money, but it was collecting lots of customers and gaining plenty of attention. Who cared if it was operating unprofitably, as long as investors didn't mind and its database grew exponentially? Everyone knew that eventually TechTarget would make a bundle by selling advertising to the growing number of Internet technology vendors. Why worry when both their audience and the number of potential Internet advertising customers increased every day?

Then came the year 2000, and the bottom fell out for the dot-coms. By summer, dot-com companies were dropping like flies. Those still around were competing like crazy for more capital to stay in the game. TechTarget was just one of thousands of floundering companies on the Net.

Like everyone else in the dot-com business, Strakosch was sure that the key to success with this new technology was gaining a larger and larger audience. One day, the audience would hit a critical mass and TechTarget would cash in. Until then, it just had to hold on. So Strakosch focused on building market share at an even faster rate. To do this, he pulled out all the stops. He sunk more and more money into improving and expanding TechTarget's product line. And he was successful! Going nose-to-nose with the competition, Strakosch built the audience for his sites to an incredible 2.6 million.

However, much to his amazement, nothing changed. Even with such a growing army of nominal site users, he couldn't raise the money he needed from investors. Dot-coms were still convinced that the secret to both survival and success was in market share. But the inevitable results were that no matter how successful they were in building share, they went under, one after the other.

Strakosch realized that he wouldn't get enough money to stay afloat unless he did something different. If he could prove TechTarget would eventually make money, he could get the capital he needed. However, he was years away from being able to make money with Internet advertisers. He was basically using the sales model that everyone knew was the only way to succeed on the Net—get loads of customers and worry about making money sometime in the future. What to do?

Much to the surprise of competitors and everyone else, TechTarget defied the conventional wisdom about what it took to win in this new, technology-driven business. Strakosch quit trying to increase his audience. Moreover, he quit trying to sell to the thousands of smaller potential Internet advertisers and concentrated on the larger technology companies, such as Oracle, IBM, Sun Microsystem, and Intel.

Competitors thought that TechTarget had made a major mistake. They knew Strakosch would lose customers and market share, and he did. To them, this was a sure sign of imminent failure. TechTarget's total number of customers went down significantly, and some of his advertisers left to find companies that still followed the old, standard dot-com business model. However, unnoticed by everyone, TechTarget started to slowly move toward profitability. This all paid off in 2001. TechTarget attracted $30 million in venture capital funding, and it achieved profitability early the next year. Most of TechTarget's former competitors were no longer around. No doubt if asked, they would have still expressed surprise that what Strakosch followed was a conscious strategy, and not dumb luck.[1]

## Surprise Can Make Up for a Deficiency in Resources

In Chapter A, we saw how the Carthaginian general Hannibal decisively defeated his Roman opponent, Terentius Varro, although the Romans outnumbered the Carthaginians four to one.

Varro expected that Hannibal would put his best troops at the front center of his line. In those days, that's where the best troops of every army in battle were positioned. It was where the fighting would be the toughest. But Hannibal surprised Varro. He did the unexpected. Hannibal deployed his best troops on his flanks. By using surprise, as well as other principles of strategy, Hannibal won an amazing victory over his competition.

Hannibal's victory demonstrates one of the reasons why surprise is such a key strategy principle in competing with others—it can make up for a deficiency in resources. And, who ever has enough resources? But even more important, when combined with secrecy, speed, deception, originality, and audacity, doing the unexpected and surprising your competitors can shift the balance of power decisively in your favor, and it can result in success far out of proportion to the energy and effort expended. In other words, small companies can defeat larger competitors, and it won't necessarily cost an arm and a leg.

## Surprise Works for Everyone

It doesn't make any difference whether you are a large organization or a tiny one—or even a political candidate. You can use boldness and creativity to create surprise, and win.

In the preliminaries to the California recall election in the fall of 2003, it was obvious that Arnold Schwarzenegger would be a major candidate if he decided to run. Still, the word went out that his wife, Maria Shriver, didn't want the actor and famous bodybuilder to be a candidate. For several weeks, the media published stories that Schwarzenegger would announce his decision not to run on an upcoming *Tonight Show* appearance on NBC, and he would endorse fellow Republican and former Los Angeles mayor Richard Riordan as a candidate. Friends and foes alike set their plans on this as a certainty.

On the night of Schwarzenegger's appearance, *Tonight Show* host Jay

Leno made the introductions and the expected jokes. Then, all grew quiet as the cameras focused on Schwarzenegger. He began explaining that it had been a difficult decision. As he started to state what this decision actually was, the screen went blank, and one of the old, black-and-white NBC logos from the 1950s appeared with the caption: "We are experiencing technical difficulties, please stand by." When Schwarzenegger appeared again, he was concluding, ". . . and that is why I made the decision that I made."

Of course, the whole thing was a joke. Schwarzenegger made others before making the surprise announcement that he was a candidate, after all. According to the *Los Angeles Times:* "The result: His announcement landed with the force of an explosion from a Schwarzenegger movie."[2] The resulting excitement brought the new candidate tremendous media attention and the lion's share of media coverage in print, radio, and television, much to the consternation of his rival candidates and the sitting governor, Gray Davis, who was trying to avoid a recall election. Schwarzenegger rode this wave of excitement all the way to the statehouse.

Employing the principle of surprise can help companies succeed, even in areas where their competitors have gained the upper hand. In the late 1950s, Volkswagen had invaded the American market and won a significant, but small, following. This was with the original Beetle. In 1959, the Big Three American companies, Ford, General Motors, and Chrysler, came out with their own small cars to compete with Volkswagen—the Ford Falcon, Chevrolet Corvair, and Plymouth Valiant, respectively. First-year sales for all three weren't bad, but as the years went by, all offered more luxuries and options, and the weight of the cars went up. In the minicar segment, Volkswagen continued to grow. Sales of all three American cars declined, and the three companies eventually withdrew from the small car market. However, Ford analysts noted that while sales for the Falcon declined, demand for certain options increased. These options were the padded dash, bucket seats, and the four-on-the-floor gearshift. Ford leaders used their creativity, and in 1965, they boldly introduced the Mustang. This vehicle created an entirely new automobile category. It took Ford's competitors years to catch up.

## PERFORMANCE SUPERIORITY: NOT NECESSARY

You don't even need a better product to create a decisive victory through surprise. Apple, pioneer of the personal computer, had dominated the market for several years when IBM decided to enter the fray. Steve Jobs even took a full-page advertisement in several newspapers welcoming IBM to the business!

IBM entered the marketplace with a product that was technologically inferior to Apple's. However, IBM boldly not only allowed, but encouraged, anyone and everyone to write software for its operating system. Apple had maintained strict control over the totality of its product and kept its software proprietary. You know the result. In short order, there was a hundred times the software available for IBM's system as there was for Apple's. The customer decided that this was more important than Apple's technical edge. IBM took over the market, in large part due to its surprising software strategy.

## SURPRISE USUALLY INVOLVES SOME DEGREE OF RISK

Of course, employing surprise almost always involves risk. This is because surprise involves actions, which may be untested, may not have ever been done before, and may be considered foolish, or impossible. But the shrewd and successful strategist assesses the risks in the situation, and he does what he can to minimize them, swallows once or twice, then maintaining secrecy, forges ahead. He acts boldly.

On October 30, 1974, former heavyweight champion Muhammad Ali fought the then-champion George Foreman in Kinshasa, Zaire. Foreman had cut a fearsome path through the heavyweight ranks. He had knocked out most of his opponents in the early rounds, including a two-round annihilation of Ali's old adversary Joe Frazier the year before. Most people, in and out of boxing circles, gave Ali no chance. Foreman was eight years younger and much stronger than the former champ. Many thought Ali could be seriously injured by the power of Foreman's punches. If Ali had the slightest chance, it would be to use his foot speed to dance away from the larger man, not allowing Foreman to solidly connect.

Ali didn't run, and he didn't dance. Instead, he stunned the world and, more important, his opponent by staying in one place, letting Foreman pin him up against the ropes and throw punch after punch at him. None of the blows hit Ali's head, as he leaned way back over the ropes, but Foreman landed numerous punches to his midsection. Observers felt it was just a matter of time before Ali wore down from Foreman's barrage. Instead, it was Foreman, not used to such exertion and so certain of victory, who wore out.

Once it was obvious that Foreman had nothing left and could barely lift his arms to defend himself, Ali moved in for the kill, knocking Foreman out in the eighth round, the first time Foreman had ever been knocked down in the ring. Ali's surprising strategy not to evade Foreman's punches, instead letting Foreman wear himself out, came to be known as the "rope-a-dope." It was a convincing example of how the strategy of surprise can overcome a more powerful opponent.

## ▌ SECRECY IS ESSENTIAL

Surprise can only be achieved if your competition does not realize or understand what you are doing. This does not mean that you must forever maintain absolute secrecy about everything. It is only necessary that your competitor be kept in the dark long enough so that he cannot do anything to stop you from achieving the outcome you desire.

Strakosch's competitors knew what TechTarget was doing in dropping the fight for Web site customers. They just didn't understand why, until it was too late. By then, TechTarget had the money to stay afloat, and they did not.

Varro didn't know what Hannibal had in mind. His cavalry screened the actions on his flanks. He assumed that Hannibal's best troops were front and center. He assumed wrong. When Hannibal's center retreated, Varro thought he was winning. Not until the two flanks closed like large doors did he comprehend what Hannibal had done. At that point, it was too late to do anything at all, except fight it out at a tremendous disadvantage. Varro did and left most of his army dead on the battlefield.

## ▌ TOTAL SURPRISE IS UNNECESSARY

Even achieving total surprise isn't necessary. Again, it is only necessary that the surprise be such that the full significance of the action isn't grasped until it is too late for a competitor or adversary to do anything about it. This was brought home to me during some strategy research I did, looking at a personal, rather than an organizational, setting.

One of my respondents at the university told me this story. He had been an all-league swimmer in high school but could never quite beat one competitor from a rival school, who was league champion. However, in studying this "unbeatable" champion, he noticed that his time was directly related to how hard he was pushed by his competitors. When he competed against poor swimmers, he never had a particularly good time, even though he still always won.

My subject was a very strong finisher, maybe the best in his league, but was never quite good enough to nose out this champion after having gone all out in a race. So my research subject decided on an unexpected strategy. He would not go all out! At least, not at first. Instead, he would pace the champion, not push him. He would stay just far enough back to remain in striking distance, but in the number two position. However, just as they approached the race's finish, my research subject poured on the steam with every ounce of energy. It was totally unexpected, and he had actually bettered this "unbeatable" champion and handed him the only defeat of his career.

## IF YOU WOULD BECOME A HANNIBAL, ADOPT THESE FIVE CONCEPTS

If you want to be a Hannibal, or survive when the chips are down (as TechTarget did), use the principle of surprise to your advantage. Here are five ways you can accomplish this:

1. Do what is not usual.

2. Choose the least likely path.

3. Execute what has never been done before.

4. Opt for the impossible.

5. Change your pace.

### Do What Is Not Usual

We do some things a certain way year after year and never think about them. It is the usual way of doing things. Then, someone does things differently. These successful strategies get our attention because they work. And we wonder, "Why didn't I think of that?"

## Sushi, Anyone?

What started on the West Coast as a unique food preparation not for everyone soon spread across the country. At first, eating raw fish was seen as moderately repulsive. Then it seemed as if people everywhere were doing it. Creative thinkers soon rushed in to exploit the demand. Why not sell premade sushi through supermarkets? How hard could it be? After all, fresh raw fish is fresh raw fish, and rice balls are rice balls. People could enjoy sushi in the privacy of their own homes, and it could be guaranteed fresh.

Many supermarkets rushed in to cash in on the sushi bonanza. The competition included not only the other supermarkets, but also the sushi bars and restaurants that were already selling the Japanese product.

This proved to be easier said than done. Supermarket customers weren't buying, despite a clear price advantage. The more astute supermarket strategists did some research. They discovered two things. First, part of the reason for the success of the product was the atmosphere of the restaurant, complete with a grunting sushi master with razor-sharp knives. The supermarket strategists realized there wasn't much they could do about that. However, they'd faced the same obstacle with other specialty foods and overcome this disadvantage, so that aspect didn't disturb them.

There was another important factor in dealing with sushi, not true with other restaurant foods with which supermarkets competed. One half of the product component was fresh, raw fish, and the product was eaten in that state. Customers simply did not believe the supermarket product was as fresh, and, therefore, it could not be as good.

In Denver, Colorado, Brand Management Inc., a food-branding consultancy, was hired by a supermarket chain to convince potential customers that its take-home sushi was as good as what could be found in a sushi bar.

Led by Shultz Hartgrove, their president, the consultancy team struggled to come up with a solution. They conducted focus groups and went through intense, brainstorming sessions, all to no avail. Then, as recalled by Hartgrove, "My partner and I stopped at a local sushi bar, and every few minutes we'd hear a sushi chef shout out, 'Sushi ready!' to alert waitresses their order was ready."

With this in mind, Brand Management came up with three basic recommendations, which the supermarket chain followed. First, the product was branded by calling it "Sushi-Redi." Next, a sushi menu board (just like in a sushi bar) was hung in the stores. Finally, Sushi-

Redi ads were placed in the restaurant sections of local newspapers. The headline? "No reservations? No problem."

This latter recommendation was truly brilliant as it connected the supermarket's sushi directly to restaurant sushi and positioned it as being of equal quality. Doing what was not usual worked wonders against both of the supermarket chain's two main classes of competitors. It put Sushi-Redi head and shoulders above other brands of prepared sushi, and it took business away from sushi bar competitors, as well. The results were truly outstanding: a 30 percent increase in sales in the first six months.[3] This was an excellent example of doing what is not usual—pitting supermarkets directly against sushi bars, making sushi bar sushi available, without waiting, at a supermarket. ▪

## Choose the Least Likely Path

Everyone knows that there are certain ways we are supposed to do things. There are other ways, but no one does them. But, when we choose the least likely path, we can frequently surprise the competition, and our customers, and score a major victory.

### The Crazy Path to Distribution Success

In 1997 Eric Poses invented a board game called Loaded Questions. It tests players on how well they know each other. Every time Poses got people playing, they loved his game. So he founded his company, All Things Equal, Inc., and put the game into production. The only problem was he couldn't get distribution for it. And with no distribution, there were no sales.

This is a traditional problem with many small companies that produce new items that they must get to market. Their competitors, the major manufacturers, have their own sales forces, which dominate the market. To get to the consumers, small companies have to get to the retailers. To do this, they must go through one (or more) intermediary agents. However, even those independent distributors willing to carry the single line of a small company really can't spend a lot of time selling only one item. It's much more productive to sell the multiple, proven product lines of a major player. As a result of this situation, Poses' sales were just about zero. The competition was just too strong.

So Poses did something different. He took the least likely, totally inefficient, crazy path. He loaded his car with product and, over the next four months, took off from his Santa Monica, California, home base and drove all around the country visiting small retail stores, promoting and selling his games face-to-face, one or two at a time. He stopped at nothing. He sold products out of his car, performed in-store demos for customers, and even made many stops at campsites and coffee shops countrywide to get the word out. Amazingly, he was able to sell over 1,000 games this way. And his promotion paid off, too. He got media attention because of his crazy method of getting to market. Plenty of it. *BusinessWeek, The Wall Street Journal, USA Today,* and CNN were just a few of the media outlets that carried stories about him; his company; and, of course, his game, Loaded Questions. As a result, Toys "R" Us contacted him and ordered 6,500 games.

Poses even gained a unique differential advantage by his least attractive path. Says Poses: "Instead of just trying to work with a buyer to get the game on the shelves, I'm supporting sales by meeting with customers who are looking for a good board game. Now, from the thousands of products on the shelves, mine stands out."4

Flushed with success, he hit the road again and his sales kept growing. To date, he has sold $5 million in product while outperforming competition from some of the largest names in the business. Traveling 50,000 miles on the road may sound like the least likely path to successful distribution. No one, least of all his competitors, thought anyone was crazy enough to do it. But, apparently Eric Poses was, and it brought him success against all odds. Now his company has a product line of five games and All Things Equal continues to grow.5 ❚

## Execute What Has Never Been Done Before

If something has never been done before, it is unexpected. Maybe you should think about doing it.

### This Man Sold Land That No One Could Live On

A large construction company threatened to take over the land of a small farmer in Iowa. The company was building a highway, and it was easier to build directly through the farmer's property than to go around it. The farmer pleaded with the company. The rerouting was minimal. The farmer's lawyer told him that if his case were brought to trial, he would probably win. The problem was that this would cost money that the farmer didn't have, and there always was the chance that the construction company would win and the court would force the sale of the farmer's property for the public good.

The farmer may not have had the financial resources to bring the construction company to court, but he did know how to think, and he thought of something that hadn't been done before. The enterprising farmer subdivided a small, but strategically situated, portion of his land into one-inch-square lots. He sold as many of these miniature lots as he could at one dollar each to prospects he found through clever advertising. Now if the construction company wanted the land, it had to deal with and sue many different property owners, instead of just one. It decided to reroute the highway slightly to avoid the trouble. ∎

## Going Where No One Has Gone Before Brings Victory in Harlem

Some years ago, Calvin Copeland was making a living with a fast-food restaurant he had started in Harlem. His hard work led to success—a little too much success. Fast-food giant McDonald's perceived a major opportunity, and golden arches were built right next door to Copeland's establishment.

McDonald's probably assumed that any competition, like Copeland, would be driven elsewhere, or out of business. But Copeland thought about his problem, then applied the principle of surprise to contend with the king of the fast-food chains. He dropped the fast food, which had made him a success, and he concentrated on something that no one else, including McDonald's, had ever heard of—fast soul food. With his unusual concept of fast soul food, not only did Copeland hold his own against McDonald's, but his success led to the Reliable Restaurant chain, which soon grossed $2 million a year—about twice what he did in sales before McDonald's came on the scene. ∎

## Opt for the Impossible

Opting for the impossible means thinking outside the box and doing things in a way you, and your competitors, have not thought of previously. It means taking creative risks, and it may mean doing the previously unthinkable.

In my book *The Stuff of Heroes*, I gave the example of a great warrior who was also a scholarly professor, Joshua Lawrence Chamberlain, who, without question, opted for the impossible in battle. He did the unthinkable, and he taught hard-bitten veterans a lot about both uncommon commitment and using the principle of surprise as a strategy. Professor Chamberlain was teaching at Bowdoin College in Maine. Then, war came when Fort Sumter was fired on by Confederate forces in 1861. Chamberlain believed strongly in the Union cause, and he resolved to fight for it. He enlisted as a private in the Union Army. Soon afterward, he obtained a commission from the governor of Maine. Two years later, he was a colonel commanding the 20th Maine regiment in the Army of the Potomac.

On July 2, 1863, the 20th Maine was in the little town of Gettysburg, Pennsylvania. The battle fought there is one of the most famous and bloodiest battles in American history.

On the second day of fighting, the 20th Maine was assigned the mission of defending a wooded knoll known as Little Round Top. Little Round Top was located at the most strategically important position on the battlefield on the extreme left end of the Union line.

What the Federals didn't know was that Confederate general Robert E. Lee had concentrated some 15,000 battle-hardened troops, under Lieutenant General James "Old Pete" Longstreet, to attack precisely at that part of the Union line. If they could capture Little Round Top, the Confederate forces could move their artillery to the knoll and fire parallel along the unprotected Union line. That is called enfiladed fire, and it is deadly. They could then outflank the entire Union line and cut off the Union troops in the center and on the right from their line of supplies. Many military experts feel this action would have been decisive, and the United States would have lost the battle.

This battle occurred at a critical time. Because of previous Union defeats and other problems, the war had already become extremely controversial and divisive in the North. A good part of the country wanted to make peace with the Confederacy.

England awaited a single decisive Confederate victory to recognize the Confederate States of America as an independent country. Had Longstreet been successful on that hot July afternoon, it might not only have ended the battle, but the war. The United States might have been permanently divided.

Longstreet's corps attacked with great determination and ferocity led by the 15th Alabama, commanded by Colonel William Oates. The 20th Maine held their position. The Confederates charged Little Round Top again. Once more, the 20th Maine beat them back. However, ammunition was running low. Chamberlain hoped that the Southerners would not attack again. Both sides had suffered greatly. Many Confederate dead and wounded marked the route of their previous assaults. But once again, the Confederates attacked. After a gallant effort, they were again forced to retreat.

Chamberlain found that few of his troops had bullets left to shoot. They had no hope of resupply. There was nothing with which to defend Little Round Top against another Confederate onslaught.

Chamberlain's officers advised him to withdraw at once to prevent capture. Chamberlain looked around at his battle-weary troops. The 20th Maine had suffered many casualties. Many of the survivors were wounded. The situation was critical, and it seemed hopeless. Then, Chamberlain opted for the impossible. His surprise move changed history.

"Tell the men to fix bayonets," he ordered. His officers looked at him incredulously, but they carried out his orders. "Did the Colonel think he could scare off the attackers by merely a show of 'cold steel'?" they thought. "What did he have in mind?"

Chamberlain looked down the hill toward the Confederate lines. He could see that Longstreet's men were in the process of forming their ranks for yet another attack. Chamberlain again looked at his men. He pointed his saber at the grouping Confederates and commanded: "20th Maine . . . Charge!"

There is (and was) no tactics manual that advised an action like this. It was an impossible move. But, the 20th Maine charged down from Little Round Top with bayonets fixed on their mostly empty rifles. They yelled and screamed like madmen. The Confederates were totally surprised by this move. Recall Xenophon's words: "The less a thing has been foreseen, the more it frightens." Brave as they were, the Confederates fell back. Opting for the impossible, Joshua Chamberlain saved the entire battle of Gettysburg at this critical juncture.

Joshua Chamberlain was a remarkable leader. In very real terms, his spiritual use of the lesson of surprise substituted for physical bullets. He opted for the impossible and thought outside the box. He may be the only commander in history who ordered an attack with bayonets when he no longer could defend a position with bullets.

## Change Your Pace

Most strategists understand that performing much faster than a competitor expects can lead to success, and many will concede that the resulting surprises can paralyze a competitor and play an important part in achieving final success. But acting slower than expected can be just as surprising, and just as successful. This concept is less understood and less known.

There can be significant advantages to holding back and allowing a competitor to beat you to the marketplace. These include the following:

- Competitors who rush in are already committed to their previous investments. On the other hand, you can include the latest technological improvements in products and processes.

- You may be able to achieve greater economies of scale than competitors who went first because size of market and demand are more accurately established.

- You may be able to get better terms from suppliers, employees, or customers since your competitors will be locked into higher costs that were negotiated when the market was still at risk.

- You'll probably have lower research and development and marketing costs, with less of your resources wasted. So you'll have a better profit margin, and you can offer lower prices.

- You'll also be able to pick the weak link in your competitor's program at which to concentrate, and then attack.[6]

Peter Drucker recommends two strategies—"creative imitation" and "entrepreneurial judo"—which grow from this concept of doing the unexpected by changing your pace and intentional, or even unintentional, lateness to market.

**Creative Imitation.** Creative imitation is a notion thought up initially by Theodore Leavitt of Harvard. The idea is to imitate in substance, but to make better use of the original concept than the one initially introduced.[7] Several years ago, a number of books hit the market in two areas: fitness and sex. (Come to think of it, what's changed?) One of the most popular fitness titles was a book that made the *New York Times* bestseller list called *How to Flatten Your Stomach* by Coach Jim Overroad.

An entrepreneurial publisher by the name of Melvin Powers put the two, proven-demand concepts of fitness and sex books together in a single, humorous volume that he wrote in less than two days. He called it *How to Flatten Your Tush*, by Coach Marge Reardon. He sold 250,000 copies in less than six months.

**Entrepreneurial Judo.** In competitive judo, one of the basic strategies is to use your opponent's own force and aggression against him, turning it to your advantage by throwing him off balance. According to Peter Drucker, entrepreneurial judo means catapulting your company into a leadership position by sidestepping the competitor's strength after allowing it to make the first move. He cites the example of the transistor. Bell Labs developed it in 1947. Akio Morita, president of Sony, then flew to the United States and negotiated a license for only $25,000. Well-entrenched and larger companies in the United States had their own programs for this technology. They struggled on, thinking to achieve a higher profit margin with their own innovation. Two years later, the first Sony portable transistor radio entered the market, and within eight years, the Japanese had captured the radio market all over the world.[8]

| STRATEGIST'S LOG | DOING THE UNEXPECTED |
| --- | --- |

The principle of surprise has worked time and again across the ages in all walks of life. In the business arena, doing the unexpected can have a terrific impact on success, regardless of your company size, location, or the competitive situation. In fact, when combined with secrecy, speed, deception, originality, and audacity, doing the unexpected results in surprising your competitors to such an extent that it can decisively shift the balance of power in your favor. As a result, you can achieve a victory far out of proportion to the energy and effort expended.

To best use the principle of surprise, look for opportunities in the following areas:

- *Do something that is not usual.* A move unexpected by your competition will not only catch them by surprise, it will garner attention in the marketplace.

- *Take the least likely approach.* You don't have to just do things the way they've always been done. There are always alternative options.

- *Try something that's never been done before.* This doesn't mean to just throw all caution to the wind, attempting something with little chance of success. But if you weigh your options beforehand, you may find a totally new approach holds great promise.

- *Attempt the impossible.* Naturally, you can't do something that is literally "impossible." But, in many cases, you'll find that doing the previously unthinkable is well worth the risk.

- *Slow your pace by holding back and letting your competition go first.* There can be many substantial advantages for your company in allowing a competitor to beat you to the marketplace. ▍

## CHAPTER 6

# Keep Things Simple

*"The simplest moves are the best."*
—NAPOLEON BONAPARTE

*"To be simple is to be great."*
—RALPH WALDO EMERSON

The more clear and concise your strategic plan is, the easier it is to implement and the less that can go wrong along the way. In fact, the phrase "Keep it simple, stupid!" has now worked its way into virtually every aspect of life. But the first time I heard the phrase, it didn't come from an American corporate executive, a football coach, a software developer, or a political consultant. It was used by an Israeli general during an interview about the reasons for his recent victory against overwhelming odds.

In the spring of 1967, Egypt, Syria, and Jordan joined together "to liberate Palestine." In those days, the three countries made no bones about their intentions. They were going to destroy Israel and "throw the Jews into the sea." Jordan held the land today claimed by the Palestinians on the West Bank of the Jordan River. These Arab countries declared that the strip of land called Israel was actually Palestine, and Israel had no right to exist as a country. They announced that they intended to rectify that situation.

On the face of it, there was no doubt that the three Arab states could defeat the Israelis and eradicate their country, exactly as they threatened to do. The combined standing armies of the three Arab countries were several times the size of Israel's. They outnumbered the Israelis in planes, tanks, artillery, and ships. Moreover, the Arabs boasted first-line MIG fighters from the Soviet Union. Israel flew mostly older aircraft bought from many sources. The only U.S. aircraft Israel owned were relics from World War II.

Russian advisers were embedded in both the Egyptian and Syrian armies. Until only a few years before, a British general had commanded the Jordanian Army, which still had embedded British Army advisers. The Jordanians used recently manufactured British equipment and aircraft. Jordan's King Hussein had attended Sandhurst, England's West Point.

With heavy financial backing from the oil-rich Arab states, the three Arab allies faced an Israel that had little capital and a population of only a few million people. All things considered, Israel was likely to be overwhelmed.

There was sympathy in America for Israel, but officially the United States remained neutral. Interviewed by American media, King Hussein stated that if the United States prevented the three Arab countries from doing "this thing," the Americans would forever be enemies of the Arab people. Nevertheless, the United States did try to persuade the Arabs not to attack, and it attempted to get the United Nations (UN) to help. American diplomats achieved little success. U Thant, then secretary-general of the UN, ordered troops to withdraw from the Sinai desert, which separated Israel and Egypt. This permitted the Egyptian armies to move in and advance right up to the Israeli border. With a large caucus of Arab countries now in the UN, it appeared that this organization, which in 1948 had voted to support the establishment of Israel, now intended to support its destruction. President Lyndon Johnson instructed U.S. government agencies to begin planning how to handle whatever Israeli refugees survived the inevitable Arab onslaught.

On June 4, everything changed. The Israeli Armed Forces launched a preemptive attack that took their enemies completely by surprise. The Israeli Air Force spearheaded the assault by striking the vastly superior enemy air forces at their bases, destroying most of the Arab planes while they were still on the ground. From the first day, Israel dominated the skies, and this helped it to win a decisive victory on all fronts.

The resulting Six-Day War was an incredible turnaround, with repercussions that continue to this day. Since 1967, Israel has been seen as the dominant military power in the Middle East. As a result of the war, Israel not only fended off its attackers, but it also occupied lands belonging to Egypt, Syria, and Jordan. Israel refused to return this land except in exchange for a peace treaty. Syria has still never signed a peace treaty with Israel. Such a treaty was eventually signed with Egypt in 1979, and the lands captured from Egypt were returned. Many years later, in 1994, Jordan also signed a peace treaty with Israel, but it did not want the West Bank returned. Jordan had itself previously expelled Yasser Arafat and his armed forces from the same territory in 1972. Jordan now declared that the West Bank belonged to the Palestinians, and essentially told Israel to work out its problems with the Palestinians on its own.

The world was amazed. How did Israel accomplish such a feat? Military analysts from many countries poured over maps and studied the war, particularly the air attack that gave Israel air superiority over the battlefield from the first day. What highly sophisticated, well-rehearsed, and complex plan could enable the tiny country of Israel to defeat its far more powerful, wealthier, better-armed, and more numerous foes?

The U.S. military, at the time bogged down in the Vietnam War, questioned Major General Motti Hod, then commander of the Israeli Air Force, about this wonderful plan and sophisticated strategy. What were the components? How did Israel integrate and coordinate all the elements? What were the secrets of the perfect timing and coordination? Hod responded that while they did have a plan, it was simple. Identify the proper targets, take off, keep your mouth shut, and hit the enemy as hard as you can. "We have a motto in the Israeli Air Force," he said. "It is 'Keep it simple, stupid!' And that's what we did."

## SIMPLICITY APPLIES TO BUSINESS STRATEGY

The concept of simplicity is just as valid in planning business strategy as it is in conducting military campaigns. An analysis conducted by the prestigious Booz Allen Hamilton consulting firm showed that in one industry after another, large traditional companies faced the identical problem: overcomplicating their business. The strategies they developed to run their businesses had become so complex that profit margins had almost disappeared. Naturally, this left them vulnerable. As these previous market leaders struggled under the burdens of the complicated business models they themselves had devised, smaller, nimbler competitors with less complex strategies swallowed up market share by meeting customer needs at a lower cost.

According to the Booz Allen Hamilton analysis, this is best illustrated by the large U.S. hub–and–spoke airlines. As a result of their complex strategies, it costs these carriers twice as much per seat mile as low-cost carriers to complete a 500-mile flight. This is because their solution to the goal to take anyone anywhere led them to massive physical infrastructures, fleets of dissimilar models of aircraft, expensive information systems, and large pools of labor.[1]

 ## KEEP IT SIMPLE, STUPID!

Whatever actions strategists decide upon must ultimately be implemented, or nothing happens. But the more elements that make up each action, the greater the likelihood that one or more will fail. The National Aeronautics and Space Administration (NASA) once noted that if every single part in one of their space systems was 99.9 percent reliable, they couldn't launch it because the overall reliability would be less than 50 percent! That's because of the huge number of necessary parts and the resultant complexity of the overall system. The 2003 space shuttle *Columbia* disaster proved once again that in a complex system, it doesn't take much to cause everything to go awry and fail completely.

If the actions you must take to implement a strategy are overly complex, you may have difficulty keeping them straight. Others may have difficulty following their part of the plan. The more complex the plan, the more problems can crop up. Complexity has caused many brilliantly designed plans to fail when executed. Thus, simplicity itself is powerful and compelling.

Failure to incorporate the principle of keeping plans simple has caused failures in all fields of human endeavor. An entrepreneur lost a multimillion-dollar contract to a competitor even though he was the inventor of the product, and he held patent protection on it. His complex pricing formula resulted in his costing an order for thousands of units of his product at the same rate at which he sold a unit one at a time! This drove the customer, which happened to be the U.S. government, to do business with a competitor that could supply the product for 60 percent less. The U.S. government doesn't enforce patents. That's up to the individual who holds the rights to the patent. Although a lawsuit was possible, the entrepreneur's attorney advised him that even if his patent were declared valid in the courts and he won his case, the award would be based on a percentage of the price paid, not his price. As a result, his award would be less than the cost of the legal action.

## Your Author Fails Pricing 101

I must confess that at one time I fell victim to a similar error in pricing. Increasingly, corporations and professional associations had called upon me to give speeches. At first, I had a simple pricing system based on the length of the speech. However, I had read an article in an academic journal that had developed a sophisticated pricing model for services. In my enthusiasm to be on the cutting edge, I decided to implement the model. As I recall, this required quite a few entry variables, which considered not only the length of the speech, but the number of attendees, the size of the organization, annual sales, etc.

In any case, I prepared myself to use the model, and I tried several examples. They seemed to work. The next time I received a call about speaking and was questioned about my fee, I was ready to show what a sophisticated guy I was. I asked for the required variables, plugged them into the model, and before I stopped to consider the results, I reported them to the caller. There was a stunned silence on the other end of the line. The amount I had quoted was so low that it was a joke. My would-be client finally gasped something about "having the wrong Dr. Cohen." She hung up. I tried some more examples and realized that the model may have worked well for some service businesses, but not for professional speaking engagements. I returned to my former method of pricing. ▮

## KEEPING THE MESSAGE SIMPLE

Most people, even professionals, don't read textbooks, even though they are much more comprehensive than regular books, and even though almost every statement in these books is both thoroughly researched and documented. Why don't people read them? Instead of making these books easy to understand, many textbook authors actually make them more difficult. Why? Perhaps this is because of the belief that if material is difficult to understand, it must contain something of substance.

Students rarely agree with this kind of assessment. Complicated textbooks are both difficult to comprehend and more difficult to apply to practice. But students have little choice. Others (authors and publishers) make the decisions. Not so in the real world. That's probably why one of the most popular management books of all time is about as far removed from being a textbook as it could possibly be, with a simple, easy-to-follow message, large type, and only about 100 pages. The book is

*The One Minute Manager* by Kenneth Blanchard and Spencer Johnson (New York: William Morrow, 1982). Since its publication, this book has sold over seven million copies. There are hundreds of textbooks on the same subject. They contain much more information, but they are lucky to sell a few thousand copies each, and probably wouldn't sell that many if it were up to the students who are required to buy them.

## SIMPLICITY IS VITAL FOR ALL SUCCESS

This essential strategy principle demanding simplicity is itself quite simple. It is also vital for success. You can see the importance of simplicity in the coaching of team sports. I was amazed to hear about (or read) in the biography of almost every highly successful coach in every single sport that each and every one of them seemed to emphasize a single characteristic in their coaching. They believed in focusing not on fancy, complicated plays, or on complex moves by their players, but on the fundamentals. They insisted that their players practice the fundamentals over and over and over again. In other words, all of these coaches believed the same thing: The road to victory was founded not on the complex, but on the simple. It was their version of "Keep it simple, stupid!"

### Superior Web Design Strategy

Several years ago *Inc. Magazine* announced the winners of its annual competition for best Web site design. In an article announcing the results, *Inc.* said, "Effective Web design is not about creating flashy graphics and piling on the features. The best sites appreciate the value of simplicity."

Three entirely different Web site entrants took top honors in the design category that year. And very different they were. Yet all shared the common characteristic of simplicity.

One, a scooter manufacturer and retailer from New Hampshire, got the nod from the judges by creating a strong brand image and an easy-to-use format. In Massachusetts, a "techie" information portal for network-storage professionals received top marks, primarily because of its clear organization. The third top winner was a ceramics wholesaler located in Boulder. Judges liked the wholesaler's warm color palette and minimalist display of its product line in its online catalog.

These were all very different companies with different products, in different industries, and with different objectives. But according to *Inc.*, all three had the same philosophy when it came to creating a Web site. "Each followed the golden rule of Web design: "Keep it simple."[2]

*Inc. Magazine* needed only to add the additional word "stupid" to be completely in accord with what General Hod had said about Israel's victory in 1967. ▪

## HOW TO KEEP YOUR STRATEGY SIMPLE

The secret of keeping your strategy simple can be summarized by only four (simple) actions. These are:

1. Minimize the major actions and organizations you must coordinate.

2. Develop simple organizational relationships.

3. Simplify your directives and orders.

4. Avoid complex actions or solutions.

### *Minimize the Major Actions and Organizations You Must Coordinate*

One of the major military disasters that the United States has suffered in the last fifty years had a clear objective; well-led, superbly trained troops that were totally committed to the outcome; technologically superior equipment; and the advantage of surprise. Yet, the operation was a complete disaster, not only in failing to achieve the objective, but in the American lives that were lost. A failure to keep things simple was the major cause for failure. The operation I speak of was "Eagle Claw"—the attempt to rescue the American hostages in Iran.

**Iran Takes American Hostages.** On November 4, 1979, more than 3,000 Iranian militant "students" stormed the U.S. Embassy in Tehran, Iran. They occupied it and took sixty-six Americans hostage. After months of fruitless attempts at negotiation, President Jimmy Carter ordered the United States armed forces to implement a rescue.

The plan was an extremely complex, two-night operation involving all four military services—Army, Navy, Air Force, and Marines—and a variety of equipment and techniques, some of which had never been tried before. The Army's contribution alone included members of three different special operation commands: Delta Force, Special Forces, and Rangers.

The Army rescue team was to be brought into action with a combination of eight RH-53D Navy helicopters, flown by Marines and launched from the carrier USS *Nimitz* in the Arabian Gulf, and Air Force C-130 transport aircraft from the country of Oman.

The staging area for the assault was in the Iranian desert. It was known as Desert One. The C-130s would refuel the helicopters at Desert One. Then the rescue team would embark on the same helicopters, which would fly forward to hide in areas about fifty miles outside Tehran. That action in itself—desert flying at night, landing right "on the deck," and using special goggles which had never been used previously—would have been quite a trick. Remote refueling from C-130s in the middle of the desert had also never been tried before. And there was the fact that the marines would not fly their own helicopters, on which they had maintained and practiced the difficult flight techniques for some months in the United States. Instead, they were to fly unfamiliar helicopters provided by the Navy. They knew none of each helicopter's individual quirks and idiosyncrasies.

The next day, prepositioned American intelligence agents would drive the Army team to the embassy in trucks. The rescuers would disembark and launch a surprise attack on the embassy, rescue the hostages, and move them to a nearby soccer stadium. The helicopters would pick up the rescue team and hostages at the stadium and evacuate them to Manzariyeh Air Base, about forty miles southeast of Tehran.

Meanwhile, MC-130s, a specialized version of the C-130, would fly Army Rangers and Air Force combat controllers into Manzariyeh. The Rangers would capture the airfield and hold it for the evacuation. At the same time, AC-130Hs, a gunship version of the C-130, would fly cover over the embassy and the airfield to provide ground support against resistance encountered. Finally, C-141s, another larger Air Force transport would arrive at Manzariyeh to fly the hostages and rescue team to safety.

That was the plan. Pretty neat, huh? It was almost as if the plan were designed to be as complex and unwieldy as possible, with as many different organizations, which had never worked together before, involved. To work, everything had to work perfectly. Of course, with so many possibilities of things that could go awry, bad things were bound to happen.

They did. The helicopters ran into a blinding sandstorm. As a result, they were six hours late at Desert One, and the pilots were greatly fatigued from their experience. Moreover, one helicopter had to be abandoned in the desert due to mechanical failure. Another had to return to the *Nimitz*. On the ground, the troops first ran into a bus and had to take forty-four passengers prisoner. Then, an Iranian tanker truck approached and had to be destroyed. It was soon discovered that a smaller truck followed it, and before anyone could stop this truck, it got away.

Surprise was compromised, but it was decided to proceed anyway. The six remaining helicopters were refueled. As one prepared for take-off, it was discovered that it had hydraulic problems. It wouldn't be able to make the next leg of the journey.

Earlier, planners had calculated that they needed a minimum of six helicopters to complete the mission. They now had only five. The decision was made to abort the mission. In the poor visibility and confusion of unloading the fuel, packing up and getting out, a helicopter collided with an EC-130, yet another specialized version of the C-130 aircraft. Both the EC-130 and the helicopter burst into flame. Eight Americans died.[3,4]

Another rescue mission was planned almost immediately, but was called off before it was executed. However, with a private mission under the command and with the planning of one retired Army Special Forces colonel (Colonel "Bull" Simmons), Ross Perot managed to extract a couple of his employees successfully from an Iranian jail. This was done without the tremendous resources of the U.S. military. You've got to keep it simple.

## Develop Simple Organizational Relationships

We noted Booz Allen Hamilton's analysis of the woes of the airline industry earlier. Here's how one Canadian airline company simplified strategy. Many consider Bill Lamberton, vice president of marketing and sales at WestJet Airlines Ltd., to be Canada's number-one salesman. But Lamberton is actually more than a salesman. As a key member of the top executive team, Lamberton runs the department that designs the low-fare airline's route network and then figures out how to sell its service to the masses. In essence, his department determines the company's strategy and its tactics: where WestJet should fly, how often it should fly, and what prices it should charge.

Lamberton's marketing and sales department is unique because it incorporates functions typically performed by corporate strategists, be they planners or line managers. According to Lamberton, this organizational relationship provides a vital link between the research involved in identifying a new destination and the subsequent creative task of marketing it (for example, promoting WestJet as the low-fare leader in a new market). Lamberton refers to the two tasks, the first more strategic, and the second more tactical, as the "hardball" and "softball" functions of his department. It's a simple way to plan and implement strategy, and it works.

As proof of the value of this simple, but effective organizational relationship, WestJet is growing by about 50 percent a year. Its operating margin for 2002 was 12.7 percent, the third highest of any independent carrier in North America. Moreover, while most airlines in both the United States and Canada were losing money, WestJet recently posted its twenty-fourth consecutive quarter of profitability. Lamberton knows intuitively that a major key to the success of his strategy is its simplicity. He sums it up this way, "Good fares, good service, and good routings."[5]

## A Simple Purchasing Change Saves Harley-Davidson

Harley-Davidson is an American icon. For a hundred years, The Harley-Davidson Motor Company's motorcycles have roared across America's highways and byways. Hollywood recognized the company's preeminence. Marlon Brando and Peter Fonda played "wild ones" or "easy riders" on Harleys in the movies. However, in the early 1980s, the company was in severe straits and fighting for survival. Competition from Japan was growing exponentially, and it had become staggering. At the same time, the company's engineering expertise had been allowed to atrophy, and they simply weren't able to develop the products that customers wanted at a price they were prepared to pay. Sales plummeted as customers looked elsewhere for their bikes. And economic conditions didn't help. Inflation was high. Unemployment was high. Interest rates were high. It wasn't all that clear that Harley-Davidson would make it.

According to Jeff Bleustein, chairman and CEO, "We spent a lot of time putting together our business process, our values, issues, mission statement, all those things we believe in. We wanted to get everyone pointed in the same direction." But the real key was a new and simpler relationship with the company's suppliers. A close examination of the engineering department revealed a system in which the developmental engineer did his own purchasing. He would have to survey the supply base, identify a supplier who could best make the parts, and then confirm that the supplier had the needed technical capabilities to support the design. However, these engineers had neither the training, nor the experience, nor the time to act as buyers. They frequently picked suppliers that were good at innovation, but lousy at producing in high volume, or at keeping to a delivery schedule. The company suffered mightily.

So Harley-Davidson changed all that by simply assigning a specialist with the title of purchasing engineer to do all the buying and to handle these relationships. Soon, everything began to turn around. CEO Bleustein describes it as adopting beneficial relationships with Harley-Davidson's suppliers and taking a strategic approach to purchasing. But, no matter what you call it, the effects of this simple change have been dramatic.

In one year, the production of Harley-Davidson motorcycles increased by 17.5 percent; earnings were showing a compound annual growth rate of 37 percent; and consolidated revenues grew 18.8 percent, to $2.45 billion.[6]

In 2000, *Purchasing Magazine* awarded the company its Medal of Professional Excellence, and in 2002 shareholders realized a 242 percent return on their investment.[7] ▐

## Simplify Your Directives and Orders

To implement any strategy, you must communicate it to those who are going to execute it. This means that you must communicate your strategy so that it can be easily understood. This is especially important under pressures of time, competition, and limited resources. It doesn't take rocket science to understand that you must keep it simple. Yet, many directives on strategy seem to be so complex that even well-experienced, highly educated managers and workers can't understand them. If they cannot understand them, they cannot execute them properly. Conversely, communicating your intentions clearly and simply can have a major impact on their successful execution.

### Simple Communication Critical in the Hotel Industry

An article in *Hotel and Motel Management* reported that simple communication is one of the most important considerations when planning and developing extended-stay properties. Of course, zoning laws, which vary from location to location, are critical, but simple communication is vital in order that those who have the authority to approve your concept understand what you are trying to do.

The problem is that some city and county leaders almost routinely deny or limit building permits for extended-stay hotels. Why? Although more apparent than real, there are concerns that the units will bring more crime and transient individuals to the area. Nevertheless, convincing civic leaders isn't rocket science. Simply communicating with those who have the power is all it takes.

Says Jim Anhut, senior vice president of Six Continents Hotel's Staybridge Suites and president of the Extended Stay Lodging Council of the American Hotel & Lodging Association:

> Communication is key . . . for anyone considering building extended-stay in a municipality. . . . Do your due diligence on the people who make that decision [whether to approve or not]. . . . Educate them: "Here's who we are, what we're trying to do, our enterprise, and our track record and history." Sometimes it's easy for people to make a negative decision about something they don't understand very well.[8] ❚

## Avoid Complex Actions or Solutions

Strategists who go for the complex over the simple make things more difficult for themselves and others. This approach is almost invariably counterproductive. In an interview with an *IndustryWeek* editor, Gwendolyn Galsworth, who heads Quality Methods International, a Dayton, Ohio–based consulting firm, called simplicity "the wave of the future" and "the coming revolution."

Of course, success strategists have known about the principle of simplicity for thousands of years. Nevertheless, demonstrating that we must frequently relearn what we already know, Galsworth devoted an entire, much-needed book to the concept. In *Smart Simple Design* (Wiley, 1994), Galsworth gave an outrageous example of product variety, certainly a viable strategy as a general concept, but in this case, gone mad. During a sales slump, one automobile manufacturer offered customers 87 different styles of steering wheels, 300 ashtrays, 437 dashboard meters, 1,200 carpets, and 110 possible radiator models. Sales declined even further.

According to Galsworth, some companies, attempting to build their reputations on providing the widest possible choice to customers, often create nightmares in their management information systems (MIS), production systems, and in everything else. "Even when hot new products give a company an unassailable market presence, the same products can produce soaring cost, complication, and confusion inside its walls," she said.[9]

Years ago, as a neophyte entrepreneur, I read every book I could lay my hands on as I attempted to master the rudiments of selling directly from an advertisement. I was amazed to discover that one book (written more than seventy years earlier) had urged marketers to resist the temptation to give customers too many options, or to attempt to promote too many different products in a single advertisement. The author maintained that such an approach would only confuse the prospect and reduce sales in response to the ad. "Focus on a single product with only a couple of options, and promote the heck out of it," he recommended. Others writing on direct-marketing methods recommended the same approach. The strategy was to create a satisfied customer by first promoting one product, then sending her a catalog with other offers and selling similar and ancillary products.

The key is to avoid complex actions or solutions, no matter their form.

| STRATEGIST'S LOG | KEEPING THINGS SIMPLE |

In any field, overly complicated plans often fall apart due to their own complexity. The age-old strategic principle of keeping things simple works equally well on the battlefield, in sports contests, in the corporate boardroom, on the factory floor, in sales and marketing, and in every other human endeavor,

Strive to keep things simple, and you'll be pleased with the results. Your people will be better able to follow your plan. And the simpler the strategy, the fewer variables there are to go bad.

To simplify your strategic plan, follow these four actions in developing your strategy:

1. *Start by minimizing the major actions and organizations you must coordinate.* The less complicated your overall plan, the better its chance for success.

2. *Establish simple, clear-cut organizational relationships.* Trying to figure out the corporate structure at some companies is like trying to read hieroglyphics. This is a recipe for disaster.

3. *Make sure your orders will be easily understood by those who must implement them.* If your strategic directives cannot be understood, they cannot be executed properly—especially when you throw in the pressures of time, competition, and limited resources.

4. *Seek simple solutions to whatever problems arise.* In every area of competition—warfare, politics, sports, business, etc.—success goes to the leaders who find simple solutions to complex problems.

And, above all else, remember to "keep it simple, stupid!" ❚

## CHAPTER 7

# Prepare Multiple, Simultaneous Alternatives

*"If thou wilt take the left hand, then I will go to the right; or if thou depart to the right, then I will go to the left."*

GENESIS 13:9

*"To achieve victory we must as far as possible make the enemy blind and deaf by sealing his eyes and ears, and drive his commanders to distraction by creating confusion in their minds."* —MAO TSE-TUNG

There is a famous story in game theory known as "The Prisoner's Dilemma." It goes something like this. Two men are caught after committing a mugging. The district attorney (D.A.) knows that these two men are guilty. They were arrested in the vicinity of the crime with the victim's wallet. They fit the description of the robbers. They both have done time in jail for similar crimes. Unfortunately, the victim fails to correctly identify either in a police lineup.

The D.A. goes to one robber and offers him a deal. If he will identify the other man as the one who committed the crime, he will be rewarded with release (since he himself has not been positively identified). His partner, of course, will go to jail.

The prisoner is left alone to consider the offer. If he does nothing, both he and his partner stand a chance of being convicted and going to jail. If he identifies the other man as a thief, at least he will go free, even though his accomplice will go to jail. He is about to accept this alternative, when he realizes that the D.A. has used a strategy of multiple, simultaneous alternatives. It is likely that the D.A. has made the same offer to his partner! If both identify each other as involved in the theft, they will both go to jail. If he does not identify his partner as a robber and his partner identifies him, he will go to jail and his partner will go free. The D.A., a clever strategist, has arranged things so that he wins, no matter what the thieves do.

## EVERY STRATEGY NEEDS MULTIPLE, SIMULTANEOUS ALTERNATIVES

Suppose you're going to drive to the store to pick up some groceries. At the corner where you turn to get to the store, there's been an accident. Emergency vehicles and police cars are blocking the road, and nobody can get past. Do you turn around and go back home? Of course not! You know several different ways to get to the store. You simply take an alternate route to avoid the accident scene. Or, you can go to a different store.

We've all heard the old clichés of going to the "backup" plan, or having to switch to "Plan B" when things go wrong. Unfortunately, these expressions are often used humorously—indicating that there is no backup plan, or that Plan B is an impossibility. But the truth is, to be successful, every strategy, no matter how good, should have multiple alternatives operating at the same time.

Doesn't this principle fly in the face of principle 6 (Keep things simple)? Not at all. Each of your alternative approaches can be just as simple as your overall strategy. You're just giving yourself more than one way to succeed.

## WHY MULTIPLE ALTERNATIVES ARE NEEDED

Every strategy should incorporate alternative, simultaneous approaches to reach an overall goal or objective. These may be alternative approaches or alternative, intermediary objectives. Multiple alternatives are necessary for four reasons:

1. Things rarely go as planned.

2. Competitors are always out to get you.

3. Your main effort isn't working as well as you had planned.

4. Maximum effort can mean maximum impact.

## Things Rarely Go as Planned

Some would say that things never go exactly as planned. Every strategist encounters roadblocks. Unexpected obstacles appear. People do things that you never imagined they would. The weather gets in the way. A planned alternative approach allows the strategist the flexibility to continue toward the goal without a major delay. You can see this conceptually in Figure 7-1.

### Figure 7-1

---

ON THE ROAD TO REACHING AN OBJECTIVE, THE STRATEGIST WILL
ENCOUNTER ROADBLOCKS

---

*Roadblocks are a fact of life for strategists. Expect the unexpected. Humans are often unpredictable, so the human factor must be considered. Weather can be an influencing factor. Economies can take unanticipated turns. A planned, alternative approach allows the strategist the flexibility of continuing toward the goal without a major delay.*

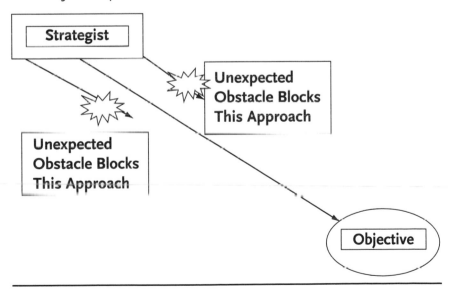

## Trouble Getting Started

Nicole Dionne had just eight months of experience in the sound design industry. She was only twenty-six years old and was employed by a company that creates sounds to fit the moods of commercial advertisements on TV and trailers that advertise movies. She had some radical new ideas for improving the business, so she put together a thirty-page business plan. When her boss ignored her plan, she took an alternative approach for which she had already prepared and laid the groundwork. She and a partner, who was an expert on the technical side, left the company to implement the plan themselves.

Unfortunately, the required funds were more than she had anticipated. So she approached venture capitalists, dozens of them. Many venture capitalists won't touch a start-up. A few that she talked to said they would, but they wanted 60 percent of the profits and total control of her business. Dionne didn't want that. Fortunately, she had taken another, simultaneous approach.

Nicole's alternative approach was to obtain a small business loan. She contacted sixty banks from all over the country. Most told her that she had to be in business for two years and have collateral. She had neither. So she and her partner put a third alternative into motion. They cashed in their retirement plans, emptied their savings accounts, and together came up with about $30,000. It still wasn't enough, but at this point luck intervened. Someone recommended a specific loan officer at an unknown bank. This bank loaned her an additional $30,000, and she and her partner were set to go. Within three months, she paid off the loan.

Eight months later, Nicole was able to expand the fledgling business into a music company with a 4,000-square-foot studio in a good location. She won two Clio awards (the "Oscar" of the advertising industry). Within two years, she was considered tops in the field, and her company's annual sales exceeded $1 million.[1] ❚

## Selling to Two Different Markets

Upjohn, once a well-known chemical company—now a part of Pfizer, Inc.—dominated the market with a medicine that cured mastitis in cattle. Because there were dangers in its use, the drug was distributed only through veterinarians. After several years of development, the company came up with a new product that not only provided a cure, but also could be given safely to bovine patients by anyone. This meant a considerably larger potential market since Upjohn would be able to sell the product not only to veterinarians, but also directly to farmers and cattlemen through feed stores.

Fortunately, Upjohn strategists decided on an alternative, simultaneous approach, because they encountered serious, unexpected resistance to the product from veterinarians (who no longer had an exclusive on the cure) and unforeseen problems due to their own inexperience in selling direct to farmers and cattlemen. Sales of the new medicine were a fraction of those of the product it had replaced, despite the fact that the potential sales were so much larger.

The alternative approach Upjohn used was to simultaneously introduce a drug that was similar chemically, but sold under a different name. This "different" product was reserved exclusively for veterinarians, and it allowed the company to retain its historic market while learning to sell to the farmers and cattlemen. ▪

## Competitors Are Always Out to Get You

Sometimes the situation can be even worse. The strategist encounters both unexpected environmental obstacles and a competitor concentrates his resources against the planned, primary approach of the strategist. An alternative, simultaneous approach permits immediate refocusing on the part of the strategist to go straight on to his objective (see Figure 7-2).

A more sophisticated method of dealing with competitors, using multiple, simultaneous alternatives is to position a competitor on the "horns of a dilemma." That means that no matter what the competitor does, he suffers negative consequences. Positioning the competition in this way is an elegant action in any competitive situation. That's what Hannibal did to Varro at Cannae. No matter what Varro did, he was likely to lose, even with superior resources, because Hannibal had prepared alternative actions. Had Varro chosen one approach, Hannibal would have selected another. The results would have been the same and resulted in Varro's defeat. Having our competitor on the horns of a dilemma is always an outstanding position to be in. As shown in Figure 7-3, if the objective is not your final goal, you can also have an alternative objective.

*Figure 7-2*

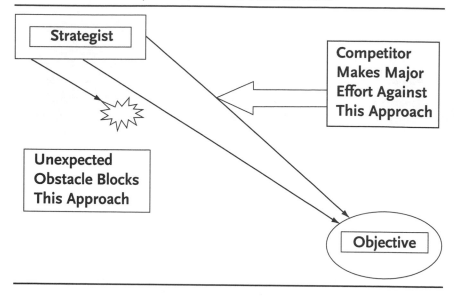

AN ALTERNATIVE SIMULTANEOUS APPROACH PERMITS IMMEDIATE REFOCUSING, SO THE STRATEGIST CAN GO ON TO HIS OBJECTIVE, DESPITE COMPETITION.

Strategist

Competitor Makes Major Effort Against This Approach

Unexpected Obstacle Blocks This Approach

Objective

## A Mail-Order House Puts a Competitor on the Horns of a Dilemma

Drew Allen Kaplan, president of DAK, a mail-order house selling electronics products, found a radar detector in Korea called Maxon, which he could buy and sell at less than 50 percent of the price of the biggest name company that produced radar detectors. Moreover, with a little testing, he discovered that in performance the Maxon could equal, or exceed, the pricier model sold by the large company.

Of course, Kaplan could have simply promoted his product at a much lower price than this expensive model and let it go at that. Instead, he decided to put this bigger company on the horns of a dilemma. He did this by challenging this company to a performance test. At first, he was ignored. Then, as Kaplan turned up the heat with magazine interviews, this large company found itself on the horns, as Kaplan intended. If they didn't accept his challenge, they looked as if they agreed that their product was not only more expensive, but inferior technically. That way DAK would continue to score points in the market. If the other company accepted DAK's challenge and lost . . . well, it was a losing situation no matter what they did.

*Figure 7-3*

## HOW MULTIPLE ALTERNATIVES CAN POSITION OUR COMPETITORS ON THE "HORNS OF A DILEMMA"

*No matter what our competitor does, he suffers negative consequences when multiple alternatives are deployed. Note that this can also be accomplished with an alternative objective.*

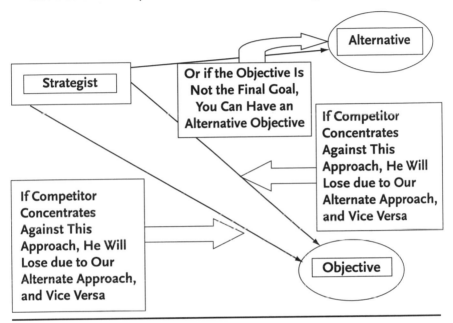

The bigger company's model may have been built better and been more reliable overall, but DAK's challenge only addressed the performance issue. We can Monday-morning quarterback the situation and suggest that the large company should have made a counterchallenge. But even that action would have given DAK more free publicity. ∎

**How Lincoln Put Douglas on the Horns of a Dilemma.** We looked at Abraham Lincoln's application of the lesson of commitment in Chapter 1. However, there is more to that story. Lincoln was an expert strategist. That's probably why he was ultimately successful in becoming president and saving the Union. He gave the impression that he just sat, uncaring one way or another, and let things happen before reacting. This was patently untrue. His law partner, Billy Herndon said, "That man who thinks that Lincoln sat calmly down and gathered his robes about him, waiting for people to call him, has a very erroneous knowledge of Lincoln. He was always calculating and always planning ahead."[2]

Moreover, Lincoln was a master at positioning his adversary on the horns of a dilemma. He demonstrated this repeatedly in his senatorial campaign against Stephen Douglas in 1858. George B. McClellan, later a Union general, but then chief engineer of the Illinois Central Railroad, favored Douglas. He put a railroad car at Douglas's disposal at no cost. This put Lincoln at a big financial disadvantage.

However, Lincoln came up with a strategy. He got Douglas's train schedule and bought his own ticket, usually on the same train. Douglas got the crowds together and spoke at each stop. Lincoln managed to speak almost immediately thereafter to the crowds that Douglas had drawn! In this way, Douglas was put on the horns of a dilemma. He could stop speaking, or put up with Lincoln's following him around and challenging his every word. Clearly, Douglas couldn't stop. So Lincoln followed him and spoke after him—relentlessly.

Lincoln's strategy gave Douglas an additional problem. Lincoln wanted to debate. Douglas did not. Douglas was the incumbent and well known. Lincoln was unknown in many districts. It wasn't in Douglas's interest to debate. However, once again, Lincoln had forced Douglas's hand. Lincoln's follow-up speeches were thrashing him, and he had little chance to respond. At least, he reasoned, he would get this opportunity with debates. So Douglas agreed to debate in the seven districts where the men had yet to speak.

Lincoln, however, had not yet finished using this principle of strategy. During the debates he asked Douglas, "Can the people of a United States Territory, in any lawful way . . . exclude slavery from its limits prior to the formation of a State Constitution?" Lincoln was thinking ahead. If Douglas answered "No," it could cost him the Free-Soil voters of Illinois. If he answered "Yes," he was sure to be rejected by the South in the future presidential election of 1860. Douglas apparently decided that one election in hand was worth two a couple of years down the road. Douglas answered, "Yes." He won the senatorial election in 1858, but Lincoln won the presidential election of 1860 because Douglas had hurt himself on the horns of a dilemma.[3]

## Your Main Effort Isn't Working as Well as You Had Planned

The principle of multiple, simultaneous alternatives also teaches us to be flexible in how we reach our objective, even as our objective remains constant. If the strategy we are employing is not working, or not working as well as it should, it is foolish to continue it. We must find another way. It pays to have alternatives ready to go.

## The More Radical Alternative Wins Out

A Californian company, Sierra Engineering Company, developed a valve required for oxygen-breathing masks used by pilots in the U.S. Air Force. The valve specifications had very high tolerances, so high that it was clear that normal quality control methods would be obsolete.

The company's strategy for meeting this challenge was one of multiple, simultaneous approaches. The first approach could be termed the standard one. It focused on how many valves selected at random from each batch would need to be tested to ensure that the entire batch, consisting of thousands of valves, were within tolerance. To do this, the production process had to be optimized to the extent that the number of out-of-tolerance valves was minimized.

The second "fallback" approach was more radical. It assumed that the standard approach would not work and that the production process could not be controlled to this extent. In this alternative approach, every single valve would be individually tested. Here, the focus was on optimizing the method of testing to lower its cost, rather than on production methods to lessen the incidence of out-of-tolerance valves.

The second alternative was deemed an unlikely alternative, but as luck would have it, normal methods of inspection simply would not work. Production could not make valves of the required tolerance in a sufficiently high percentage. Sierra Engineering Company optimized the second approach. So successful was this alternative approach that for almost twenty years Sierra was the sole source for supplying these valves to the government. Every single competitor tried the single approach of trying to optimize the production line, testing only a representative number of valves. They never imagined that anyone would actually test every single valve. Consequently, they never succeeded in winning a competitive contract against Sierra Engineering. (This concept is shown in Figure 7-4.) ▌

## Maximum Effort Can Mean Maximum Impact

Finally, multiple, simultaneous approaches are used to create a maximum effort for maximum impact and maximum sales. (This concept is

*Figure 7-4*

---

### FLEXIBILITY AND ALTERNATIVE APPROACHES

---

*The strategist must be flexible in reaching the objective, even as the objective remains constant. If the strategy employed is not working, or not working as well as it should, it is foolish to continue it. Use an alternative approach.*

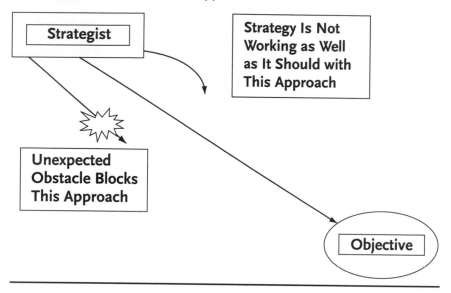

---

shown in Figure 7-5.) You may want to do this (1) when introducing a new product to establish yourself before the competition can enter the marketplace; (2) when you know that the life cycle of the product is extremely short, and you want to maximize your profits during the period of growth; or (3) when you control the market to the extent that you are unaffected by rivalry between different channels of distribution. When you are able to do this, it also provides you with considerable flexibility in the face of obstacles or competition. However, there are reasons why using multiple approaches for maximum income may not be possible, even for the short term. We'll look at this issue more closely later in this chapter.

## Maximizing Results with Multiple, Simultaneous Alternatives

Joe Cossman was a tactical marketing genius and an incredible strategist. I've written about some of his exploits previously. However,

*Figure 7-5*

MULTIPLE, SIMULTANEOUS APPROACHES TO CREATE A MAXIMUM
EFFORT FOR MAXIMUM IMPACT AND SALES

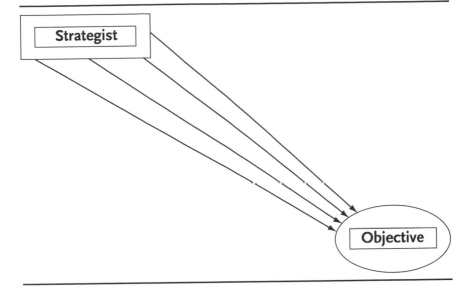

results are what count, and the results he achieved in almost every business venture that he entered were absolutely phenomenal. It seemed that no matter what product he introduced, he would soon dominate the market. For example, Joe developed a child's educational toy, the Ant Farm. He sold 3,118,000 of them. He introduced an insect poison. He sold 5,824,000 units. He came out with rubber "shrunken heads" to hang on the rearview mirror in cars and sold 1,600,000. As he frequently pointed out, "Others look for only one or two markets for a product. I look for every one I can find."

You're probably familiar with his garden sprinkler, a plastic hose with holes in it. Joe not only sold this through supermarkets and garden supply stores; he sold the sprinklers to poultry farmers to air-condition their chicken coops during the summer, and to show dog people to wet down dog runways.

He sold through mail-order houses, magazine advertisements, and on commission through radio and television stations. He appointed sales representatives throughout the country. He sold at trade shows and even hired commission salespeople for house-to-house calls. He partnered with retailers, wholesalers, and sold direct to the consumer. He found agents to sell his product overseas.

With so many alternative approaches to marketing his products,

Cossman was unbeatable. He used the principle of multiple, simultaneous alternatives to create a maximum effort for maximum impact and maximum sales time after time. ■

## LIMITATIONS ON MULTIPLE, SIMULTANEOUS ALTERNATIVES

You may now be convinced that the use of multiple alternatives is always a good idea. And this is generally true. However, there are certain situations in which multiple, simultaneous approaches may not be desirable, or even possible. For example, the economics of a given situation may limit what you should do by what you can do. Because resources are always limited, you may only have the resources to pursue a single approach, or a limited number of approaches, as opposed to all available approaches (as Joe Cossman frequently used in advertising and distributing his products). When this is the case, sometimes the strategist can threaten multiple approaches, or give the appearance of taking more than one approach simultaneously, even though she actually doesn't have the resources to do this. However, as soon as possible, additional approaches should be incorporated into the stratcgy.

Thus, one tactic that has been employed is distribution through a limited number of channels and subsequent expansion through additional channels, using the profits from initial operations. A company may distribute locally and later expand nationally, even though immediate national distribution was the preferred approach.

Another reason why multiple alternatives may not be desirable is due to conflicts between these alternatives. In the case of Upjohn, it could not successfully sell its product through feed stores and veterinarians under the same name at the same time. A standard drugstore outlet selling your brand of toothpaste at the recommended retail price will hardly be delighted that the discount store across the street is selling it at 10 percent to 20 percent less. A newspaper purchasing a column from a syndicated journalist does not mind if other papers around the country print the same column, as long as the other newspapers in its geographic area do not print it. A mail-order house selling your product does not want to see the same product sold in retail stores.

In every case, the channel distributor would like to have exclusive rights to sell. As a result, using multiple, simultaneous approaches, a channel may not push your product or service aggressively. In fact, unless they have "an exclusive," some channels may refuse to sell your product at all. These types of problems don't only exist with products and channels of distribution. Multiple approaches may not be desirable if different managers responsible for each approach are likely to engage in a destructive rivalry that you cannot control.

These are the situations for which you must make the decision as a leader, and as a strategist. At some times, the desires or even demands of the actors in potential approaches, or your own limited resources, outweigh other considerations and limit your possible actions so you are unable to pursue all potential approaches, or even more than one approach. In other cases, use of multiple, simultaneous approaches can be maintained in the face of these types of problems.

| STRATEGIST'S LOG | PREPARING MULTIPLE, SIMULTANEOUS ALTERNATIVES |

You should prepare more than one way to reach your objective in advance. That means, when formulating strategy, you must consider alternative, simultaneous approaches. And in most cases, you should incorporate these multiple alternatives into your strategic plan right from the start.

Why are multiple, simultaneous alternatives necessary? There are several reasons:

- Things rarely go exactly as planned, so you need to have alternatives not only ready to use, but actually in use. When unexpected obstacles block one approach, an alternative approach is already at work.

- Your competitors will take measures to thwart your efforts, so multiple approaches enable you to bypass these obstacles. In the best-case scenario, you put your competitors on the "horns of a dilemma" where, no matter what they do, they will suffer negative consequences.

- Your main plan may not work as well as you had hoped. Rather than start from scratch, you can push one (or more) of the alternate approaches.

- Exerting maximum effort through several different approaches at once can mean maximum impact to achieve your objective faster, or more completely.

Of course, there are situations in which multiple, simultaneous alternatives may not be possible, or desirable. These are rare. But they do exist. As a leader and strategist it is your responsibility to determine when these cases occur, and what to do about them. ∎

## CHAPTER 8

# Take the Indirect Route to Your Objective

*"Avoid a frontal attack on a long-established position; instead, seek to turn it by a flank movement. . . ."*
—B. H. LIDDELL HART

*"You can tell a man's character by the way he makes advances to a woman."*
—ADMIRAL ISOROKU YAMAMOTO

Chris Zane is the founder of Zane's Cycles, a bicycle store near New Haven, Connecticut. As he was trying to get established, the competition was tough and he had to fight hard for every customer. How to compete against Wal-Mart, Kmart, and other giants, much less the established independent dealers, was a major challenge for this small retailer.

Zane soon decided that he couldn't compete directly. For example, he couldn't offer a substantially lower price, a more extensive cycling inventory, better products, or a phalanx of products that had nothing to do with bicycles.

Because direct competition having to do with the product, price, and distribution were standard, he decided he'd have to differentiate his business in another way by taking an indirect approach. Zane decided to emphasize customer service, specifically the length of time that the service was to be provided.

Of course, everyone says they offer superior customer service, including extended guarantees of one time period or another. In his business, the norm among all his competitors was to offer a thirty-day guarantee on routine parts and service. Zane decided to jump up his guarantee to one year. It took his competitors two years to realize they were losing market share to Zane's Cycles, due to this indirect approach on "the flank" of the mainstream way of competing.

Competitors finally caught on and eventually matched Zane's one-year guarantee. Unfortunately for them, Zane immediately doubled his guarantee to two years. When competitors tried to play catch-up and followed him again, he went to a five-year guarantee. In the end, Zane offered a lifetime guarantee. Competitors thought that at last this was as far as he could go, but it wasn't. Those competitors that could reluctantly extended to a lifetime guarantee. However, even that wasn't the ultimate. Zane soon extended his lifetime guarantee to everything in his store! By then, he had plenty of additional cycling products to offer. By taking an indirect approach, Zane had found a way to compete at which his competitors were always behind, and at which he had the advantage, even though his competition in some areas was far stronger and more powerful. As a result of his indirect strategy, Zane grew pretty powerful himself; soon he was the number-one bicycle retailer in size for his geographic area.

## ▌ ZANE'S INDIRECT APPROACH: AN ANALYSIS

If you think that Zane's approach was sheer bravado and terribly risky, better think again. This strategy may have involved some risk, but it was perfectly calculated. Early on, Zane noticed that few buyers brought their bicycles or accessories in for repair after the second year of purchase. An analysis of sales data showed that even for those who did come in for repairs after two years, Zane still made money.

In addition, Zane calculated what any customer was worth to him over a buying lifetime. That's why when a customer came into Zane's store with a six-year-old pump that was completely worn out from use, Zane happily gave him a brand new pump. Let's look at his economic analysis for this pump. This six-year-old, worn-out pump was a top-of-the-line item originally costing $60. So you might jump to the conclusion that Zane was out $60. However, the pump's cost to Zane was only about $30. Moreover, in this case, because of his relationship with the manufacturer, he was credited with the $30, so giving the customer a new pump actually cost Zane nothing.

Even if the pump had cost Zane $30, replacing it for free still made economic sense. The next two times this customer came in to his store, he bought $200 in accessories. Zane netted about $100. Moreover, when the customer decided to buy his next bicycle, where was he likely to go? So, Zane made even more. And, what about word-of-mouth advertising to other prospects? That's probably worth a lot more.

Conceptually, what Zane's Cycles did is shown in Figure 8-1. Zane's Cycles did not meet the competition head-on, but maneuvered around the competition's flank to strike in an area of Zane strength against competition weakness.

As this is written, Zane's Cycles has grown to become one of the top five bicycle retailers in the nation. No wonder that Texas A&M invited this Connecticut Yankee to come out to Texas to teach as part of the college's executive-in-residence program![1,2]

The shortest distance between two points may be a straight line, but that is in geometry, not strategy. It isn't necessarily the best direction to take to reach your goal when facing competition. Any football, basketball, hockey, or soccer player or coach can tell you that. Feinting in one direction and going toward another, drawing off the competition in one direction and then passing to someone unexpected to score the goal is standard fare in team sports. It would be utterly foolish and predictable to simply head directly toward a goal, especially if it's in a direction where the competition's concentrated, simply because it involved a shorter measurable distance.

## The Indirect Approach Mystifies Until It Is Too Late

If you have ever seen a magician's performance, you may have wondered at his ability to perform what appear to be impossible feats. In fact, his

*Figure 8-1*

ZANE'S INDIRECT APPROACH

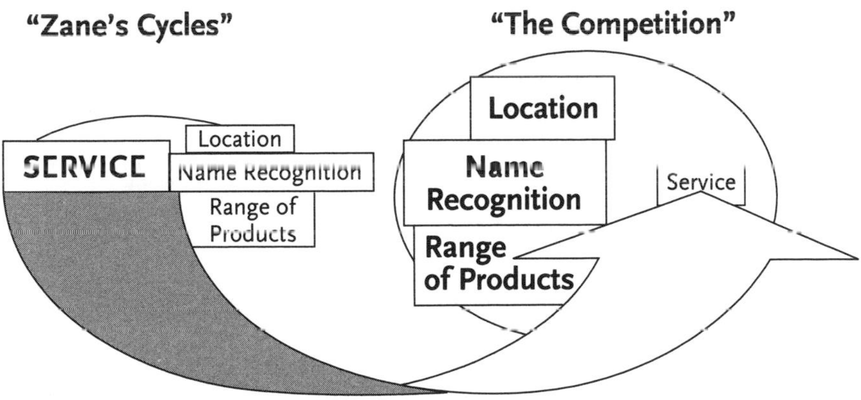

ability to "do magic" is based on an application of the indirect approach. While you are being misdirected by him to focus on something unimportant, he accomplishes something that you may well have noticed if you had not been distracted.

For example, consider the simple trick of rubbing a coin into one's elbow until it disappears. One easy way of doing this is to announce what you are going to do. You then begin to rub. You "unintentionally" let the coin slide off your elbow and fall to the floor. You pick the coin up and begin to rub again. You again "unintentionally" drop the coin. You can repeat this clumsiness a third time. However, this time, as you pick up the coin, you look directly at your audience and comment that this is a slippery coin. You begin to rub again. Suddenly, the coin is gone. What happened? While you looked at your audience and distracted them with your comment, no one noticed that you picked up the coin with your other hand!

**Liddell Hart's Analysis of Successful Strategy.** Basil H. Liddell Hart was one of the leading military strategists of the twentieth century. Some would go further and say that he was one of the greatest strategists of all time. Liddell Hart spent a lifetime studying the strategy of war and wrote numerous books on his analysis of the subject. Leading practitioners on both sides of many conflicts acknowledged his contribution to their successes, and his fellow theorists from many countries recognized and acclaimed his brilliance.

The central theme of all of Liddell Hart's work was that of the primacy of the indirect approach to achieving any goal. Liddell Hart concluded that the indirect approach was a law of life in all spheres and a truth of philosophy.[3]

He went on to show that in all areas of life related to the influence of mind on mind, direct confrontation only encountered, and in some cases actually provoked, a stronger and more stubborn resistance. However, resistance could be diminished, and thus success was far more likely, if an approach was taken that avoided the areas of strongest resistance. In most cases, this means sidestepping the position where the competition is the strongest and making your approach where it is weaker. Although, as we'll see shortly, there is more to it than simply going where your competition is not, that indeed is one consideration.

**The Indirect Approach Applied to a Strategy for Romance.** Some years ago, while conducting research into strategy, I heard a story during an interview that tended to confirm Liddell Hart's contention that the indirect approach is the basis of successful strategy in all human endeavors involving mind-to-mind confrontation.

One executive told me that he had competed for his wife with another suitor. Alas, the other suitor was wealthier and was able to take this young woman on more dates and to better places than he could afford.

Rather than go head-on in a competition he knew he could not win, this man took the indirect approach by signing up for a community college real estate course that he knew his future wife was also taking. His competitor could not take the same course, because of his business schedule. Sitting next to this woman in class, and taking her home afterward, allowed the man to spend a lot more time with her, at no additional cost. "It only took one semester," he said, "and we were engaged." Thus, the power of the indirect approach is confirmed for romance, as well as in warfare and business.

## How You Can Apply the Indirect Approach in Your Strategy

The indirect approach requires more than merely avoiding a competitor's strength to approach a goal in an indirect manner. If this alone were all that were required, applying this concept to strategy would be routine and simple. But, it is not.

If all you do is avoid a competitor's strength and avoid approaching a goal directly, an adversary may spot your intentions, and he will take steps to redeploy his resources to counter your strategy, if he can. You will gain nothing. Taking advantage of this principle means that your indirection must have some finesse. You must distract your competitor and get him to focus on something else of lesser or no importance—just as the magician does with his audience.

**The Story of the Smuggler.** There is an old story about a customs inspector stopping an expensive, brightly painted yellow car at the border to his country. The car and the man in it looked suspicious. The inspector made a search of the vehicle but could find nothing, so he let the car pass.

The next week, the man and his car were at his inspection point again. This time he made a more thorough inspection. He could find nothing. Every week, the same car came to his post. Every week, he searched the car more thoroughly than the previous week, but every time he came up empty-handed. Finally, the customs inspector received permission from his superiors to pull the car out of the line. He had mechanics waiting, and they completely disassembled the car. They spent several hours doing this, but they could find nothing. The man returned with his car the following week, and for several more weeks after that, but eventually, the man and his yellow vehicle were no longer seen at the border.

Years later, after his retirement, the former customs inspector saw the suspected smuggler in a bar. After these many years it still bothered him that he could not discover what the man was smuggling. He approached the smuggler, who recognized him right away.

"I know you are a smuggler," said the former customs inspector.

"Not anymore," replied the smuggler.

"I know you were smuggling something through my post," said the ex–customs inspector. "If this is true, would you please tell me what it was you were smuggling and how you concealed it? It's driving me crazy not knowing."

"Certainly," said the smuggler. "The fact is, I didn't conceal what I was smuggling. I was smuggling yellow automobiles." The smuggler was a master of the indirect approach.

## ▌ BUSINESS "BATTLE MAPS" BEGIN WITH MAPPING THE INDUSTRY

Using the indirect approach requires a thorough analysis and calculation of the possible results of your action, and your competitor's ability or inability to react.

One way of doing this is through business "battle maps." It was probably William E. Rothschild of General Electric who first suggested some sort of mapping to investigate competitive positions. With what Rothschild called a competitive arena map, an entire industry could be plotted out. First, define your business in terms of the need you intend to fill. For example, it might be an educational need, a transportation need, a computer need, a food need, and so forth. Next, develop a matrix, or map, of this business arena. The vertical axis documents the products and services that fill your arena. Along the horizontal axis, various types of customers in your arena are designated. In Figure 8-2, the horizontal axis may be categorized by land, sea, air, and space customers, or by Army, Navy, Air Force, NASA, or Department of Energy custom-

*Figure 8-2*

## COMPETITIVE ARENA MAP

| | Company A | | Company B | |
|---|---|---|---|---|
| | U.S. Army | U.S. Navy | U.S. Air Force | U.S. Marine Corps |
| **PRODUCTS** | Ground-Air; Short Range<br>Ground-Air; Medium Range<br>Ground-Air/Space; Long Range<br>Ground-Ground; Short-Medium Range | Sea-Ground; Long Range<br>Air-Ground; Short Range<br>Air-Air<br>Sea-Sea; Short-Medium Range | Ground-Ground; Long Range<br>Air-Ground; Long Range<br>Space-Ground; Long Range<br>Air-Ground; Intermediate Range<br>Air-Ground; Short Range<br>Air-Air<br>Space-Space | Air-Ground; Short Range<br>Air-Air<br>Ground-Air; Short Range<br>Ground-Air; Medium Range<br>Ground-Ground; Short-Medium Range |
| **SERVICES** | Consulting<br>Feasibility Studies<br>Trade-off Studies<br>Applied Research<br>Pure Research<br>Development<br>Testing | Consulting<br>Flexibility Studies<br>Trade-off Studies<br>Applied Research<br>Pure Research<br>Development<br>Testing | Consulting<br>Feasibility Studies<br>Trade-off Studies<br>Applied Research<br>Pure Research<br>Development<br>Testing | Consulting<br>Feasibility Studies<br>Trade-off Studies<br>Applied Research<br>Development<br>Testing |
| **COMPONENTS** | Warhead<br>Guidance<br>Air Frame/Space Frame<br>Propulsion<br>Defense<br>Launch | Warhead<br>Guidance<br>Air Frame<br>Propulsion<br>Defense<br>Launch | Warhead<br>Guidance<br>Air Frame/Space Frame<br>Propulsion<br>Defense<br>Launch | Warhead<br>Guidance<br>Air Frame<br>Propulsion<br>Defense<br>Launch |
| **PARTS** | Electrical<br>Mechanical<br>Hydraulic<br>Fuels<br>Armor<br>Explosive | Electrical<br>Mechanical<br>Hydraulic<br>Fuels<br>Armor<br>Explosive | Electrical<br>Mechanical<br>Hydraulic<br>Fuels<br>Armor<br>Explosive | Electrical<br>Mechanical<br>Hydraulic<br>Fuels<br>Armor<br>Explosive |

*Source:* Adapted from William A. Cohen, *The Practice of Marketing Management, Second Edition* (New York: Macmillan, 1991), p. 154.

ers for government marketers. The competitive arena map encompasses the entire industry.

## Constructing a Segmentation Matrix Map

The competitive arena map encompasses the entire industry. The next step is to construct a segmentation matrix business battle map. Here we get down to the specifics. First, select those products and services you are going to analyze, along with those of your competitors. Then determine how they can best be described. This may be by pricing, company size, quality, complexity, function, or positioning. It is what you feel is the most important product breakdown in this particular situation. This description goes on the vertical axis. The horizontal axis is used to segment the customers into groups, but the segmentation is more precise than with the competitive arena map. You can segment your customers any way you want. Again, select what you believe is important, given the situation you face. While there are an infinite number of ways to segment your customer, typically you can do this by geography, demographics, psychographics (i.e., how your customers think), or lifestyle. A fictitious segmentation matrix battle map for toothpaste is shown in Figure 8-3.

If you construct one of these "battle maps" over a period of time, say one per year, you will gain tremendous insights regarding your competition's intentions, coming potential threats, and potential opportunities for the future. Of course, these maps shouldn't be the end of your analysis, only the beginning.

## Creating a Three-Dimensional Battle Map

Perhaps the ultimate in business or marketing battle maps is shown in Figure 8-4. You can add a third dimension to show more information, to make the map more useful in planning, to analyze the strategies of the competition, and to analyze both the threats and the opportunities in every situation, so that you can develop an effective, indirect approach.

In Figure 8-4, the dimension that has been added is *total market potential*. Total market potential is calculated by multiplying the number of potential customers in the segment by the average price of the product sold. Thus, if a certain segment has a potential of two million customers, and the average product price is two dollars, the segment would encompass a total market potential of $4 million.

Each segment is identified in Figure 8-4 only by numbers—1, 2, 3, 4,

*Figure 8-3*

## SEGMENTATION MATRIX MAP

|  | Children/Teens | Age 19–34 | Age 36+ |
|---|---|---|---|
| **Plain Toothpaste** | Colgate—Palmolive Procter & Gamble | Colgate—Palmolive Procter & Gamble | Colgate—Palmolive Procter & Gamble |
| **Toothpaste with Fluoride** | Colgate—Palmolive Procter & Gamble | Colgate—Palmolive Procter & Gamble | Colgate—Palmolive Procter & Gamble |
| **Gel** | Colgate—Palmolive Procter & Gamble Lever Bros. | Colgate—Palmolive Procter & Gamble Lever Bros. | Colgate—Palmolive Procter & Gamble Lever Bros. |
| **Striped** | Beecham, Inc. | Beecham, Inc. | |
| **Smoker's Toothpaste** | | Topol | Topol |
| **Pump Packaging** | Ora-B | Colgate—Palmolive Procter & Gamble | Colgate—Palmolive Procter & Gamble |

PRODUCT SEGMENTATION

CUSTOMER SEGMENTATION

*Source:* Adapted from William A. Cohen, *Winning on the Marketing Front* (New York: John Wiley & Sons, 1986), p. 63.

etc.—for both customers and products, and it can be indicated by a different code, color, or other distinguishing feature. In Figure 8-4, a segment of less than $5 million in potential sales is left blank. Potential sales of $5 million to $10 million are indicated by a series of diagonal lines, $11 million to $20 million by a series of horizontal lines, and $21 million to $30 million by vertical lines. A small rectangle outlining the area indicates the competitor's (or your own) activity in a particular segment. The rectangle is divided by a line going from the lower left corner to the upper right. The upper section of this division shows a percentage. This percentage is the market share of that segment for the company outlined by the rectangle. The figure in the lower right part of the rectangle (separated by the diagonal) is a quantitative representation of the assets committed to doing business in this segment in millions of dollars. Using overlays, even additional information can be shown on these three-dimensional battle maps.

*Figure 8-4*

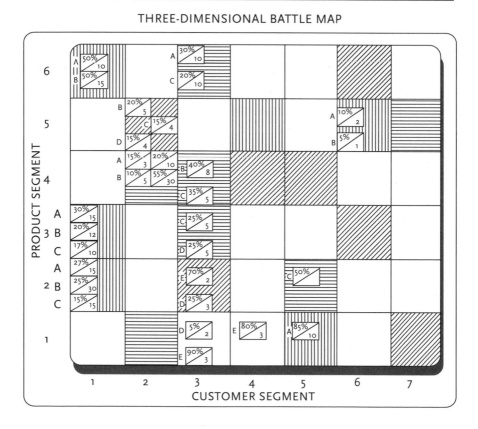

THREE-DIMENSIONAL BATTLE MAP

Doing an analysis for an indirect approach may not be easy, but battle maps will assist you greatly.

## ▌ WHERE TO BEST USE THE INDIRECT APPROACH

The approach you select to compete indirectly may involve one or more of the essential principles outlined in previous chapters. The key is to know where to use the indirect approach to get the best results. In general, look for situations where:

1. You can apply a strategy, but a competitor cannot.

2. A competitor cannot easily duplicate your actions.

3. You can fly under the competition's radar, until it is too late.

4. Whatever happens, you will have the advantage.

These situations might involve products, pricing, market segments, geographical locations, distribution methods and systems, sales methods, advertising, promotion, business—in fact, the possibilities are infinite.

### *You Can Apply a Strategy, but a Competitor Cannot*

In every situation, there are advantages and disadvantages for all organizations, regardless of their size or power. For example, a large organization may have tremendous marketing and financial muscle, plus name brand recognition and a greater number of resources. How can a smaller company compete?

This is a perfect place to apply the principle of the indirect approach because there are actually many approaches that can be taken by a smaller company. A smaller company can make decisions and implement strategy faster; concentrate in market segments that would be unprofitable for a larger company that carries a bigger overhead; and even do things that a larger company may feel is detrimental, or inappropriate, for its image.

Remember the famous Avis advertisement slogan: "We try harder." Avis tried harder because it was not the number-one car rental agency. That honor belonged to Hertz. This approach put Hertz in a bind. How could Hertz, number one in the rental car industry and all-powerful in that industry, counter that slogan? Avis found a way to avoid the direct approach of competing as an equal. Instead, Avis actually made being number two an advantage. Because Avis was not the top company in its field, the implication was that it had to try harder to compete by providing better service, better prices, and better extras. Hertz could not say, "We're number two." In fact, there wasn't much Hertz could say.

## A Cheesecake Entrepreneur Goes Where the Competition Cannot

Debbie Patt of Clarendon Cheesecakes in Clarendon, New York, was a small entrepreneur with little money available to compete with the larger bakeries selling cheesecakes, no matter how delicious or delectable her product. With no money for advertising or promotion, she sought other means of advertising, marketing, and just getting the word out.

First, she went online. This got her some additional business, but she soon realized that the competition there was very strong. She had to do more. What could she do that larger competitors could not?

Patt hit on the idea of putting brochures on top of the boxes holding her cheesecakes, which were sold in every local supermarket. She also put her brochure in every piece of mail leaving her home or office, even including utility bills. She didn't stop there. Patt convinced everyone she knew to put promotional magnets on their cars and to wear company-branded hats and shirts. She also persuaded everyone she knew to call their local stores several times a week, to inquire if they were carrying Clarendon Cheesecakes yet. Larger bakeries belittled what she was doing. They were unwilling to take any such actions. This kind of persistent, personal-touch marketing campaign was "beneath the dignity" of her larger competitors. It would have affected the image they had so carefully cultivated. So, they were unable to follow in her footsteps. Patt had taken an indirect approach that her competitors could not copy.

Next, Patt started looking for partnerships among bakeries that didn't compete directly with her products. For example, she approached a local bakery that was well known for decorating, and she began selling their wedding cakes along with her cheesecakes. National cheesecake brands can sell similar products, but they do so in an almost generic, limited fashion. Patt didn't compete directly with them. She took the indirect approach and went where they could not (or would not) go by partnering with other local bakeries.

Finally, she took the time to personally talk to local store and restaurant owners about carrying her cheesecakes. For large bakeries to
do this wouldn't be cost-efficient, due to overhead limitations. This
didn't bother Patt, and it didn't affect her overhead.

As a result of this and other indirect strategies that Clarendon Bakeries adopted, Patt's cheesecakes are currently sold in fourteen stores
(and counting), plus numerous local restaurants. Stores are now calling her and begging to let them sell Clarendon Bakeries cakes![4] ▌

## A Competitor Cannot Easily Duplicate Your Actions

There are situations where a competitor could redeploy resources to
counter your actions if he chose, but it just is not worthwhile to do so.
This isn't as strong a scenario as in the previous example, but it is still
pretty strong in giving you an advantage when you take an indirect approach.

One common way of taking this indirect approach is to bite off a tiny
bit, or niche, of the market, and to dominate it. This can work for any
organization, regardless of size. As we've seen in earlier examples (such
as little ICS, Inc. taking on giant IBM in the narrow area of typewriters
for the teaching field), it is one way for a weaker company to emerge
victorious against an overall stronger competitor.

### A Speaker Finds a Niche

William Bachrach of Bachrach and Associates, Inc. in San Diego, California, was a successful financial adviser and a good speaker. He had
heard that the speaking profession could be very lucrative, and he
thought that he had developed some special techniques and insights
that would enable other financial advisers to increase their business
significantly. He asked established speakers for advice, and they all
told him the same thing: "That market is too small. You've got to gen-
eralize your presentation so it will be more useful to larger groups of
people. Otherwise, you just can't succeed."

However, Bachrach knew the financial adviser business and felt
that this was the group he could best help. Rather than take the more
established route of giving generic presentations to larger groups, he
chose a more indirect path where he would have the field to himself.

Ten years later, by specializing in this one area of speaking, Bachrach not only dominates the niche he chose, but he is considered a major speaker, when compared with all speakers in the industry. Last year, he earned almost $1 million in speaking fees. ▮

## You Can Fly Under the Competition's Radar, Until It Is Too Late

Another situation where the indirect approach can be successfully taken is when your intentions won't be known, or they will be perceived as unimportant, until it is too late for the competition to do anything about it. The competition either is ignoring what you are doing, or simply sees no threat in your actions. By the time they recognize what you've actually been up to, you've won the day.

### Selling Ant Farms

My friend Joe Cossman was in the toy business in the early 1960s. This was the era of Sputnik and high technology spawned by the vision of space exploration. President Kennedy had announced the intention of the United States to put a man on the moon within ten years. Large toy companies sought to capitalize on this mood. They eagerly competed in developing toy robots that walked under their own power, rockets that could actually be launched and would ascend several hundred feet into the air, and telescopes through which authentic celestial observations could be made.

These large companies had equally large research and development budgets and large sales forces. Joe never had more than thirteen employees. How could he compete amid this frenzy to mimic our explorations in space with limited resources against much larger competitors? The answer was not to compete directly. Instead, Joe looked for old products that he might be able to make attractive with a new twist and a small investment.

After some weeks of investigation, he came up with a toy product that had been around for more than fifty years and was still selling on the toy market, albeit poorly, in 1961. This was the ant colony container for children. What someone had developed in the 1890s was essentially a wooden box frame with glass windows in the front and back.

The box was filled with soil. Kids would collect ants and put them in the box with food. If they caught the right kind of ants, the ants would eventually colonize the box. Because of the glass windows, all of their activities could be observed.

However, there were problems with this product. The glass windows made the product hazardous for children and unwieldy as a toy. The fit between the wood frame and the glass was imperfect, and frequently the ants escaped. Finally, because the ants had to be captured by the children themselves, it took a number of tries before the correct ants would be captured and the container colonized. Of course, stores were unwilling to sell live ants along with the container, so the toy was mainly sold in limited numbers to teachers who used them in the classroom for educational projects.

Joe had an idea how to solve all of these problems. The development of plastic, and specifically clear plastic, meant that the container could be made very cheaply out of 100 percent plastic. Moreover, Joe had an idea how to handle the problem of the ants, too. Each container would be sold with a "stock certificate." Buyers would mail it in to a central location that then would send the correct ants to stock the container with no guesswork. Joe called his product an "ant farm."

Most of Joe's competitors knew what he was doing. But they were focused on high-technology space toys. Moreover, they looked at previous product sales and "knew" that this was a very limited market. They didn't know Joe Cossman or his incredible ability to not only find new and unique methods of promotion, but to use every single one.

For example, when his dog had nine puppies, Joe called the *Los Angeles Times*. "What's special about your dog having puppies?" a reporter asked. "She has nine puppies, but only room for eight," he answered. The reporter said he would bring a photographer over and do a human interest story. Cossman, the promoter, redecorated his dog's basket . . . with strategically placed flyers illustrating the ant farm!

He announced to the world when the White House ordered an ant farm for Caroline Kennedy, the president's daughter. Several weeks later, he received a letter from the White House asking, "Where's the ant farm?" In all the excitement over getting the order, someone had forgotten to send it. He spread the story of his faux pas as well, providing even more publicity.

Despite all the interest in space and the millions of dollars spent by toy companies in developing cutting-edge toys, Cossman's Ant Farm was the number-one selling toy that year, and he sold almost a million of them. There were no patents on the product, and other companies easily could have copied him. They knew what he was doing, but by then, it was too late. Cossman was established and dominated this market. Ultimately, millions of this product were sold and are still being sold to this day by Cossman's brother-in-law. ■

## *Whatever Happens, You Will Have the Advantage*

As we've seen earlier in this book, too many dot-com companies became fascinated in fighting nose-to-nose within the single dimension of gaining more customers. Yet, while hundreds of companies got on the Web and duked it out with this direct approach, few noticed, or cared that all this activity wasn't producing profits. Eventually, and almost simultaneously, many simply ran out of money.

**Making Money with Dot-Coms the Easy Way.** During the days of the great California Gold Rush in the nineteenth century, you were far more likely to make a fortune by servicing those engaged in the violent and frantic competition in the goldfields than by struggling there yourself. That's how Levi Strauss got established in the jeans business. It's been the same story on the Internet. More e-commerce entrepreneurs won on the Internet through indirect strategies than those fighting it out for sales to consumers.

Consider Judy Estrin. Estrin is not a business novice. Previously, she made a fortune by starting companies and then selling them off. That's what many companies wanted to do eventually with their dot-com companies, but they never got the chance.

3Com purchased Estrin's first company, Bridge Communications, for $235 million. Precept Software, another company she started, went to Cisco Systems for $84 million. Then she and her husband, Bill Carrico, started a new company, Packet Design. Packet Design is involved with the Internet, but not in the way you might think.

While other e-commerce companies battled for profits on the Web in time-honored fashion, Estrin sidestepped all that competition. Instead, her company's business is to help Web service providers manage increasingly complex systems with fewer employees, keep the Net running smoothly as traffic backs up, and solve other security and networking problems. Gamblers may win or lose, but the house providing the service to gamblers always wins. They outmaneuver the competition by taking the indirect approach to profit. That's Estrin's way of taking the indirect approach. In 2002, she was inducted into the Women in Technology Hall of Fame.[5]

| STRATEGIST'S LOG | TAKING THE INDIRECT APPROACH |
|---|---|

As we've seen, you can gain the advantage in competitive situations by taking the indirect approach over the direct one. All you need to do is look at the variables in every situation. These critical variables may be almost anything, including products, pricing, market segments, geographical locations, distribution methods and systems, sales methods, advertising, promotion, business, and more. Then, find a way to sidestep the competition. You want to go with your strength against your competition's weakness.

Using the indirect approach requires that you calculate the probable result of your action, and analyze your competition's ability (or inability) to react. You'll find that it helps to picture the situation graphically. Therefore, the technique of developing battle maps can be of enormous help in your advance preparation.

It is also vital that you recognize where to use the indirect approach to get the best results. In general, look for situations where you are able to use a strategy that your competition can't use, where your competitors can't—or won't—duplicate your actions, where your intentions won't be known, or they will be perceived as unimportant until it is too late, or where no matter what happens, you will have the advantage.

Combining the indirect approach you have selected with the lessons from previous chapters on concentration, economy, surprise, etc. will give you a tremendous advantage over your competition, even if on paper he is a lot stronger. ■

## CHAPTER 9

# Practice Timing and Sequencing

*"There is a tide in the affairs of men, which taken at the flood, leads on to fortune."*  —WILLIAM SHAKESPEARE

*"To every thing there is a season, and a time to every purpose under the heaven . . ."*  —ECCLESIASTES 3:1−8

An article in a leading business magazine entitled "Timing Is Everything" advised: "No matter what size your business is, the best time to buy advertising is in the first quarter—always. The next best time is the third quarter. These are the months when most radio and TV stations are hungry and offer low rates and special packages to lure advertisers who may not otherwise bother to advertise . . . and that spills over to print media." The article goes on to say, "Inventory needs to be filled to make budgets, and the buyer is really in the driver's seat. Rates can drop by half in the first quarter. . . ."[1]

This is all true if you look only at "buying advertising." However, if you are deciding *when* to advertise, the logistics are much more "situational" and you have to consider whether your prospects will buy during that quarter, no matter your cost of advertising.

For example, if you sell snow shovels or Christmas ornaments, advertising in spring or summer would be ill-advised, as would running a promotional campaign for a sprinkler system in the dead of winter in most parts of the United States. Entrepreneur Robert Ramsay soon discovered that March is not a good time to run a direct-mail campaign to certified public accountants (CPAs). After spending all his money and getting zero leads, he figured out that his prospects were busy doing taxes. Moreover, Ramsay's company, CXWeb, was a Web design and hosting company. Later, he did spend his scarce resources to promote his service at a better time of year. However, most CPAs weren't interested in being on the Web back in 1999. So, even when they had the time to read his advertising material, Ramsay lost money and failed again. He no longer had the resources left to keep going, and his business went under. Ramsay learned the lesson of timing, however, and today his advertising strategy with his new company, SmallBizPlanet.com, Inc., is more productive.[2]

## IS THE AMOUNT OF MONEY SPENT LESS IMPORTANT THAN WHEN IT IS SPENT?

Timing is critical in so many fields—sports, politics, and military strategy all come to mind immediately—but it is especially important in business. Doing the "right" thing at the wrong time can result in a great waste of money, time, and effort, with no results to show for it. To some, this may seem like a no-brainer. Yet many otherwise savvy businesspeople are convinced that it is the amount of money spent that is more important. Even if they recognize that timing is more important in some areas, like seasonal advertising, they maintain it is not generally true overall. They couldn't be more wrong.

Let's look at something entirely different, say, a simple strategy for motivating employees: Reward them with money. Which is more important in this situation, how much you give them or when you do it? William T. Quinn, Jr., owner of a publishing company in Somerset, New Jersey, wanted to motivate his employees in this manner. He discovered that when handing out bonuses for extra or exemplary effort, it was timing, not the amount of the bonus, that mattered most. The key was to dispense his motivational dollars when his employees were most stressed, and to do so on the spot, not to wait for some collective time to reward everyone together in the future.[3]

This finding is psychologically sound. If you want to motivate someone, the desired action and the motivator should be as close together as possible. I witnessed the importance of this in the military in the awarding of decorations for bravery or accomplishment. In combat, these medals were frequently awarded only a few days after they were earned. In these cases, they had the greatest positive effect on the morale of the awardee, and everyone else in the unit. They motivated the individual and the rest of us to even greater efforts. In peacetime, however, I've sometimes seen months, or in one case three years, pass before a deserved event receives recognition. Such delay between the accomplishment and the recognition had the exact opposite effect. In one case, the recipient even refused a medal he had earned. It should be no surprise that timing is far more important than money when considering motivators in business.

 ## DOING THE RIGHT THING AT THE WRONG TIME CAN CAUSE A DISASTER

Although it may seem obvious that a company should not expand exponentially until it is ready, companies sometimes try to exploit their success before they have built the necessary base or the time is right, or they take the right steps, but in the wrong order.

A health-food store in Los Angeles was so successful in building sales that the manager opened fourteen stores within eighteen months. However, with insufficient financial resources, no brand name, and no mastery of the intricacies of the supply chain within the industry, he was bankrupt in the nineteenth month. Many e-commerce companies learned this same lesson, and like the health-food store manager, also found that future potential didn't count for very much if you couldn't pay your current bills.

Webvan, the largest online grocer, went under despite 750,000 loyal customers, $800 million in investments, and the acquisition of its rival HomeGrocer in a $1.2 billion deal. In very simple terms, Webvan expanded exponentially without ever having established that the business was in a position to make money. It exploited its failure, not its success.

## TIMING IS ALWAYS IMPORTANT . . . BUT SO IS SEQUENCING

Planning and implementing a strategy is like preparing a recipe for a special dish, or the formula for dynamite. Do something at the wrong time, or put things together in the wrong sequence, and you could end up with a disaster, even though the right things were done or the correct ingredients were used. Certain of the ten essential principles of strategy must be accomplished in a specific sequence in order to be effective. The objective must be fully defined, and you must gain full commitment to it before you do anything else. Next, you must identify the decisive point and move to economize to mass at that point. Only then are you ready to take the indirect approach to actually accomplish your objective. Although you must exploit your success, this can only be done when you have real success to exploit.

Specific strategies for timing and sequencing must be carefully calibrated for the situation at hand. For example, Edward Tse, a vice president of Booz Allen Hamilton and the managing partner of its greater China operations, recommends the following sequential approach for companies desiring to enter and do business in China:

- Articulate a China vision, commit to the vision, and understand its implications.

- Develop superior consumer insights.

- Transform consumer insights into superior product market strategies.

- Effectively manage sales and distribution capabilities.

- Achieve operational excellence.

- Build a strong local organization and capabilities platform.[4]

Other strategy situations in other countries or geographic regions may emphasize slightly different elements or require a different sequencing of overall strategy to maximize the effect in achieving goals.

## FOUR ASPECTS OF TIMING AND STRATEGY

Clearly there must be a strong link between timing and strategy if you wish to maximize your resources and the innovative strategies that you may have developed. There are four important aspects regarding timing and strategy that we must consider within this principle to secure this linkage:

1. When should you take a specific action?

2. In what sequence should the actions be taken?

3. Will the actions taken be continuous or discrete functions?

4. Are the actions going to be repeated?

The answers to each question will usually differ depending on the situation.

Understanding the major elements of timing contributes to our ability to introduce them into our strategies for maximum effectiveness, and not simply to take actions as we happen to think of them, or when we have the necessary human, capital, or equipment resources.

Let's look at each in turn.

## When Should You Take a Specific Action?

Knowing when to take a certain action is of primary importance. Take the introduction of new technology. You make think that if you develop something, you should just rush to introduce it. This is rarely the case.

If your company is known for being first with the latest and cutting-edge technology, that may be your competitive advantage. If this particular advantage is important in your industry, and you have the resources to support it and the risk involved, by all means introduce the technology as soon as you develop it. Clearly in this case, it even makes sense to invest the necessary resources to ensure that you are the very first to develop the innovation and introduce it into the marketplace.

However, if you haven't got the resources that guarantee you an immediate impact, maybe it's better to let someone else get in first and make the mistakes that you can learn from. Then you can introduce something even more advanced with less risk and a lower resource commitment.[5]

The fact is, you can sometimes be the leading-edge technology company, miss the boat in being first, and still come out smelling like a rose. IBM was the technology leader in computers when someone at the company did a flawed marketing research study that concluded that if IBM decided to develop the technology for personal computers, a mere 1,000 customers a year would be interested in purchasing the resulting product.

Of course, this was utter nonsense, which Steve Jobs proved when he founded Apple Computer and created an industry in the process. However, as we all know, IBM did finally enter the market, with a technologically inferior product no less, and took over the field by spotting the weaknesses in Apple's strategy of maintaining strict control over who could write computer software for its hardware. Actually, IBM wasn't just late to market; it was very late with a host of other companies getting there first.

This doesn't mean that being late is always the thing to do. It does, however, show that in industries in which the state of technology is not the big differentiator, hanging back may have advantages.

## First, Early, or Last in All Present Strategic Possibilities

Under the principle of timing, being first, early, or last to market can all be correct strategic choices. For example, being first to market offers the greatest payoff, if you are successful. It is possible to establish yourself, your brand, your contacts, etc. This will make it extremely difficult for anyone else to break into the market, and you have the possibility of dominating it, perhaps forever.

Polaroid was the first to enter the market for instant photography with Edwin Land's technology. Despite the efforts of other major corporations and the expiration of Land's early patents, Polaroid was able to dominate this market until the era of digital photography.

But being first incurs the greatest risks and the highest costs. You are the pioneer. You make the most of any mistakes as you learn what your market likes and dislikes, where to advertise, what features of a product or service are desired, and which should be eliminated.

Being early, but not first to market, isn't so bad, either. It also has timing advantages. Your risk is much reduced. You know the concept, product, or service will work. You get to see what mistakes your competitor made, and yet it may cost you very little. Your competitor may have paid in blood for lessons that you get without paying or risking a cent. Also, your competitor may have made commitments for distribution or other matters which cannot be so easily discarded. If the first entry failed, you get to see where things went wrong and how you can make them right.

In the early 1980s, RCA spent millions of dollars trying to introduce the videodisc player and videodiscs. This disc was the size of an old vinyl record, but it was cheaper and easier to store than videotapes. The company developed a library of discs, conducted a major advertising campaign featuring movie personality Gene Kelly, and eventually it cut prices. Yet despite advantages over the VCR and videotapes, all was for naught and RCA wrote off a $580 million investment. The videodisc was ahead of its time, and it was a case of the player attempting to drive the market, rather than the videodisc itself.

Five years later, it was a different story and the timing was right. In the interim, the vinyl record industry had collapsed with the introduction of the audio-laser compact disc (CD). There were millions of CD players in the market based on laser technology. The time was ripe for the introduction of a new videodisc based on the same tried-and-true technology. When Philips, Sony, Toshiba, and Warner all sought to enter the market with movies on CDs, they were well aware of RCA's earlier failure. They did everything to ensure success, including first agreeing on a common standard format. The very successful result for a second-place entry was the DVD.

What about a company that is not early, but may be even late? I do not believe it was IBM's intention to be late in the personal computer market, but it certainly worked to its advantage. Although Apple dominated the market at first, IBM, though late, learned from Apple's missteps, and those of other companies that had entered the fray. Using its tremendous resources and the shrewd strategy of letting anyone create software for its system, IBM was able to forge ahead and take control of the market, despite the fact that it was neither first, nor early, to market. ▦

**Piecemeal Commitment Is Bad Strategy.** A major issue for strategists is what to do if all the resources necessary for implementation of a particular strategy are not presently available, but will soon be available over a period of time. Many leaders think that the best move is to begin implementation anyway and to simply add resources when they are ready. In an article on strategies for starting an e-business, *Microsoft Central* advises against this:

> Biding your time and working out a structured IT strategy, rather than grabbing stuff off the shelves piecemeal, will pay huge dividends in the long term.[6]

For e-businesses, this is confirmed by conclusions in many articles on e-business strategy: "An unconnected or piecemeal system will be a strategic setback—and a major expense."[7] "[W]e can too easily fall into the trap of reacting in a piecemeal fashion to a haphazardly presented series of apparently unrelated technology concepts."[8] "Benefits: . . . Identification and resolution of issues at a strategic level, instead of piecemeal."[9]

Those seeking to minimize the cost of success open their campaign with the minimum resources calculated to do the job. They slowly increase the necessary resources (as perceived) to overcome the competition's efforts. Usually, both methodologies are exactly the wrong things to do in any situation where competition is a major factor.

This tends to happen because you have insufficient resources to get the job done, so your competitor is able to concentrate his resources at the decisive point. As you keep adding resources, he keeps overwhelming you. In military strategy, this is aptly called committing your forces piecemeal.

**Vietnam: Why the Piecemeal Approach Fails.** Failure is exactly what occurred in Vietnam when the United States adopted a piecemeal strategy to try to reach the objective of a noncommunist South Vietnam. At first, the United States sent a small advisory force of about 500 men. This was augmented by President John F. Kennedy to 15,000 and then, as results still were unfavorable, by President Johnson and his Secretary of Defense Robert McNamara to nearly a half million men. However, this was not one dramatic increase, but a gradual increase over a period of time.

The bombing campaign over North Vietnam was slowly escalated in a similar manner. McNamara announced that we would keep "raising the ante" until North Vietnam backed down. North Vietnam never did. It fought on until America was forced out of the country by politics, and a shrewd application of the indirect approach.

To their great shame, military leaders knew piecemeal escalation and commitment would not, and could not, work. They expressed their ideas to their civilian bosses, but were told to keep quiet. If they weren't going to be team players, they were off the team. Many military leaders today feel that they should have resigned in protest. Instead, they rationalized the situation. Someone else would carry out this foolish policy anyway, and perhaps piecemeal commitment could work—this once.

This approach to strategy has been tried many times in military history. It has never worked when facing a determined adversary. The problem is that "the competition" meets the raised ante with superior forces, and if it doesn't chew its adversary up, at least it fights it to a stalemate. In the case of bombing, the enemy gets accustomed to handling the new, higher level of force. Eventually, it is the attacker that gets weary of the situation, not the defender.

By contrast, when overwhelming resources are committed up front, the defender has no opportunity to succeed. He is simply overwhelmed. In the long run, this strategy costs less. Best of all, it succeeds, whereas committing resources piecemeal never does.

## *In What Sequence Should the Actions Be Taken?*

"To every thing there is a season, and a time to every purpose," says the Bible (Ecclesiastes 3:1–8). For the strategist, this emphasizes that even positive actions should at times be deferred until the right time. For example, there is a time to reveal to competitors, prospects, vendors, and others just how strong you are and what you have accomplished. Then, your strength may act as a barrier to discourage others from competing against you. Your strength will also attract business to you. However, if you reveal this information too soon, it can have the opposite effect. Instead of discouraging competitors from entering the market, it may encourage them to do so. "If this company can do so much so fast, we can do the same." Even potential customers may be unconvinced, feeling you may be just a "flash in the pan," and have little staying power. On the other hand, the right actions, taken at the right time can lead to success, even with modest resources.

### The Shooting of a Pizza Man Saves Almost 1,000 Lives

Richard Davis was the owner of a small pizzeria in Detroit. While making a pizza delivery one hot summer night in 1969, Davis was attacked and shot. Davis was in a dangerous area, so he was also armed. He returned fire and wounded two of his three attackers. This probably saved his life. While recovering from his wounds, Davis began thinking about a means of personal protection. To date, the inspiration from the Davis shooting has saved the lives of almost 1,000 policemen and women. The body-armor company he founded is the leader in its field. And action sequencing was an important part of Davis's success.

Davis found that although the police were given body armor that would stop many types of bullets, in the final analysis, it provided no protection at all. The reason was that the armor was heavy, rigid, and bulky. So, it remained in the trunk of the police car, and when police were shot, they weren't wearing it.

Investigating different options, Davis found that a flexible body armor vest using ballistic nylon had been in use by the military since the Korean War. It was also heavy and bulky. However, this was because it covered the entire upper torso. This was necessary because although the vest wouldn't stop the high-velocity rifle bullets prevalent on the battlefield, it would stop grenade and other shell fragments traveling at a lower velocity, which, though not specifically aimed, could do damage anywhere on the upper body. However, these military vests would stop most pistol bullets, which was, and is, the main threat facing police.

Davis reasoned that two rectangles of the ballistic nylon material would protect the front and back of the torso, and they could even be worn under a police shirt. The two parts could be held in place by Velcro straps. This was a brilliant innovation that no one had thought of before. Davis proved it would work by firing at a telephone book protected by his armor. The bullet didn't penetrate. Moreover, the design was easy to manufacture, and the materials were relatively inexpensive.

But in this early design, there was little that could be protected by patent. This meant that if Davis was successful in introducing the product, say through official police channels, not only would there be great delay in gaining approval, but it was very likely that once approved, the police would simply publish his specifications and go out for competitive bid. Davis would be in for a lot of frustrating work convincing officialdom for very little, if any, gain. ▪

## As Part of His Strategy, Davis Shoots Himself

Davis hit on a simple, but effective strategy that required both courage and commitment. First, he demonstrated the effectiveness of his armor by shooting at it while it protected objects such as telephone books and sandbags at police departments in Detroit. At the same time, he prepared promotional materials aimed at individual police officers, and he began selling his armor directly to them for under fifty dollars a set.

Davis knew that eventually he would be challenged to put himself on the line to prove his armor, but he didn't do this until he was ready. In his words, he performed an act "in the name of science," and shot himself while wearing his armor. The first time he did this was an important step in his overall strategy. The other 192 times he did this, he says, "was simply show business."[10]

His shooting demonstration was so dramatic that he was soon asked to repeat it all over the country. He sold enough body armor to individual policemen that by the time police departments got around to ordering it and paying for large buys, Davis's company, Second Chance, was the industry leader. ▪

## Davis Took Each Key Action in Sequence

Today, Second Chance supplies armor to the police and military all over the world, and it is a major corporation in the industry. Second Chance has produced 700,000 units of body armor, and Davis was awarded a Lifetime Achievement Award by the American Society for Law Enforcement Training in 2002."

But back in 1973, within three years of the introduction of Davis's armor, there were nineteen different companies that had entered the market and were competing with Second Chance with similar products. By then, Davis was in a position to sell to police departments as well as direct to the user, and his ongoing research and development efforts had placed him ahead of the competition and resulted in numerous patents.

Davis's strategy of first selling direct to the individual user and only later, when the organizational customer became more sophisticated, selling to departments was an important strategy sequence decision. Even his decision as to when to use himself as part of his demonstration was "on target." If he had offered to shoot himself first, before demonstrating the efficacy of his innovation, he would have probably been perceived as a crackpot. He may have even been prevented from using himself for promotional purposes, though he knew it was safe to do this. By following a step-by-step action plan, Davis started a new business in a completely new field, and he beat out the competition using the principle of timing and sequencing. ■

## *Will the Actions Taken Be Continuous or Discrete Functions?*

If we look back to our advertising example again, we can see that certain types of ads can be maintained at almost a constant level and produce profitable results, whereas others are best done periodically by season, or by previously established demand.

This concept should be applied to strategies in other functional areas. Is it best to add new products to a line on a continual basis, or to do so at fixed, or random, periods? Assuming the needed resources are available, do we open at new locations without pause, or do other factors regarding demand or competitor response drive this decision? When his Model T dominated the automobile industry, Henry Ford refused to introduce a new product. General Motors captured Ford's dominance of the marketplace by doing exactly that and forcing a strategy that exists in the automobile industry to this day: the introduction of new models every year.

## *Are the Actions Going to Be Repeated?*

An important aspect of the principle of timing and sequencing is knowing if your action is a one-time-only event (where you make your move, achieve whatever degree of success, and then go on to the next action). Or, if the action is to be repeated, you must determine how often it should be repeated to remain effective, and how strongly it should be emphasized when repeated.

Direct marketers who sell by catalog to established customers track customer purchase patterns on a continual basis. For any individual customer, they continue to mail new catalogs, old catalogs with a new cover, or even identical catalogs which have previously been sent, so long as the customer keeps buying from them. Because they track this information, they know whether to mail to a customer weekly, monthly, bimonthly, annually, or by some other period. Moreover, because they also track the items selected and their prices, they know what products to emphasize and at what price. The same principles should be applied to all strategies.

---

**STRATEGIST'S LOG** | PRACTICING TIMING AND SEQUENCING

It is absolutely crucial that the strategy recipe be put together properly. This involves both timing and sequencing. Doing the right thing at the wrong time can be as bad (or worse) as taking an action which is not the right thing to do under any circumstances.

To incorporate this principle of strategy, consider four key questions:

1. *When should you take a specific action?* There are certain situations where you should try to be first, others where you're better off simply being early but not first, and still others where you actually have an advantage entering a market later than your competition.

2. *In what sequence should the actions be taken?* Taking the correct actions in the proper sequence can give a powerful boost to your overall strategy and propel your company to success.

3. *Will the actions taken be continuous or discrete functions?* Some actions must be maintained at a constant level to produce profitable

results. Others are best done periodically, based on previous results.

4. *Are the actions going to be repeated?* If so, with what frequency and relative emphasis will they be repeated in order to remain effective? ▦

# Exploit Your Success

*"Once the enemy has been thoroughly beaten up, success can be exploited by attempting to overrun and destroy major parts of disorganized formations. . . . The enemy must never be allowed time to reorganize."*

—FIELD MARSHAL ERWIN RUMMEL

*"When we have incurred the risk of a battle, we should know how to profit by the victory, and not merely content ourselves, according to custom, with possession of the field."*

—MAURICE DE SAXE

By June 1940, the German armed forces had succeeded in defeating Poland, in forcing the allied evacuation of Norway, and in making France submit to a humiliating surrender. England had not surrendered, but British forces had been driven from the European continent. England stood alone against Germany. The United States had not yet entered the war. Hitler prepared to invade Britain and his plan had a name: Operation Sea Lion. Only the Royal Air Force (RAF) and the British Navy stood in the way of the plan's execution. So Hitler told Herman Goering, commander of the German Luftwaffe (Air Force), to destroy the RAF. Then they would go after the Royal Navy, invade England, defeat the British, and end the Second World War with a German victory.

The Germans had superiority in numbers of aircraft, with 900 fighters and 1,300 bombers against 650 operational RAF fighters. They had more pilots, and many experts said they had technologically superior munitions. To that point, the Germans had been victorious over all who had opposed them. The German Army was on a roll; the Luftwaffe had played a significant role in these victories. So pleased was Hitler that he created a new rank to reward Goering for the Luftwaffe's success. Goering became the first officer to hold the rank of Reich Marshall in German history. It was expected that the Luftwaffe would eliminate the RAF in short order. Yet, in what came to be called the Battle of Britain, this did not happen.

Goering's aerial onslaught began on August 8, 1940. The objective was to knock out RAF Fighter Command so that the German bombers could then be used against the British Navy and the British ground defenses. The strategy was to attack RAF bases and seaports and force British fighters to rise up in defense against the German aircraft. With Germany's overall superiority in numbers, the British fighters would be destroyed.

The Luftwaffe opened its attack with raids of up to 500 bombers. RAF fighters took off from their airfields in response, as the Germans had anticipated. However, the Germans were surprised by the effectiveness of British defenses, and resistance was much stiffer than they expected. This included the use of radar and early warning to warn of the approach of a formation of German bombers. This enabled the British to rapidly concentrate against German attackers whenever they appeared. As a result, it was the British, rather than the Germans, who had superior numbers at a particular location. After a few weeks, with their losses much heavier than expected and mounting rapidly, the Luftwaffe shifted the emphasis of its attacks to RAF airfields and communications and control centers. This was a smart move and proved far more effective, though German losses continued. The pressure on British defenses was enormous, and the tired English pilots and those supporting them on the ground began to show signs of stress.

With British defenses and RAF Fighter Command severely strained and only days, if not hours, from collapsing, the Luftwaffe suddenly stopped its assaults against airfields and communication targets. In an effort to destroy civilian morale, the focus was shifted to the far less costly night bombing of London. German losses decreased rapidly and London was in flames, but this shift of strategy was still a major mistake. Throughout the day, the overloaded British defenses got the respite they needed to recover, and recover and rebound they did. The RAF was never defeated, and Hitler abandoned his plans to invade England.

Said Winston Churchill, "Never in the course of human history have so many owed so much to so few." As an aside, one RAF pilot jokingly responded, "He must have been talking about our bar bill." Nevertheless, the Battle of Britain was won, and England was saved.

## █ MAKE SURE THE FAT LADY GETS TO SING

An anonymous philosopher is frequently quoted as saying, "It ain't over until the fat lady sings." This apparently refers to the fact that an opera does not end, even when you think it is over, until a hefty soprano (who is often near death) sings in the final act. The principle for the strategist is that we don't want "it" to be over until the fat lady sings, meaning that we have exploited our success to the fullest extent.

To truly understand and apply this principle—the necessity of exploiting our success—we must understand how success occurs. The process is always the same, taking place in two stages, although the time periods of the two phases may differ, and this can sometimes discourage us and cause us to stop the process. While it's true that it isn't over until the fat lady sings, sometimes she never gets to start her song.

### *The Success Process*

To reiterate, the success process always involves two phases. First, a critical mass either exists, or it is created. This critical mass is the environment in which we are trying to achieve the success. Building this mass into the critical phase may take years, a few months, a few days, or even a few hours.

As we continue to pursue success, at first nothing or very little is likely to occur. Suddenly, the second phase comes and everything seems to happen at once. Like a nuclear chain reaction, our environmental mass becomes supercritical. And just as the chain reaction results in a nuclear detonation, if we manage our success correctly at this point, a complete triumph results. That is why Hannibal was able to not only achieve success against his Roman enemies in the face of overwhelming odds, but why this success was so complete, with the superior Roman force completely overwhelmed and destroyed. Note that this did not happen all at once, but that in the final phase when the Romans were crushed, it happened very quickly, far too quickly for the Roman commander to be able to do anything about it.

Because things happen so rapidly in this second phase, the perception may be that success is instantaneous. However, a closer examination of any achievement will show that only just before the triumph occurred did the pace speed up to near light-year velocity. Whether the earlier phase lasted years or days, the pace of the first phase would have appeared to be slow.

Unfortunately, because of this variance in time between the phases, there are two traps that we can fall into that can block the very triumph we seek (see Figure 10-1). First, because the initial phase may be glacially slow, we may not realize that the mass is becoming supercritical. In this case, we may abandon the process before the chain reaction can occur. This is what I call a Type 1 Error.

## Type 1 Error—Quitting Before Success Is Achieved

Motivational speaker Tony Robbins says, "God's delays are not God's denials." He is cautioning his listeners not to abandon the process before it becomes supercritical. That's one reason that Winston Churchill admonished, "Never give in! Never, never, never, never, never, never, never. In nothing great or small, large or petty—never give in." It's not only defense against an adversary that he is referring to, but also the striving to reach success. You must never give up your strategy unless you are 100 percent certain that it is not working. One also doesn't abandon the objective. Instead, a new strategy is found for achieving that objective.

In analyzing the Battle of Britain, strategists have found plenty of errors made by the Luftwaffe, including a failure to properly appreciate the role and application of strategic airpower. However, I believe the major error was abandoning a strategy that was working (concentration against airfields and communications) for a strategy (night bombing of London) that meant the rejection of the original objective—eliminating RAF Fighter Command. We'll examine how to recognize when a strategy should be abandoned or modified shortly. First, let's look at the second error frequently made by strategists that causes them to fail to achieve overwhelming success. I call this a Type 2 Error.

## Type 2 Error—Failing to Exploit Success for Maximum Gain

The second trap we can fall into is also due to the relatively long time period of phase one of the success process. We can be so happy to achieve a modicum of success that we stop the process before a full triumph is attained. It's as if Hannibal called his forces off as soon as the Romans got the worst end of the deal, happy to have stopped his numerically superior adversary and survived the encounter. This happens all the time, in all spheres of human endeavor, at all levels.

## A Job Hunter Blows Off an Additional $20,000 a Year in Salary

After many months, an out-of-work man accepted a job at $80,000 a year, which was the same amount he had been paid at his previous job. But the individual who hired him told me that he would have gladly paid this man $100,000 a year! The $80,000 he offered was his opening bargaining position. The employer was desperate for the expertise that this man had. All the man would have had to say was five words: "Can you do any better?" But he accepted the $80,000, without trying to test how final an offer it was. He achieved a modicum of success, but he did not exploit it for maximum gain—that is, the additional $20,000. We must exploit the success we achieve. ▪

## HOW TO KNOW WHEN TO CHANGE, MODIFY, OR ABANDON A STRATEGY

When Churchill told us to never give up, he was referring to our ultimate objective or goal. He was not talking about abandoning our strategy. If we know our strategy isn't working, it would be foolish to keep beating our heads against the wall. Tony Robbins, whom I quoted ear-

*Figure 10-1*

THE TWO TRAPS THAT CAN BLOCK THE PATH TO COMPLETE VICTORY

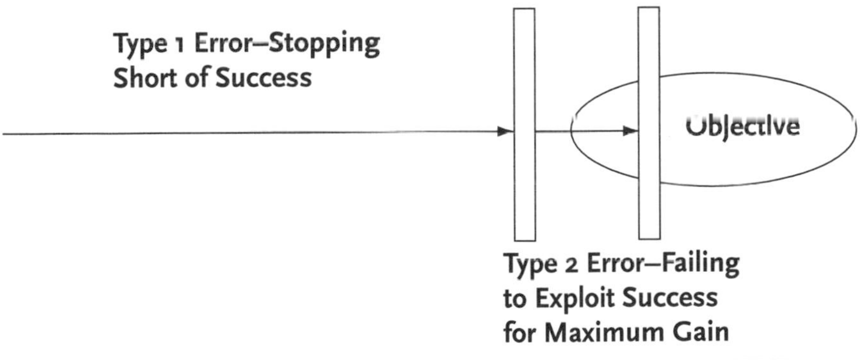

**Type 1 Error–Stopping Short of Success**

Objective

**Type 2 Error–Failing to Exploit Success for Maximum Gain**

lier, also says that one definition of insanity is to repeat the same strategy, but to expect different results. The problem is, how can we tell if our strategy is getting us to our goals or not? If the Germans had known they were literally hours away from achieving their goal of eliminating RAF Fighter Command, it is doubtful that they would have abandoned their strategy. Nevertheless, they did abandon their strategy. This implies they did not know that their strategy was working.

There are a number of ways that strategists can determine, or at least approximate, if their strategies are working or not within an acceptable cost and time frame. From this, the leader can make a decision whether the strategy should be continued, changed, or abandoned. Among these strategy-assessing methods are:

1. Reliable intelligence

2. Judgment

3. Metrics

4. Analysis of similar or past events

5. The Delphi Method

Let's look at each of these in turn.

## Reliable Intelligence

If you know what's going on, and you're getting where you want, you don't need to worry. You know you are progressing toward a goal, and you know the results of your actions; you don't have much to worry about. Had Goering known that British defenses were about to collapse, he would have been less concerned with his losses, knowing that a few more days, or as some say, even a single day, would bring complete success. The problem is that reliable intelligence is sometimes pretty hard to obtain, or isn't really all that reliable. So we frequently don't know how close we are to achieving our ends.

### Direct Marketing's Advantage in Obtaining Reliable Intelligence

Direct marketing is a method of selling that uses advertising through an interactive medium to elicit a direct and measurable response. As such, it has major advantages over other types of retail selling, like a store. If a customer buys through a store, the customer purchases the product, leaves, and that's usually the end of the transaction.

However, the measurable response component of direct marketing gives reliable intelligence to the seller. Depending on the method of advertising—direct mail, space advertising, or through the Internet—the seller has the buyer's name, address, phone number, and e-mail address. Moreover, the seller knows what is purchased, and its price. As the buyer returns to purchase more, the seller has records of types of products, prices, frequency of purchase, and how recently the last purchase was made. This information can be used in developing new products, offering items in certain price ranges to different customers, and more.

By sending direct mail to different lists of prospects segmented, say by profession, or advertising in magazines read primarily by specific groups, the direct marketer has reliable intelligence as to who will buy his product, and who will not.

Marketer Joe Sugarman, who for years was on TV hawking his BluBlocker sunglasses in an infomercial, was the man who introduced the handheld calculator to buyers in the United States. It was only after Sugarman's success that Sears offered this new product. Others followed soon afterward. But, if Sugarman didn't have reliable intelligence that told him how he was progressing toward his goal, the introduction and general use of this product may not have been so swift.

In 1972, Sugarman borrowed money to sell an early model of the handheld calculator to prospects through the mail. He obtained several lists of prospects and did his mailing. It was not a success. Most people did not respond, and Sugarman lost all the money he had borrowed. However, he carefully analyzed this reliable direct-marketing intelligence. He discovered that while he had failed miserably in four of the six lists he had used, two of the lists were highly successful. In fact, had he only mailed to these two lists, he would have made money. He took these results to his creditors and borrowed more. His second effort increased the numbers of letters mailed, but he only sent letters to the two previously successful lists. Sugarman knew he would succeed due to the reliable intelligence from his first mailing.

Today, many strategists have adapted direct-response techniques to obtain reliable intelligence to tell them how they are progressing with their strategies toward their goals. ▪

## Judgment

Some strategists are afraid to exercise judgment. This is a mistake. The gut feeling of judgment can work quite well. Judgment is formed over a period of time from past experience, training, education, and everything that has occurred up to the time that it is needed and exercised. The strategist may or may not spend a lot of time thinking the situation through. It all depends on the time available. If there is little time, the integration of these many sources of input is done almost automatically, in the blinking of an eye, and without thinking deeply. Yet the strategist, using judgment to determine progress toward the achievement and what (if any) actions need to be adjusted to bring this about, is frequently successful.

Many business and other leaders throughout history have succeeded in proceeding to ultimate success through judgment alone, and often, expert judgment works just fine. But this is not always so, and that's its limitation. Judgment should be part of the strategy equation, but it should not be the sole component.

**A Cautionary Tale on the Use of Judgment.** Although judgment works in many cases, solely relying on it can get you in trouble.

There was a young American cavalry officer during the American Civil War who relied exclusively on his judgment. So well developed was his ability in this regard that he was successful in engagement after engagement. And he was so highly thought of by his commander that although only a captain, he was ordering colonels as to the proper action to take on the battlefield with the full authority and approval of his superior. He would size up the tactical situation point to where he knew a cavalry charge was needed and say, "The general desires that you attack that position immediately." The colonels knew better than to dispute the captain's instructions, even though they knew that "the general" had not yet been apprised of the situation. On his general's recommendation, Abraham Lincoln jumped the promotion of this young captain over thousands of other officers, and at age 25, only two years out of West Point, this *wunderkind* was made a brigadier general.

Exercising outstanding judgment, he avoided ordering his commands into impossible situations, and he was victorious in every single battle or engagement he fought. He was the first Union cavalry general to get the better of Confederate cavalry wizard General James "Jeb" Stuart. In the Northern news media he was compared with Napoleon's great cavalry general Marshal Joachim Murat. A year and a half later, he was promoted again. At age 27, he became the youngest major general in the U.S. Army.

At the end of the Civil War, not only did President Lincoln commend him, but General Sheridan gave him extraordinary credit for the Federal victory. He presented the young general with the very table on which General Robert E. Lee and General Ulysses S. Grant had signed the terms of surrender at Appomattox.

Queried by newsmen as to how he was able to repeatedly achieve victory under all circumstances, this officer said that he would size up the situation based on everything he knew, experienced, or had read in military history, and then make his decision. In other words, he relied solely on his judgment.

After the war, the young general was sent out west. He soon mastered this type of warfare, even though it differed greatly from his Civil War battles, and over the next eleven years he again gained victories over the Ku Klux Klan and in the Indian Wars, never losing a single battle or skirmish. Yet, this strategist finally did lose a battle, and it was for this one battle that this general is remembered today. This, the general's final fight, and his only loss, was the Battle of Little Big Horn, and though George Armstrong Custer lost only this one time, his judgment, which had never failed him previously, has been called into question ever since.

I call a continual and sole reliance on judgment (no matter how good or accurate it has previously been) "the Custer syndrome." Obviously, it is to be avoided.

## Metrics

Metrics are means of measuring success. These quantified methods should be decided upon before the undertaking begins. In other words, the strategist needs to plan his actions all the way from start to the final triumph. The metrics that he has calculated ahead of time will tell him if he is achieving his goals and is on schedule (or not) every step of the way. That's part of what's in a flight plan. If something goes amiss, the pilot can tell by consulting preplanned metrics whether he has enough fuel to his preplanned destination or whether he must turn back or seek an emergency landing field. We need to do the same in business.

For example, breakeven, defined as the number of units or dollar sales needed before you recoup your investment and are no longer losing money, is an important metric for a new product or service. So are others—including payback, return on investment, and turnover. All are important indicators that can help to tell the strategist how things are going, or whether some deviation from the plan is required to reach his goal and attain ultimate success.

A woman taught ballroom dancing, mostly with part-time instructors. She did nominal advertising and offered a free introductory lesson. Over time, she built up to a group of clients who took regular dancing lessons. She wasn't getting rich, but she was doing okay. One day she went over her records. She learned an amazing fact from the metrics these records provided. A student spent, on average, $3,000 over time for dancing instruction that cost her less than $500 to provide, including the cost of getting the student, paying her instructors, and overhead expenses for renting the studio. This told her that she could easily spend much more to recruit each student and still make money. She significantly increased her advertising and paid her instructors a bonus to bring in additional students. Within six months, her profits increased by 500 percent.

Of course, it is critical to pick the right metric that is appropriate for your situation. For example, if staying "in the black" is crucial while reaching your objective of capturing a certain market share, you'd better look at both sales and profits. Otherwise, you may be driving yourself into bankruptcy, even while you strive toward your goal.

## Analysis of Similar or Past Events

Looking at what happened in the past and comparing this with the present can give you some insight as to how you are doing. Like other means, it's not perfect, but you can see whether or not you are getting where you want to be.

For example, every product has a life cycle. In simple terms, the product life cycle represents the fact that a product is introduced and eventually it "dies." That is, the product is no longer very profitable, so it is withdrawn from the marketplace. The first handheld calculator I owned was the size of a small brick and had no memory. It was manufactured by Commodore and sold for $29.95. You could buy a ten-year warranty for another $10. A year later, I gave it to the kids as a toy. By then, not only was there a smaller model with a memory, but the price had dropped by 50 percent. Today, you get the whole works the size of a credit card for less than $5.

Some years ago, someone took this concept and actually graphed the life cycle of products. Varying shapes resulted when sales and profits were plotted against time. About 26 percent looked something like Figure 10-2. Of course, you can arbitrarily divide the stages of a product life cycle any way you want. In this case, the researcher named four:

*Figure 10-2*

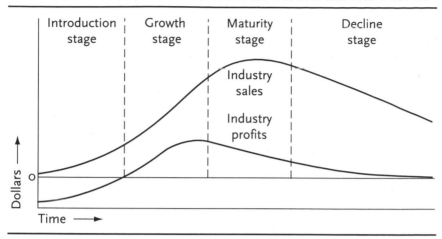

A PRODUCT LIFE CYCLE PLOTTED WITH INDUSTRY SALES AND PROFITS

introduction, growth, maturity, and decline. These four stages have come to be generally accepted to represent what actually happens with every product or service. That's good for theory, but what about practice? In practice, every product is different. In fact, no product cycle is exactly the same. Still, by quantifying dollars and time, you've got some basis of comparison.

If you are striving to get out of the growth stage where you are making little money, and into the stage where you are practically minting it, a comparison with a similar product's life cycle in the past may give you a basic idea of where you are and how you are doing.

## The Delphi Method

Delphi refers to the location of the most revered oracle in ancient Greece. In ancient times, forecasts and advice from gods were sought through intermediaries called oracles. The Oracle at Delphi was apparently one of the best. She was on target often enough to be in considerable demand. Wouldn't it be wonderful for the strategist if the Oracle at Delphi could be summoned to tell us how we are progressing and how close we are to achieving success in a particular situation with our strategy today? Believe it or not, something along these lines is possible.

**A World War II General Seeks an Oracle.** During World War II, General "Hap" Arnold, commanding general of the U.S. Army Air Forces, sought an oracle to predict technological advancements. He approached research scientist Theodor von Karman and asked him to prepare a forecast of future technological capabilities that might be of interest to the military. Von Karman's ideas were apparently promising, because shortly after the war ended, Arnold got the Douglas Aircraft Company to establish Project RAND (an acronym for research and development) to study the "broad subject of intercontinental warfare other than surface." Since then, RAND has grown into one of the leading think tanks in the world, doing research in a variety of subject areas, some far removed from warfare.

But back to our story. Twelve years after RAND's founding in 1958, two RAND researchers published a unique paper, "On the Epistemology of the Inexact Sciences."[1] The paper provided scientific evidence and logical thinking for something we may consider a no-brainer. According to these eminent researchers, in fields where scientific conclusions cannot be derived, the testimony of experts is perfectly permissible. Well, thanks a lot. We've been doing that anyway.

This result from "On the Epistemology of the Inexact Sciences" may elicit a reader response of "So what?" Nonetheless, there were problems emanating from this simple conclusion in the RAND paper. The problem is that different experts come up with different testimonies. Which do we believe? Remembering that expert opinion or judgment is one of our recommended solutions, previously we've assumed that the past equals the future. That is, there is a presumption that if an expert has been successful in the past in his "expert testimonies," he will continue to be so in the future. So, we listen to this expert over others. The problem lies in "the Custer syndrome" we looked at earlier. No one's judgment is 100 percent accurate on all occasions.

Moreover, individual experts can suffer from a variety of biases. If testimony is given in group settings, there is a tendency to agree with the opinion of the individual with the greatest reputation, or the one who is most persuasive, or to follow the opinion of the majority. Once an opinion has been stated, there is a psychological reluctance to abandon it, even if it is completely wrong.

To overcome these shortcomings, two thinkers at the RAND Corporation, Olaf Helmer-Hirschberg and Norman Dalkey, recalled the ancient oracle at Delphi, Greece, and developed the Delphi Method.[2]

**How the Delphi Method Works.** The Delphi Method is a structured process for collecting and distilling the knowledge from a group of experts by means of a series of questionnaires interspersed with controlled opinion feedback that overcomes the psychological obstacles previously mentioned.

Here's how it works in a nutshell. The three basic principles of the Delphi Method are these: (1) a structured method of information flow, (2) feedback to the participants, and (3) anonymity for the participants as to who gave what opinion.

In actual practice, the procedure might go as follows. Let's say that we want to know when our new product, the Universal Terminological Integrator, will reach breakeven and begin to turn a profit.

First, we gather a group of experts together and ensure they have all the information they need to proceed. Then we ask the question. Our group of experts may be in the same room and respond simultaneously on a scrap of paper. Or, they may be in different locations and respond by mail or e-mail. Our experts must not only predict when the event in question will occur, but explain why they responded, along with the date that they answered the question.

A neutral facilitator organizes the results, giving feedback as to the extremes of the dates given by the experts and the reasoning that led to these assessments. However, anonymity is maintained, and no one knows who said what, or why he or she said it.

The facilitator then initiates the process again, and the identical steps are repeated. If done correctly, as the process is repeated, the extremes tend to move toward agreement on a single date.

The Delphi Method can be amazingly accurate. In one study of sales forecasting, actual results achieved were compared with several other methods of forecasting. When compared against actual sales for the first two years, errors of only 3 percent to 4 percent were reported for Delphi, 10 percent to 15 percent for quantitative methods, and approximately 20 percent for judgment.[3]

## ▌ WHICH METHOD IS BEST?

We've examined several means of determining our progress with our present strategy toward a goal: reliable intelligence, judgment, metrics, analysis of similar or past events, and the Delphi Method. Which method is best? As they say, it all depends. It depends on the situation; it depends on the time and information available; it depends on personal preference and a lot more. You have to make the call. My advice is to use all five methods, or as many as you can.

## If the Strategy Is Working, Exploit Your Success

Once you've determined that your strategy is succeeding, you should take action to exploit your success. A race care driver doesn't ease up on the pedal when he takes the lead. He usually floors it and tries to leave his competitors in the dust.

As described previously, a Type 2 Error is failure to exploit the situation for all we can get out of it, even when we are otherwise successful. There is a danger here that not only will we suffer in failing to achieve maximum gain, but worse, in a competitive situation, there is a danger that the competitor, whom we might have dealt with previously, will come back to do us harm.

Why do strategists fail to follow through and allow this to happen? Some become fatigued with the process. They feel that they've won. There is no need to continue to keep the pressure on. Others become complacent due to their success. They feel that there is no way that their competitor can recover. Some strategists don't want to appear too greedy, or to "tempt the gods." Some just don't have the additional resources readily available for a complete triumph, and they don't want to expend the energy to get them. Whatever the reason, a Type 2 Error is just as serious as a Type 1 Error (quitting before success is achieved), and this error can occur in any industry at any time.

## Henry Ford Fails to Be All He Could Be

Henry Ford was a genius in many ways, and his use of the assembly line to reduce the time and cost of manufacturing was brilliant. However, he was so focused on cost reduction that he insisted that his famous Model T be painted in one color and one color only: black.

Consumers who complained were told by the determined Mr. Ford, "You can have your car in any color you want, so long as it is black." Frequently this intransigence is looked at as a lesson in consumer behavior. That is, consumers wanted a choice of colors, and Henry Ford didn't have the smarts to understand this. This is untrue. Henry Ford was very intelligent and understood that many potential customers wanted a choice of colors. He could have added this option and charged for it. However, the Model T was a tremendous success story. Why did he have to change things just to satisfy this additional market segment?

An automobile company that was much smaller at that time, General Motors (GM), saw the opportunity and went after this consumer segment, which soon expanded to include a majority in the marketplace. By the time Ford reacted, GM had grown larger than Ford. It took Ford fifty years to recover from this "small" error in strategy and overtake GM's lead. Today's companies are liable for the same mistake. ■

## How Apple Failed to Exploit Its Success

Steve Jobs and his associates were brilliant in introducing the technology represented by the personal computer. However, like Ford, Apple erred by not exploiting its success. By the late 1970s, Apple had defeated all comers and dominated the market for new computers. It could have had even higher sales, but for one factor. Apple would allow no one else to write software for its operating system. Never mind that doing this could build a barrier that could keep out even giant IBM, which was threatening to enter the market. Apple blindly stuck with what had worked in the past and refused to further exploit its success. Jobs was convinced that Apple was so far ahead technically that he would continue to control the market and reap its benefits at will.

IBM spotted this weakness. When it entered the marketplace and gave anyone a license to develop software for its operating system, thousands of hungry computer software developers came out of the woodwork. So unaware was Jobs of the opening he had presented to IBM that he actually took full-page advertisements welcoming IBM to the business! In short order, consumers were switching to the technically inferior IBM system because the total capabilities of this system were so much greater due to the fact that so many software programs were available. It was as if these thousands of external engineers were all working for IBM . . . and in a sense, they were.

IBM made a serious mistake in not being first in the personal computer business. However, when it found a way to enter the market, its resources and the weakness left open by Apple in failing to fully exploit its success allowed it to quickly turn things around, and take over the number-one position. To date, Apple has not recovered from this mistake. ■

## EXPLOITING SUCCESS

The strategist must learn to fully exploit success. There are two types of errors that may impede her from doing this. The first, a Type 1 Error, is quitting before success is achieved. The second, a Type 2 Error, is failing to exploit a success for maximum gain. Both types of errors are dangerous and to be avoided. They can undo a successful strategy and leave you at a disadvantage.

To avoid either error, the strategist must know how well the strategy is working. While it is sometimes difficult to determine progress, the ability to determine the status toward achieving goals can be enhanced by all of the following methods. They can be used singularly or in combinations for maximum effectiveness:

■ Reliable intelligence, when available, can enable you to quickly see what kind of progress you're making toward your objective.

■ Judgment, either your own or that of others, is often the best guide to how a strategy is doing, when to change it, and when to keep going. However, no one's judgment is 100 percent accurate.

■ Metrics provide a quantifiable measurement of success. They should be determined before a strategy is put into operation, so that they can provide signposts along the way.

■ Analysis of similar or past events can give you some good insight into how your strategy is working, especially when you have identified a similar situation to use as a comparison.

■ The Delphi Method relies on distilling the knowledge of a group of experts, independently forecasting the results of a strategy into a single, often amazingly accurate prediction.

No matter which method, or combination of methods, you use, when you determine that your strategy is, in fact, working, keep the pressure on. Build on your success. Exploit it for maximum results. ■

# PART 3

# Putting the Strategic Principles Into Action

## CHAPTER 11

# Strategy Must Be Tailored to Fit the Environment

*"Never does nature say one thing and wisdom another."*
—EDMUND BURKE

*"It all depends on the terrain and the situation."*
—ANONYMOUS

Captain Adolph von Schell, a German infantry officer, wrote a little, ninety-nine-page book called *Battle Leadership*, relating his observations from the vantage point of a junior officer in the Imperial German Army during World War I. Wrote von Schell:

> As commanders, we must know the probable reaction of the individual and the means by which we can influence this reaction.[1] A really classical example of this art of estimating a situation psychologically was shown in the year 1917 by a brigade commander. This general said, "Each of our three regimental commanders must be handled differently. Colonel A does not want an order. He wants to do everything himself, and he always does well. Colonel B executes every order, but he has no initiative. Colonel C opposes everything he is told to do, and wants to do the contrary."

A few days later, the troops confronted a well-entrenched enemy whose position would have to be attacked. The general issued the following individual orders:

To Colonel A (who wants to do everything himself):

"My dear Colonel A, I think we will attack. Your regiment will have to carry the burden of the attack. I have, however, selected you for this reason. The boundaries of your regiment are so and so. Attack at X hour. I don't have to tell you anything more."

To Colonel C (who opposes everything):

"We have met a very strong enemy. I am afraid we will not be able to attack with the forces at our disposal."

"Oh, General, certainly we will attack. Just give my regiment the time of attack, and you will see that we are successful," replied Colonel C.

"Go, then, we will try it," said the general, giving him the order for the attack, which he had prepared sometime previously.

To Colonel B (who must always have detailed orders) the attack order was merely sent with additional details.

All three regiments attacked splendidly.

The general knew his subordinates; he knew that each one was different and had to be handled differently in order to achieve results. He had estimated the psychological situation correctly. It is comparatively easy to make a correct estimate if one knows the man concerned; but even then it is often difficult, because the man doesn't always remain the same. He is no machine; he may react one way today, another way tomorrow. Soldiers can be brave one day, and afraid the next. Soldiers are not machines, but human beings who must be led in war. Each one of them reacts *differently* at *different* times, and must be handled *each time* according to his particular reaction.[2]

Leaders and workers are all part of the environment. Strategy, whether it has to do with helping them to perform at their optimal level in implementation, or in devising the optimal strategy in a particular situation, must be tailored to fit the personnel involved. They shape strategy; strategy does not shape them. Yet they make up only a portion of the total environment of strategy.

## THE ENVIRONMENT INVOLVES MANY DIFFERENT ASPECTS OF THE SITUATION

Every strategic situation presents its own set of circumstances, encompassing several different environmental factors. A strategy that does not consider and allow for the total environment in which it is to be executed is a poor strategy, regardless of how clever it is in all other aspects. Among the many environmental variables that every leader must consider in developing the right strategy are:

1. The leader's personality, including style and ability

2. Capabilities of subordinate leaders and workers

3. Geography, climatic conditions, and season

4. Culture of the marketplace

5. Laws and regulations—the rules of the game

6. Politics

7. Available resources

8. General economic and business conditions

9. The competition

The optimal strategy is shaped by all of these factors (Figure 11-1). The leader must take all of this into account in formulating his strategy. He must analyze his own situation and that of his competition thoroughly. The great Chinese strategist Sun Tzu advised, "Know the enemy, know yourself; your victory will never be endangered. Know the ground, know the weather; your victory will then be total."[3]

## The Leader's Personality, Including Style and Ability

The leader's influence on competitive situations of all types is extraordinary. What one leader can do easily, another cannot do, regardless of the circumstances. It follows that this is the same with a strategy. All leaders have their own style, a preference for or avoidance of risk, and individual strengths and weaknesses. Moreover, the leader's reputation can have a dramatic effect on both the morale and esprit de corps of the leader's organization and that of his or her competitors. Therefore, this must be considered when formulating and deciding on a strategy.

**A Single Leader Who Was the Equivalent of 100,000 Troops.** It is said that General George S. Patton was so feared by the Germans during World War II that his mere presence on the battlefield was worth the equivalent of 100,000 soldiers. During the preparations for the

*Figure 11-1*

ELEMENTS OF THE ENVIRONMENT IMPACTING ON STRATEGY

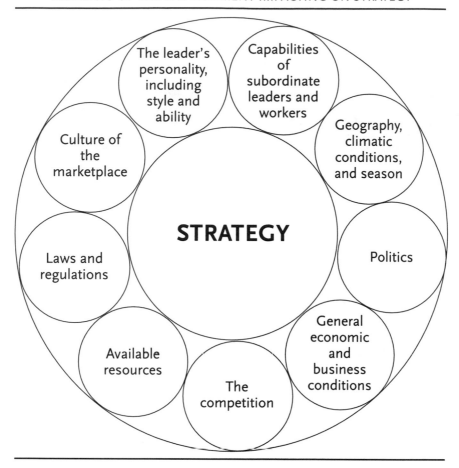

Normandy Invasion, Patton was in disgrace for misconduct, not on the battlefield, but for using profanity in a speech to a group of mothers who had lost their sons in the war. Politicians put pressure on the Army to ensure that Patton would not be given a command in the invasion. Eisenhower could not use his best general!

Not to waste Patton's reputation, Eisenhower created a phantom army group, supposedly commanded by Patton. This nonexistent army group had dummy tents, armor, and artillery pieces. Hundreds of radio signals were sent back and forth among different units of this imaginary organization. This fictional unit caused the Germans so much worry that they moved thousands of troops out of position along the French coast to oppose it, mainly because Patton was supposedly its commander, and therefore, it had to be the Allies' main thrust. Patton proved that he was, in fact, the equivalent of 100,000 troops.

**General Sheridan Won a Battle by Just Showing Up.** Another example regarding the influence of reputation occurred in the fall of 1864. Confederate General Jubal Early, commanding the II Corps of the Army of Northern Virginia, with secret reinforcements from General Robert E. Lee, surprised Union forces and went on the offensive.

General Philip Sheridan was in command of the Union Army opposing Early. He was at a commander's conference when the Confederates launched a surprise attack against his army at a point on its left flank called Cedar Creek. The attack was highly successful. One entire Union Corps was stampeded. What was left of Sheridan's army retreated and fought successive delaying actions. It was clear that Early had won a great victory, and mopping up the remnants of his adversary was thought to be his main task. Even the capital of the United States was in danger of capture by Early's victorious forces. However, though he was not present on the battlefield at the time all of this was occurring, Sheridan had a tremendous reputation among his own troops due to his previous victories.

General Sheridan, riding as fast as he could from Washington, galloped up the Valley Pike from the city of Winchester, Virginia. It was a close call, but as soon as he arrived his mere presence on the battlefield rallied his army. He regrouped his forces and drove Early from the field. His victory was so decisive that this was the last great battle fought in the Shenandoah Valley.

The poet Thomas Buchanan Read immortalized this military turnaround in a poem entitled "Sheridan's Ride." The poem was not entirely accurate. At every mile, Read threw in another stanza. He had Sheridan galloping for twenty stanzas, although the real distance was somewhat less. However, his point was well made. Even Herman Melville, the famous author of *Moby Dick,* was sufficiently motivated to write a poem entitled "Sheridan at Cedar Creek." Sheridan did little more than show up, but it was decisive for the strategy that his forces employed in their counterattack.

**The Impact of a Reputation Is a Major Factor.** You don't need to be a military man (or woman) to encounter the impact of reputation. Just imagine the difference you might feel and the different actions you might take if you must compete against a competitor headed up by an executive with a world-class reputation. I don't say that you would necessarily be shaking in your boots, but you would be foolish to ignore what this change could mean to your competitive plans, even if you looked forward to proving yourself the better businessperson. On the other hand, consider the confidence you and your subordinates would feel, even if misplaced, if you knew the leader of the competition was inexperienced and unproven, or if he had a reputation for mismanagement.

Sun Wu, celebrated as the most famous strategist in China during the period 722–481 B.C. said, "A victorious army comes into battle with a sure confidence in victory, while a declining army rushes into battle, seeking victory by sheer luck."[4] If you have a reputation based on past triumphs, flaunt it. It is far better to depend on your confidence than on your luck.

**Personality Counts!** The impact of the personality of the leader, from Julius Caesar to Norman Schwarzkopf, has always been recognized. In the early twentieth century, one of Germany's foremost military analysts, Major General Hugo Baron von Freytag-Loringhoven, completed the most extensive book ever written on the effect of the personality of the leader on strategy. The book was called *The Power of Personality in War,* and von Freytag-Loringhoven cites battle after battle in which the impact of personality was the determining factor on the outcome. He declared:

> Problems in war can never be solved like those in arithmetic, and we must be ready at all times to act properly despite uncertainties. We must not try either to reduce tactics to mere mathematical and technical formulas. This they can never become; and because they cannot is precisely why our profession is so fascinating.[5]

You need only substitute "business" for "war" to recognize the veracity of this statement. This leads to two important truths that we must recognize: first, that a strategy that one leader can successfully execute, another cannot; second, that different leaders can do better in the execution of different strategies. Remembering Sun Tzu's advice to know ourselves, including our capabilities and limitations, it is imperative to develop a particular strategy that matches our particular personality (and that of our key leaders) to the strategy's requirements.

## Capabilities of Subordinate Leaders and Workers

Top strategists and leaders of major organizations may have a limited ability to select subordinates, except for leaders at the uppermost levels of management. Still, the knowledge, capabilities, training, education, morale, health, and a number of other factors pertaining to subordinates at all levels have a tremendous influence on the execution of strategy.

Niccolo Machiavelli, the medieval Italian political philosopher, is best known for his book *The Prince*. His name has been applied to numerous devious and questionable practices that, at best, come under the heading of "the end justifies the means." However, six years before his death in 1527, Machiavelli also wrote an extensive study of strategy with the identical title that so many writers, from both East and West and ancient and modern times, chose: *The Art of War*. The book is well thought of in military circles and reflects Machiavelli's considerable intellect. He considered the question of the quality of soldiers so important that much of the first chapter is devoted to a discussion of the capabilities and condition of those who must implement a strategy, even to the point of discussing the advantages and disadvantages of keeping cavalrymen on duty after hostilities have ended.[6]

If those who must implement a strategy are incapable of doing so successfully, it makes little difference that the strategy, by itself, might be considered brilliant. It is far better to develop a simpler, less elegant, and perhaps even less ambitious strategy that can be implemented successfully. Of course, in some cases it is possible to guarantee a level of capability through selective hiring and training.

### The Lesson of Hamburger University

Hamburger University is McDonald's worldwide management training center. Ray Kroc founded Hamburger University in 1961 in the basement of a McDonald's restaurant in Elk Grove Village, Illinois.

Kroc was faced with a monumental problem. As his restaurant operations and franchises expanded, owners, managers, and employees came from a wide variety of educational, professional, demographic, and cultural backgrounds. They had varying degrees of experience in the restaurant business, or in some cases, in any business at all. With so much variance in background, experience, and ability, how could Kroc guarantee the same high, uniform quality of product? The solution was Hamburger University and the creation and teaching of standardized methods for making a McDonald's hamburger, and eventually for all McDonald's food products.

Through Hamburger University, Kroc was able to guarantee a standardized, high-quality product, regardless of the strategy he adopted in competing in the marketplace.

Although its beginnings were humble, today more than 65,000 managers in McDonald's restaurants have graduated from Hamburger University, and it is now located in a 130,000-square-foot, state-of-the-art facility on the McDonald's Home Office Campus in Oak Brook, Illinois. It has a faculty of thirty resident professors who have the capability of teaching and communicating in twenty-two languages. However, many students can attend Hamburger University in their own countries because McDonald's also runs ten international training centers, including Hamburger Universities in England, Japan, Germany, and Australia. ▮

## Geography, Climatic Conditions, and Season

We know that we cannot control the environmental variables of geography, climate, and season. A strategy that may be very effective at the seashore may be a disaster in the mountains. What works when the sun is shining may not work when it is cloudy, and certainly strategies that are successful during the summer vacation may fall flat during the Christmas season. What this means is that as we develop our strategy we must give consideration to these issues.

### A Fish Story

An entrepreneur discovered that there was a significant market for families who would like to own tropical fish, but lived in areas too far from pet stores to be able to purchase them easily. He developed an advertising campaign to reach them by mail. He thought that the biggest orders would come at Christmastime, as the fish would make unique gifts that could be delivered directly to each family, right to their doorstep through the mail.

It was a brilliant strategy. He started his advertising in the fall and guaranteed delivery at Christmas. While he had money invested in advertising, he used the customers' own money to pay for the product.

Moreover, he carried no inventory. He arranged to have his supplier drop ship this live product directly from the hatcheries. This actually permitted a slight price advantage over pet store purchase. After the first successful season, he planned on doubling his advertising the second Christmas season. But there was no second Christmas for his "tropical fish by mail."

The entrepreneur forgot that while the hatcheries were located in temperate zones, some of his customers were not. In a significant number of cases, what arrived were water Popsicles with the fish frozen inside. He had devised a brilliant strategy, but he ignored the effect of the season, climate, and the environment. That mistake caused the business to fail. ▪

## Culture of the Marketplace

One strategy does not fit all, especially not all cultures. Kentucky Fried Chicken (KFC), with so many great successes worldwide, initially faltered in Germany because Germans were unaccustomed to take-out food, or to ordering meals over a counter. Similarly, Disney, with one of the most recognized brands in the world, stumbled badly with Euro Disney when it miscalculated the behavior of French attendees, from spending habits and pricing to insufficient provisions for breakfast restaurants. Disney even underestimated the number of rest rooms that would be needed for tour bus riders, who may not have had facilities located on the bus (unlike their American counterparts). Companies that take advantages of culture, rather than fall victim to it, can frequently flourish while competitors fail.

### These Companies Survived the Dot-Com Collapse

Shrewd companies can take advantage of culture with their strategies. In the flurry of companies that faltered and fell during the great dot-com shakeout, few of the new bridal registry companies were among them.

Bridal registries have been around in the United States since the 1930s. Traditionally, they performed a useful service in helping guests choose wanted gifts for couples getting married, without duplicating their offerings. However, in the high-pressure American culture of the twenty-first century, the technology of the Internet has provided new opportunities for satisfying the wants and needs of buyers with little time and both spouses working, and also of couples seeking to maximize their receipts.

As a result, some online bridal registries offer frequent-flier miles for every dollar their guests spend on their gifts; personal wedding pages where pictures, directions to ceremonies, and seating arrangements can be posted; and even shares of stock and mortgage payments toward a planned dream house. One bridal site works as a broker for people who would like to dump unwanted gifts and receive, in exchange, something they would really like.

Other bridal registry sites are attempting to create permanent relationships with newly married couples so that future products and services may be marketed to them on the birth of babies, or when anniversaries occur. According to the publisher of *Bride's Magazine*, "If you can hook this consumer when she is in this life stage, you will fundamentally brand her for life."[7] ■

I neither commend nor condemn the fact that this situation exists as a part of American culture today. I only acknowledge that it exists, and that any strategist who ignores this, or other aspects of the culture of the consumers or business buyers in his market, does so at his own peril.

## Laws and Regulations—The Rules of the Game

Laws and regulations may seem like boring stuff to be left to lawyers, but every strategist should do (at least) a minimum investigation as to what the rules are and their impact on his or her strategy. Remember, the burden is on the strategist.

### Wine Coolers and a Strategy Gone Bad

An otherwise successful entrepreneur thought up the concept of a commercial wine cooler long before the product appeared on the market. Wine coolers had been around since before the turn of the century. However, you had to get the ingredients and mix them yourself. With parts to suit the taste of fruit juice and wine, you mixed the two, and presto—you had your wine cooler. No one had yet produced a premixed wine cooler as a commercial product.

This entrepreneur did his market research, and he realized that he had a product for which there would be a significant demand. He got hold of the cheapest wine he could find and mixed this wine with fruit juice. After a little experimentation, he came up with a recipe that tasted right.

His strategy was simple. Do the same thing in production: Buy cheap wine, mix it with the fruit juice, can it, label it, and sell it through distributors. The entrepreneur prepared a detailed business plan with full financials and had several sample cases of his concoction made up and canned. Using these samples, he presold 20,000 cases and raised the money he needed to get started.

The only problem was, he didn't know the rules. If you ferment your own wine, you pay a certain tax per gallon. However, while the law didn't specifically prohibit you from using someone else's cheap wine in some sort of mix or cocktail, and then selling it, if you did this the tax was 700 percent higher. This made the whole project unprofitable. About all the entrepreneur got out of his experience was the sample wine cooler—mixed, canned, and labeled, probably the first in the world, though it cost him several hundred dollars a can. His failure to know the appropriate laws and regulations invalidated an otherwise simple and effective strategy. ▌

## Why There Were So Many Brands of Typewriter Correction Paper

Laws can screw up what appears to be a very straightforward strategy. I can think of no case more telling, or probably more unfair, than that of the strategist who happened to be an inventor and who developed those little white rectangles of paper that allowed a typist to merely type over mistakes to make them disappear.

Before the days of computers this was pretty important stuff, because a single error usually meant whitening out the typewriting with correction fluid. Although this worked, it was messy, and it left clear evidence of the typist's mistake.

With correction paper, it was another story. This paper was impregnated with a white chemical powder. Just type over the error again using the paper and the chemical deposited exactly over each letter. The error completely disappeared.

After several years spent developing this product, the inventor applied for a patent. He merely stated that his invention consisted of paper impregnated with his chemical powder, whose main use would be to correct a typist's errors.

The patent office told the inventor that this description was too general. He needed to have a specific percentage of the chemical that was used to impregnate the paper specified in his patent. The inventor knew that between two fairly broad percentages of impregnation, his invention would work. He also knew the most effective impregnation down to one-tenth of 1 percent. Obligingly, the inventor changed his patent to reflect this optimal level of impregnation to the nearest one-tenth of 1 percent, and he was granted a patent that should have given him years of protection.

It didn't. Patents aren't secret. Others soon learned the exact name of the chemical he used after a few minutes of scanning the patent document, which is available to everyone. They also quickly discovered that they could produce a perfectly acceptable product by following the inventor's description, but deviating a couple of tenths of percent of impregnation without violating his patent. As a result, many variations of this product were produced.

Had this inventor understood the rules, he might have approached his project differently. For one thing, he probably shouldn't have patented this product at all. With a campaign to capture market share before his competition entered the market, he could have built barriers through established contacts that made it more difficult for them to duplicate his success. Moreover, potential competitors would have had to spend the time and effort on experimentation, just as he did, to develop their own products. This, too, would have kept many potential rivals out of the market. Laws, regulations, and the rules of the game are important environmental variables for every strategist. ▪

## Politics

You may be able to influence politics to some degree through lobbyists, political contributions, trade associations, or any way you can to get favorable legislation passed. However, it is foolish to assume that this will definitely happen or to base your strategy on assumptions, which if they don't come to pass, will cause your strategy to fail.

In 1934, when Harry S. Truman became a U.S. senator through the efforts of the notorious Pendergast political machine in Kansas City, Missouri, it was because numerous special interests had contributed money to the machine with the expectation of Truman's support, once elected. Many expected real economic benefits in return for their "investment." Truman was actually derided by some as "the senator from Pendergast."

These organizations may have based their strategies on the assumption that Truman would act to benefit their interests, but he didn't. In fact, he was so independent and fair that during World War II, he was appointed to head the Senate committee investigating waste and corruption in our war effort. Experts say his efforts saved the country as much as $15 billion. Truman eventually became one of the best-thought-of U.S. presidents. However, it is doubtful that those companies that invested in the Kansas City machine and based their strategies on Truman's political influence ever recouped their investment.

## Available Resources

Certain strategies are available only to companies that have, or can get, the needed resources. If you are one of those companies, that's fine. If not, what resources do you have that you can capitalize on? History is replete with examples of smaller companies or competitors that have competed against much more powerful organizations and emerged victorious. The key is to develop a strategy that capitalizes on the advantages you have, making your competitors' superior resources irrelevant.

**North Vietnam's Winning Strategy.** North Vietnam fought against the greatest superpower in the world, the United States, and won. America had the wealth, manpower, and technological superiority. The North Vietnamese developed a strategy to win the war, based on the growing antiwar sentiment in the United States. Under this strategy, the pressure on our political leaders would become too great to withstand, forcing the United States to withdraw. This worked: America withdrew, and the North overwhelmed South Vietnam, uniting the country under communist rule.

With this strategy, the very superiority of the United States was used against it, and even defeat on the battlefield became a victory. For example, the greatest defeat the North Vietnamese suffered was in their Tet Offensive of 1968. Not only was the North soundly defeated in this action and forced to withdraw, but its losses were horrendous. Yet, it was this very offensive that most influenced American politicians and the American people that the United States must get out of Vietnam at any price. This was not only because the offensive was unexpected, but because the U.S. government had been telling the American public that the war was well on its way to being won. "We can see the light at the end of the tunnel," the American commander, General Westmoreland, had said. That the enemy could launch such a massive offensive, despite our clear superiority in technology and numbers, stunned the American people.

During a conversation in Hanoi in April 1975 between Colonel Harry G. Summers, Jr., then Chief of Negotiations Division of the U.S. Delegation, and Colonel Tu, Chief of the North Vietnamese delegation, Colonel Summers said, "You know you never defeated us on the battlefield." According to Summers, Colonel Tu pondered this remark a moment and then replied, "That may be so, but it is also irrelevant."[8]

The North Vietnamese had used the best available resource—the growing antiwar sentiment in America—to its advantage in defeating a vastly superior enemy that it could never have beaten on the battlefield.

## General Economic and Business Conditions

Businesses can grow and prosper during poor economic conditions just as in times of boom. However, the strategies used are not the same, as many companies have learned to their great regret. The experience of Howard Johnson's and its eventual shift from a formerly successful strategy provides an important example.

### The Howard Johnson Story

Howard Johnson was doing very well selling ice cream from his single restaurant in Quincy, Massachusetts, when, in 1935, he persuaded an acquaintance to open another Howard Johnson's restaurant on Cape Cod under a franchise. It was a new concept in which Johnson would design the restaurant, set the standards, and deliver the food. The franchisee would own the property and receive the bulk of the revenues, paying Johnson a percentage.

Almost overnight and despite the Great Depression, the strategy worked like a charm. By the following year, there were seventeen Howard Johnson's restaurants. All were immediately successful. By 1939, Johnson had 107 restaurants generating revenues of $10.5 million a year in 1939 dollars. Multiply that figure times ten and you'll have some idea of Johnson's real achievement.

Howard Johnson's provided quality food, clean premises, and reasonable prices. Moreover, Johnson insisted on strict adherence to his standards, or the franchisee lost his franchise. However, the real key to the Johnson franchise success was the increased construction of highways all over the United States, as more and more Americans took to the road. This was confirmed during World War II when the chain contracted to open only twelve restaurants, due to gas rationing and reduced travel by the public.

With travel back on after the war, the company bounced back. By 1972, it had 1,000 restaurants and forty-two motor lodges. Then came the Arab oil embargo. Americans quit driving at a time when 85 percent of the company's revenues were dependent on automobile travel. With increased competition from the fast-food chains, even the booming 1980s failed to rescue the company's restaurant business. The clear lesson is that even when times are bad, a strategy can be constructed that can be highly successful. But like all strategies, this strategy cannot work forever, and what has made a company successful in the past may well contribute to its demise. By the way, the Howard Johnson brand name lives on under ownership thrice changed, as one of the best-known, midpriced hotels in the world, with 500 establishments in fourteen countries.[9] ▮

## *The Competition*

Competitors are usually the most serious aspect of the environment with which the strategist must deal because the competition is an intelligent entity, and by definition, it is going to work against our interests. An analysis of the total environment includes all of the previous elements—leaders, workforce, resources, etc.—but it must also take into account major competitors. One of the most serious aspects of dealing with the competition that is frequently ignored is what I call "second-stage strategy."

**Second-Stage Strategy.** Frequently, very competent leaders direct the establishment of a well-thought-through strategy. However, that is as far as it goes. The assumption seems to be that competitors are just going to sit there and take it, to lose market share, and to accept the role assigned to them in our plans. That is rarely the case. An able competitor is going to do something to counter the strategy you have initiated. As an able strategist yourself, your job is to think through how he is going to respond and to put in place, or at least develop and prepare for, your second-stage strategy to invalidate and, if possible, take advantage of his actions.

**Price Wars—The Lack of a Second-Stage Strategy.** Price wars are probably the best (or maybe the worst) example of failure to have a second-stage strategy in place. Someone gets the brilliant idea of grabbing market share from the competition by slashing prices. If competitors can't retaliate with a little slashing of their own, one may be able to pull it off. However, the strategist who proposes this move usually hasn't thought it through, and initiation of this strategy is immediately met by the slashing of prices from the competition.

The strategist now gets desperate and again slashes prices. Before he knows it, he is in a full-scale price war. Rather than capturing any market share, profits are down to zero and no one is making any money.

It doesn't matter what kind of strategy you are looking at, whether it has to do with advertising, distribution, or financing. If it hurts the competition, you can bet they're going to try to counter it, and you had better be thinking ahead of time about what you are going to do about it.

| STRATEGIST'S LOG | TAILORING STRATEGY TO THE ENVIRONMENT |
| --- | --- |

Every situation has different environmental factors. Your optimal strategy for a given situation must take into account the total environment in which it is to be executed, or it is likely to fail, no matter how clever it may be. Among the many environmental factors that should be considered in formulating strategy are:

- The leader's personality, including style and ability
- Capabilities of subordinate leaders and workers
- Geography, climatic conditions, and season
- Culture of the marketplace
- Laws and regulations
- Politics
- Available resources
- General economic and business conditions
- The competition

You have to examine each and every one of these environmental variables in the light of the strategy you propose to introduce. There is no such thing as one strategy fitting all situations. You can't keep extrapolating the same successful strategy that has worked for you in the past out into the future without eventually falling on your face. The lesson here is to work with your environment, not to ignore it. ■

## CHAPTER 12

# Crisis Strategy—What to Do When Things Go Wrong

*"There cannot be a crisis next week. My schedule is already full."* —HENRY KISSINGER

*"The crisis of yesterday is the joke of tomorrow."* —H. G. WELLS

In December 1944, the war in Europe seemed to be almost over. Allied forces were pressing the defending German armies back on every front. It seemed only a matter of time until the end. But Hitler had prepared an ambitious plan to force the Allies to retreat. After secretly husbanding reserves, he chose the weakest part of the Allied line and attacked with everything he had during a period of fog, rain, and snow when superior Allied airpower could not be employed. His plan was to rip through to Antwerp on the coast, crippling the Allied line of supply.

At first the Germans were successful, forcing a retreat. However, their complete success depended upon capturing certain strategic towns held by American General Omar Bradley. The Germans thought that these towns would have to surrender, because reinforcements would take days to arrive, and food and ammunition were insufficient. Still, they continued to hold on.

Patton's Third Army had been facing east in the area of the Saar in the south. Most thought it would take him days to disengage from the enemy, and then plunge northward to assist Bradley. However, Patton disengaged his troops, swung northward, relieved the strategic town of Bastogne, and in an amazing march taking hours instead of days, hit the southern flank of the Germans. He not only stopped the German attack, but eliminated the German gains entirely. In business terms, this was an immediate turnaround.

## ▮ A TURNAROUND SITUATION CALLS FOR A CRISIS STRATEGY

A turnaround has always been the ultimate test of a leader's strengths and abilities. My definition of a situation in need of a turnaround is a condition that is bad, and often getting worse. The leader has no alternative but to change the situation immediately, if not sooner. Unfortunately, despite Henry Kissinger's words in the opening quote, one cannot schedule for a crisis. Although the condition may have been a long time in the making, once it is recognized as a crisis situation, things are usually both desperate and unexpected. A turnaround is a crisis situation. To correct a crisis situation, you need a crisis strategy.

A crisis challenge provides strong confirmation of a strategist's worth. Were it not for the strategist, the situation would still be bad, still be in crisis. But due to the strategist's efforts, everything changes for the better.

## ▮ THE REQUIREMENTS FOR A SUCCESSFUL TURNAROUND STRATEGY

Every turnaround strategy has five requirements that the strategist must meet in order to succeed. These are:

1. Dominate the situation and take immediate charge.

2. Set a clear objective, and act boldly and decisively to achieve it.

3. Communicate your plans and progress.

4. Lead by example.

5. Hire and fire quickly, but wisely.

### *Dominate the Situation and Take Immediate Charge*

When Bernard L. Montgomery took over as commander of the British Eighth Army in Africa during World War II, it was not a plum assignment. Montgomery was then only a lieutenant general. He had done well in the Battle of France, and Churchill had especially selected him for this assignment.

Montgomery has since been criticized for many faults, but failure to take charge and dominate the situation was not one of them. He knew that he faced a crisis situation. His opponent, the German General Erwin Rommel and his Afrika Korps, had defeated the Eighth Army repeatedly. Rommel wasn't known as "The Desert Fox" for nothing. After several defeats, Montgomery's predecessor, General Claude Auchinleck, had finally won a victory at Tobruck. But flushed with success, he had attacked Rommel again and the Desert Fox had once again trounced the unlucky British commander.

The situation could only be called desperate. There was now the danger of an immediate counterattack by Rommel. With British morale at its lowest ebb, it could have resulted in total defeat and driven the Eighth Army off the African continent. The facts are the facts. The Eighth Army had an awful history in battling Rommel's Afrika Korps. It had made withdrawal after withdrawal over the previous months. In fact, Auchinleck had already issued a warning to prepare for yet another retreat should Rommel attack as anticipated.

And so, Montgomery arrived. Here's what he did immediately:

- He canceled the previous orders about withdrawal in the event of a German attack.

- He issued new orders. If Rommel attacked, there would be no withdrawal. The Eighth Army would fight where it stood. In Montgomery's words, "If we couldn't stay there alive, we would stay there dead."

- He fired his old chief of staff and immediately appointed a new one.

- From survivors of decimated units, which could no longer function independently, he formed an entirely new armored corps.

- He totally reorganized by changing his basic fighting units from brigade groups and ad hoc columns to full divisions. Some management experts maintain that reorganization is major surgery. If so, Montgomery performed major surgery, even as he faced a major crisis.

■ He told his staff to start working on plans for an offensive. "Our mandate is to destroy Rommel and his army, and it will be done as soon as we are ready," he told them.

Writing of these events years later, Montgomery said: "By the time I went to bed that night, I was tired. But I knew that we were on the way to success."[1]

I want to focus on these words: "By the time I went to bed that night, I was tired." You see, Montgomery did all of these things on his very first day.

It was only a few months later that under Montgomery's orders, the Eighth Army attacked Rommel's Afrika Korps at El Alamein. It was a major victory for the British and a turning point of the war in the North African theater of operations. Montgomery eventually was promoted to field marshal, the highest rank in the British Army. He was also awarded the title of "Montgomery of Alamein."[2] The title has a nice ring and certainly is worthy of a leader and a strategist who dominated the situation and took immediate charge.

**Take Action to Take Control.** As a strategist in circumstances where you have to implement a turnaround, you must dominate the situation, or it will dominate you. By this, I mean that you must take positive actions to gain control. You must continue to initiate actions to maintain control.

Failing to do this, you will waste your time and energy by continually responding to the actions of others, or to the crises of your environment as they crop up. You know the term for this. It is called "fire fighting." Fire fighting will steal all of your time, leaving no opportunity for you to develop the new initiatives that must be part of your strategy.

There are two reasons why you must take positive action right away, and they aren't complicated. In any crisis situation, there is a desperate need for leadership because people are scared and uncertain, and morale is usually low. If you do not take the initiative, someone must fill the leadership vacuum. Someone else will attempt to fill the role that you must. You may be the leader and this other person may not be as experienced, as qualified, or as trained as you. It makes no difference. If you fail to act at once and take the initiative, someone else will attempt to fill the leadership role, and you will have to fight to regain it.

The second reason why you must immediately dominate the situation has to do with the environment. If you fail to take the initiative, the environment tends to build up on you in a negative way. First, you have one problem. Then, you have two problems. Soon you have yet another. In a short time, the situation becomes unmanageable, and no one will be able to execute a successful turnaround.

## *Set a Clear Objective, and Act Boldly and Decisively to Achieve It*

When Montgomery was given command of the British Eighth Army, he wasn't just told, "Here's your army, see what you can do with it." He was given a definite objective by his boss, Field Marshal Harold Alexander: "Destroy Rommel and his army."

Montgomery knew that having a clear objective was critical. He said, "I hold the view that the leader must know what he himself wants. He must see his objective clearly and then strive to attain it; he must let everyone else know what he wants and what are the basic fundamentals of his policy. He must, in fact, give firm guidance and a clear lead."

Montgomery's receiving and setting of a clear objective helped turned the tide permanently for the British in North Africa during World War II. It demonstrates both the value and necessity of setting a clear objective right away in turnaround situations.

### Bold Action at Lotus

Lotus Engineering in the United Kingdom is world renowned for its technology-on-the-cutting-edge Lotus sports cars. However, a few years ago Lotus almost crashed into the wall. Only a few weeks after being hired as CEO, Chris Knight found himself and his company in the middle of a major, and unexpected, crisis. The sudden crash of the Asian stock market and poor prior cash management put Lotus days away from bankruptcy. Knight had to fashion a turnaround strategy and implement it fast.

He didn't wait to see if things were going to get better. Time was not on his side. He took charge and dominated the situation at once. The goal was pretty clear. If Lotus didn't come up with the cash right away, no more company. This was Knight's immediate objective: to find the cash to survive in the near term. Recognizing the urgent need for help, he acted on it at once. Knight hired an experienced consultant, James Basden of Corven Services.

Knight decided that the turnaround strategy had to be based on both immediate cash saving and cash generation. Both would be necessary to save the company. He formed a cross-functional team with Basden as facilitator. Primarily, the team looked for "quick wins" that would show instant results. In order to achieve this, this had to be an action team. That is, it made decisions, and then implemented them.

A typical decision leading to action was order fulfillment. Order fulfillment was slow, and it was affecting cash flow in a major way. Moreover, fixing this problem would send a strong message to everyone about the need for immediate action. And it would show that the company's leader was serious and was going to succeed in saving the company. So the team changed a fundamental policy. Cars would only be built to order. Payment was received when the car was built, not three months later. This provided additional incentive to accelerate production. Amazingly, delivery time was cut in half and both customer service and cash flow benefited.

The overall results were immediate. Lotus came up with over $64 million in forty-five days, impressing both external creditors and itself. This laid the basis for future strategies for building the health of the company.[3] ∎

**On Being a Decisive Crisis Strategist.** People do not like to follow leaders who cannot make up their minds or have trouble coming to a decision. In developing and implementing a crisis strategy, you must make decisions and communicate them as soon as practicable.

Before September 11, 2001, Rudy Giuliani was not a particularly popular mayor of New York City. He had a romantic affair while in office, and he had gone through a messy divorce. An operation for prostate cancer had taken him away from politics, and he wasn't frequently seen or interviewed on national media. Though mayor of America's largest city, many Americans had never heard of him, and others who had heard of him didn't like what they'd heard. Even in New York, many citizens were simply awaiting the end of his term of office.

Then came the terrorist attacks. There was little he didn't do as a decisive crisis strategist. Giuliani seemed everywhere at once. He communicated as few have before, or since. He was on every television and radio station. He was accessible and visible to all. Others looked to the mayor for leadership in this crisis, and he did not fail them. He listened, encouraged, helped, planned, directed, counseled, consoled and was personally on the scene to direct and to consult in rescue and cleanup efforts. He visited the injured in countless hospitals and attended over 100 funerals. He kept the city, country, and the world informed of what he and New York were doing in this critical time. He didn't always have all the facts, especially at first. No one even knew if more attacks were to follow.

However, Giuliani did not falter, and he did not hesitate. He made tough decisions, even though there was no precedent for this situation and there was limited available information about what to do. He boldly made decisions about where to put and how to use his frequently limited resources. He made decisions as to how long search teams were to continue to work in what appeared to be hopeless cases. He told the citizenry what they could expect, and what they should do, and he told his subordinates what he expected from them, as well. His bold actions and demeanor in the face of adversity gave the rest of us the courage and determination to do what needed to be done. As a result, the country got through this attack, and New York City became a symbol for America's determination to persevere. Giuliani's actions rightfully won for him accolades from around the world.

Maybe you think that you have trouble coming to a decision because you don't have all the facts. Let me assure you that you will never have all the facts. That's just the nature of leadership and crisis situations. This means that almost all of the time, you must make decisions without knowing everything that would help you to do so.

Now it is true that the longer you wait, the more you will have better facts and better information. Sometimes it is necessary to wait for important facts before making a decision. But you must weigh the delay against the negative impact. Elements of the situation can change. An opportunity may be lost. Your competition may take the advantage because of your indecisiveness. Those who follow you will, at best, be uncomfortable at not having your decision. In a crisis, you should avoid indecisiveness at all costs.

I have seen some leaders tell themselves that they are putting off a decision in order to get more facts. But the real reason is that for one reason or another they are afraid to make a decision. Failing to make a decision is also a decision. It is a decision to leave everything to chance or the initiative of others. It is not a sign of the kind of leader and strategist needed in a turnaround. And it usually results in failure.

To be a crisis leader and strategist you must be bold and decisive. Follow the recommendation of W. Clement Stone, the self-made multimillionaire who said when you feel yourself putting off a decision without reason, speak these three words out loud: "Do it now!"

## Communicate Your Plans and Progress

It is important to understand that there are many ways of communicating plans and progress. Speeches, articles, advertisements, and direct interaction with the media are the most obvious. However, there are also less obvious communication methods, which can be even more effective in carrying the message of turnaround success to both members of the organization and outside individuals and agencies. The positive effect on these various publics is returned toward the organization through their attitude, and it has a further impact on the progress in turning around the crisis.

In 1995, the American Ballet Theatre (ABT) was in deep trouble. The touring program, ABT's major source of income, had been in decline for some time. This meant less public recognition of its principal dancers, and so box office income had also fallen. Now the company owed almost $5 million, and it could not pay its bills. Fingers of blame were pointed in all directions, morale was low, and donors were reluctant to contribute to what was clearly a losing cause. The performers were also unhappy, and the press, fully apprised of the situation, made dire predictions about the future prospects of this sixty-year-old company. It was at this point that the board of directors hired Michael Kaiser as executive director.

Kaiser had a proven background in developing and implementing turnaround strategies at other art organizations. He knew that he had to take immediate action and come up with a plan. He also knew that communication was vital. Said Kaiser:

> Most turnarounds are as much a matter of changing perceptions as they are of strengthening balance sheets. Perceptions change when a continuous stream of information suggests that an organization has taken a new, vital path. This means that no one artistic initiative, positive review, or major grant is enough to change the minds of most people. The entire approach to communicating to the public—through an integrated marketing program—must be rethought.
>
> The marketing program must include both programmatic elements (marketing for individual performances or seasons) and institutional elements (marketing for the organization as an entity).[4]

Kaiser developed several important, new artistic ventures. The first was easy to do, and didn't cost much. ABT developed a master-class series when the company was not performing locally. The series allowed ABT to communicate to donors in a direct and dramatic fashion.

The first master class was presented and seen as the first public manifestation of the turnaround. Cynthia Gregory, a leading performer, taught three young dancers some of her roles in front of an audience of 500 people. Not only were they captivated by her teaching and seeing something they had never seen before, they felt that ABT had turned a corner. In fact, this modest beginning was followed by a more risky full-length commissioned ballet to a new score of *Othello*. The ABT had never done this before.

Other initiatives were also promoted, including new touring initiatives, a relationship with the new New Jersey Performing Arts Center in Newark, the creation of a junior company, the initiation of an important arts-in-education program in Harlem, and the development of a series of summer programs for teenagers.

The steady stream of new ideas and new programs, coupled with improving financial health, did a great deal to remake the image of the organization. As conditions improved, Kaiser was able to hire four new, talented, male principals. When the public perceived ABT to be the company with the best principal dancers in the world, Kaiser knew he had won.

While other factors also contributed to the turnaround strategy for ABT, Kaiser's leadership in taking new initiatives, and the constant communication of these initiatives, were the major element leading to ABT's success.

**Communicate Fast, Accurately, and Repeatedly.** Communicating fast and accurately is critical in any crisis situation. During the SARS outbreak in Canada in 2002, the need was clear. Information about the disease unfolded quickly, and bulletins were sent to physicians by national organizations and ministries of health using whatever mechanism was available in every way they could. However, getting the word to physicians in urban areas was more difficult, especially when some had no access to the Internet. Rogers AT&T Wireless experimented with using wireless technology to send information to urban physicians over their personal digital assistants (PDAs). This worked so well that some physicians are anticipating wireless telephones being used as a primary method of communication in future medical crises.[5]

During World War II, General Patton knew the value of the latest technology and was a real believer in using it. He didn't have wireless technology. But he did what he could with what he had. In training his troops prior to deployment, he kept a microphone constantly nearby. Porter B. Williamson, one of his officers reported, "Our desert radio broadcasting station had one unusual feature. There was a microphone in General Patton's office and a second microphone by his bed in his tent. Day and night General Patton could cut off all broadcasting and announce a special message or order from his personal mike. When the music would click off, we knew we would hear, 'This is General Patton.' Then clearly, accurately, and unmistakably, General Patton gave his instructions, telling everyone exactly what he wanted done."[6] I've seen other leaders in crisis and other situations do the same thing.

You cannot communicate your vision, objectives, and goals too often, or in too many different ways. The more layers in your chain of command, the more likely it is that your message will get garbled between you and the individuals who must implement what you want done. So the more often you can get your message out, and the more different media which you can use to do this, the better.

Also, by repeating and promoting your message, your subordinates will know that you really mean it, and they will begin to quote you (and promote you) themselves.

Of course, the words you choose in communicating your message can also be very important. You may be familiar with these famous words: "I have not yet begun to fight." "Don't fire until you see the whites of their eyes." "Damn the torpedoes, full speed ahead." "I shall return." All of these words were uttered by leaders, communicating with their men, and they had a tremendous impact on the leader's taking charge. There is no law against leaders in noncombat situations voicing their objectives in a dramatic way, either.

If you want your words to get out fast—to be repeated again and again and maybe to go down in history—communicate in a colorful and interesting way.

## Lead by Example

Back before 9/11, when the airline industry was strong, Continental Airlines was in last place out of the ten major airlines. It had gone through numerous CEOs. All had failed to alter the situation. *Fast Company* called Continental "a flying basket case" and "a horror show." It offered cheap fares on out-of-the-way routes, but it lacked the operational efficiency to make the lowball strategy pay off. Its jets were old, its on-time record lousy. More to the point, Continental had decimated the relationships it needed to fly high. It had reduced (or eliminated) agency commissions on low-priced routes, and it had laid off half of its sales reps. It rarely called on corporate purchasers. It had gutted its OnePass frequent-flier program.[7]

Then in 1994, the board of directors hired Gordon Bethune. Bethune turned Continental around almost immediately. Within a single year, it had gone from last place to first place in the industry in the J.D. Powers report of customer satisfaction. This was the first time in the history of airlines that this had ever happened.[8] Moreover, instead of losing money Continental was making it—and not just a little—but quite a lot. Even in these bad years for the industry, sales grew by a little over 6 percent in 2002.

What did Bethune do to accomplish this turnaround? He got Continental's employees to focus on the right things: on-time takeoffs, customer service, value for the airline dollar spent. He put in place an incentive program for aircrew, support personnel, and company executives. Continental rebuilt relationships with corporate customers and travel agents—and with its own employees. Bethune communicated to all of these constituents and let them know what was going on, as progress was made. But more than anything, this CEO led by example.

He didn't lead from an air-conditioned office. With a background in the Navy as a jet aircraft mechanic, he learned to fly, and he got the ratings that qualified him to fly the big jets his company owned. He flew on his aircraft himself so he could actually see and understand the problems. He didn't work less than his employees. He led by example, a critical action for any turnaround or crisis situation.

CEO Forum is a Web site for CEOs sponsored by Bain International in Australia. In a recent article on turnaround strategy, the authors, two Bain International vice presidents, Stan Pace and Paul Rogers, noted, "So what is the formula for successful change? First, advocates of transformation programs must be real leaders. They need to roll up their sleeves, clearly see the job, and get on with it. If you are asking the entire company to share your vision, you must begin by leading from the front. You must be seen as a person of action. You need to introduce a single set of performance and ethical standards and communicate these as simple, powerful messages to all employees."[9]

## Hire and Fire Quickly, but Wisely

In a crisis or turnaround situation, you don't have time to fool around. You must get rid of those individuals who are performing poorly, and you have to replace these people with people who can do the job.

For most people, firing is not an easy thing to do. Those you must discharge may have worked at a job or with your organization for some time. They may (or may not) have done their best. Either way, firing can mean a loss of money, prestige, security, and sense of self-worth. Still, if you are going to be true to yourself and to your organization as a leader, and implement a turnaround strategy, you have no choice.

Remember, we're not talking about ordinary, day-to-day management. We're speaking about crisis situations and crisis strategy. If your organization has a worthwhile purpose and mission, it must come first under these circumstances.

This is easier to see in warfare, where the actions and the decisions people take may mean the difference between life and death, victory and defeat. It is sometimes more difficult to understand in business situations.

What harm is it to keep people in your organization who are not performing up to standard? First, these individuals may be incapable of doing any better than they already have. Otherwise, the crisis situation wouldn't exist in the first place. Second, it is essential to get people in important positions who can implement your strategy, and do the job as you want it done. You can't do this with incumbents occupying the key positions. Finally, you can't motivate others to go all out in a crisis when you demonstrate that you are willing to except less than the very best from others. If you have the time to develop subordinates, there may not be a need for an immediate bloodletting. However, in a turnaround situation, time is rarely on your side.

Now I want to make certain that you understand fully what I am saying. Just because you are a leader doesn't mean that you fire everyone in sight that you think you can replace with someone better. That's not ethical. It demonstrates poor leadership, and it will probably interfere with the implementation of your turnaround strategy rather than help it. There may well be situations that are not crises when, for various reasons, you should tolerate people in your organization who are not performing to your standards. An individual who is no longer capable of turning in top performance, but who has done a good job in the past, may be one example. Also, if possible, you should attempt to save a person from being fired first. However, in a crisis, turnaround situation, don't waste time.

**Hiring Is as Important as Firing in a Crisis Situation.** Crisis situations in war can confirm just how important hiring is. George Washington, our first president, "the father of our country," and our first overall military commander, was appointed by the Continental Congress in a crisis situation. While he didn't exactly come out of obscurity, he wasn't a shoo-in for the job.

Washington was a gentleman farmer who had on occasion held a commission in the British Army, but not as a particularly senior officer. In the early 1960s, the wall of the office of the British military attaché in Washington, D.C. bore a portrait of Washington, beneath which the following words were humorously written: "Major George Washington, Wanted for Treason."

The rank of major is not very senior, and there were others in the American camp who had held much higher rank and responsibility, both in the English and other armies. But the Continental Congress selected Washington because they believed him to be the best, and battle confirmed the wisdom of their selection.

Other wars have shown the same concept in play. During the American Civil War, the man who led the Union to victory, and who became the first U.S. four-star general, was a former captain named Ulysses S. Grant, who had been cashiered from the Army for drunkenness. Before World War II, Dwight Eisenhower was an unknown lieutenant colonel when Army Chief of Staff General George Marshall plucked him from nowhere and skipped him over the rank of colonel (and hundreds of more senior officers) to make him a general. Marshall showed great forethought in that he actually kept a book of highly qualified officers who impressed him over the years. When crisis in the form of war came and he was in a position to make things happen, he knew just who he wanted in various critical positions. This is interesting, because Lee Iacocca did the same.

When Lee Iacocca turned the Chrysler Corporation around, it was with the help of a government guarantee on a loan. However, Iacocca handled the crisis and performed the turnaround primarily through his choice of people. Like General Marshall, he tracked the careers of several hundred executives in his former organization with whom he had previously come in contact. So important was his notebook containing the names of these individuals that he obtained special permission from

William Ford, president of the Ford Motor Company, to take the note-book with him when he left. Many of the new executives he brought to Chrysler came from this notebook.

The problem with most leaders in putting their team together in a turnaround situation is that they don't prepare at all. They ask one or two questions in an interview, and if everything seems okay, they offer the job. I mean, after all, this is a crisis situation, right? This would certainly seem to be the time to ask detailed questions concerning exactly what needs to be done in order to make sure that you are hiring the right person for the job. If you fire wisely, but fail to hire wisely, you've only done half the job, and your turnaround strategy is not likely to be suc-cessful.

| *STRATEGIST'S LOG* | IMPLEMENTING A CRISIS STRATEGY |
|---|---|

You may master the ten essential principles of strategy as presented in this book. You may be implementing them successfully at your com-pany and combining them in different ways to make them even more powerful. However, sooner or later you're going to hit a crisis. The true test of a leader is how the individual formulates and implements strat-egy when things go wrong. A good strategist knows how to correct a crisis situation—how to execute a turnaround.

These are the five essential ingredients for a successful crisis or turnaround strategy:

1. *Dominate the situation by taking the initiative.* If you don't, the situa-tion will dominate you. Don't overanalyze. Take immediate action in order to take control of things and to show your people that you are in control.

2. *Establish your objective at once and act boldly and decisively to achieve it.* This is not a time for caution. This is the time for action and risk taking. Decide now, and act now.

3. *Communicate your plans and progress.* Everybody loves a winner, so let others know that you are in the winner's category. Promote your successes so they can snowball into even greater successes.

4. *Lead by example.* The company president who forces his people to take pay cuts while maintaining his own compensation package will probably fail. One of Arnold Schwarzenegger's first acts as the

new governor of California was to forego his annual salary. True, the multimillionaire, former movie star didn't need the money. But everyone got the symbolism.

5. *Get rid of people who can't do the job and put people who can in charge.* In a crisis situation, you must get rid of the deadwood and put people in place who get the job done fast. ▪

## CHAPTER 13

# How to Apply the Principles of Strategy

*"Method goes far to prevent trouble in business; for it makes the task easy, hinders confusion, saves abundance of time, and instructs those who have business depending, what to do and what to hope."* —WILLIAM PENN

*"Statistics are no substitute for judgment."* —HENRY CLAY

The frustrated executive shook his head violently. He pounded the desk as he shut his eyes tightly in frustration. "The principles of strategy are impossible to apply," he muttered. The strange-looking man standing before him made no response.

The executive was clearly someone of importance. The jacket to his Brooks Brothers suit hung from a hanger attached to a hook on the back of his office door. In its dormant position, it revealed little. But one could judge much about the man from what was worn: razor-creased trousers, an expensive tie, loosened, but still tied around a thick neck, a broadcloth shirt, the sleeves rolled up on the forearms to reveal an expensive Rolex on the left wrist. What could cause someone like this so much discomfort?

The strange-looking man opposite him rather resembled Father Time. He was ancient. His hands trembled slightly. He had a long white beard. Wrinkles creased his skin, and his back was bent with age. He used a staff to assist his stance, but he had already refused an invitation to sit. His clothes did not match the present environment. They were ancient-man basic. They consisted of a white muslin robe, long, but not so long to conceal rough leather sandals with no socks. He wore no watch or other adornment.

The executive reached for a yellow, legal-size pad of paper. Half of the pages were curled, heavy with untidy notes. "I don't care what Hannibal did in Italy or Sun Tzu in China a couple of thousand years ago. I live in the real world of business today. You may be a seer, but you are no help. How can I economize to mass resources without everybody and his brother seeing what I am up to? There is no surprise there. And you can't approach things indirectly forever. Eventually you must reach out and touch someone. You have to do this directly. And what's this nonsense about multiple, simultaneous alternatives? I'm lucky to find the cash to fund one new initiative to approach a single objective at a time."

"Strategy is an art," commented the seer, ignoring the questions.

"Well, I don't deal with art. I'm a businessman. I run an important organization, and I am responsible for the bottom line. I know my stuff; the bottom line means numbers. I deal with numbers, with facts, not with blue-sky concepts."

"You tried formulating strategy by crunching numbers, remember?" said the seer, undeterred. "You got numbers, and graphs, and percentages, and they told you what to do. You did exactly what the numbers indicated. But your competition triumphed over you, and your strategy failed. You got your lunch eaten."

"But it shouldn't have happened! We paid a bundle to experts for those analyses. The computer programs we developed to formulate our answers were based on cutting-edge research. I put some of my best people on the project to help develop that strategy."

"The best computer is here." The seer tapped his head lightly with the handle of his staff. "But there is a methodology that will help you to use your God-given judgment, which every man—and every woman—has in abundance, to apply the principles to develop the optimal strategy you seek."

The executive leaned forward, pen in one hand, a fresh sheet of yellow paper ready in the pad clutched in the other. What the seer told the executive is detailed in the following paragraphs.

## A SCIENTIFIC METHOD WITHOUT CRUNCHING NUMBERS

Numbers are important in the development of strategy, for they may act as valuable inputs to that greatest of computers and computer programming, the human brain. Yet, it is your judgment in applying the principles of strategy that enables the development of a plan that works, not any assignment of numbers and percentages. These can never replace the incredible abilities of the human brain to integrate vast amounts of data, both qualitative as well as quantitative, and to reason things through to a solution that works.

In fact, we can induce major error into the development of strategy when we attempt to assign numbers to elements that actually cannot, and should not, be quantified. This is because assigning numbers to qualitative aspects gives the appearance of fact, when in reality we are simply cloaking judgment in a way to make it seem absolute. Thus, the tyranny of numbers.

However, this does not mean that the application of principles to strategy development is not scientific, whether quantifiable or not. The scientific method is a process that is a reliable, consistent, and nonarbitrary representation of the real world. It minimizes the influence of bias and prejudice. Because numbers are most easily controlled, we frequently assume that being scientific requires quantifiable entering arguments. This is not necessarily true. What is true is that we must approach the output we seek in a standard manner so that the output yields consistent results. In this way, we can avoid a repetition of past errors, capitalize on the greatest chances for success, and reach predictable results.

This is crucially important when employing judgment in utilizing the principles and in coordinating the many factors that must be considered in developing operational strategy. And it is painfully true when various principles conflict under certain conditions (which they often do) or when, under different conditions, one principle is more important than another, which is also true.

## ▍ PRINCIPLES, RESOURCES, AND SITUATIONAL VARIABLES

There are three key aspects to any situation we face when we apply the principles of strategy. These are:

- The principles themselves
- The available resources
- The relevant variables found in the situation faced

In Chapter 11, we looked at the application of strategy to our environment. We considered the environment to include everything but the principles, that is, both resources and all other variables found in the situation. Now we're going to separate resources and situational variables in order to apply them in a particular methodology.

We have already examined the ten essential principles in preceding chapters. The resources we have available consist of such elements as manpower, capital, equipment, special knowledge, ability and know-how, and all other assets. We have also looked previously at the environmental variables and know that they include economic conditions, business conditions, state of technology, politics, legal and regulatory requirements, social and cultural norms, and the competition.

The strategist first looks at all aspects of the situation and carefully selects the relevant variables within it. Each variable must be turned to an advantage, avoided, overcome, or ignored. The strategist's purpose is to integrate the relevant variables with the principles, and using the available resources, develop a plan to accomplish the mission.[1]

In Figure 13-1, I have prepared three lists of the aspects necessary, side by side. Rather than relying on numbers, statistics, percentages, and the like, this chart provides a quick overview of the elements that should be considered when developing an appropriate strategy for a given situation.

## CASE IN POINT: ATTACKING THE MARKET LEADER'S TOP PRODUCT

To illustrate the method for applying the principles of strategy, let's look at one of the most successful new product introductions ever undertaken against a market leader. In 1936, Lever Brothers, number two in the soap business behind Procter & Gamble (P&G), introduced Spry vegetable shortening to compete against P&G's well-entrenched Crisco brand.[2] The smart money said "no way." Having been on the market for twenty years, Crisco was firmly established. Despite the Great Depression, its sales were up. Plus, it had no serious challengers, despite that fact that lard and butter were far less expensive. The Crisco name had become synonymous with vegetable shortening and was almost generic. When women asked for "Crisco," they meant vegetable shortening. Yet within one year of introduction, Spry had captured 50 percent of Crisco's market share. Moreover, there were no new ingredients used, and Spry was made from exactly the same raw materials as Crisco.

*Figure 13-1*

| CRITERIA FOR EVALUATING A GIVEN SITUATION TO DEVELOP A STRATEGY | | |
|---|---|---|
| *Situational Variables* | *Principles of Strategy* | *Available Resources* |
| Economic conditions | Commitment to a definite objective | Manpower |
| Business conditions | Seizing and maintaining the initiative | Capital |
| State of technology | Economization to mass | Equipment |
| Politics | Positioning | Special knowledge |
| Legal and regulatory issues | Surprise | Leaders |
| Social and cultural norms | Simplicity | Other relevant resources |
| The competition | Multiple simultaneous alternatives | |
| Other relevant variables | The indirect approach | |
| | Timing and sequencing | |
| | Exploitation of success | |

## How Lever Brothers Did It

Lever Brothers was a subsidiary of Unilever of London, a giant world-wide corporation. Having been successful with a number of products in the United States, during the late 1920s, it was looking for another new product to launch in America. The company first looked at all aspects of the situation. A vegetable-shortening product seemed a good potential candidate. P&G had already proven there was a market. Although Lever's potential competitor's product was well established, its dominance also meant there were no other major competitors or competitive products to contend with. At the time of the initial decision, both business and economic conditions were good.

Lever initiated a deeper look into its competitor's product and found some weaknesses. Although women liked Crisco, there were some things that they didn't like. If refrigerated, it turned hard and was difficult to use. If left unrefrigerated, it tended to turn rancid. The color was not consistent, and while housewives would have preferred the product in a pure white colorization, it tended to be described more as a sort of dirty white color. Moreover, the packaging was not uniform in the cans in which it was supplied, and the housewives didn't like that, either.

**Integrating the Principles.** Looking at the principles of strategy, we can see how some were integrated with the situational variables to this point. Lever Brothers seized the initiative and committed to a definite objective. It planned to concentrate resources at the strategic position of vegetable shortening. P&G thought its product, Crisco, was invulnerable; thus it paid little attention and did no research with the consumer. In fact, it had even allowed quality control in manufacturing and packaging to get sloppy. As a consequence, the thought that a competitor, even a major one like Lever Brothers, would introduce a product to compete with Crisco was totally unexpected, even unthinkable. Lever Brothers capitalized on this belief. Coupled with good security, the Spry product was launched with complete surprise.

**Looking at Resources.** Lever Brothers decided which of the situational variables could be taken advantage of, avoided, or overcome. Moreover, it had the resources to do this and to support the general principles of strategy it was planning. Unilever had made major technological advances in Europe in the manufacture of soap, and the technology was directly transferable to the production of vegetable shortening due to hydrogenation, the major process common to both types of products. Thus, a vegetable-shortening product was compatible with Lever's experience, know-how, and technical advantage. The problems with Crisco noted by consumers were easy to overcome. Some simply had to do with stricter quality control. Financial resources and know-how were on Lever's side, but it even had one additional major advantage.

**Lever Brothers' Secret Weapon.** Francis Conway had become president of Lever Brothers in 1913 when sales were but $1 million. By the late 1920s, sales were over $40 million, largely due to his personal leadership. Conway had met every challenge thrown at him, and he had the confidence of the parent company leadership back in England. Unilever invested the money to build the manufacturing plants to make the product. By the early 1930s, Lever Brothers was ready to go.

**Enter the Great Depression.** The Great Depression began in October 1929 and preempted Lever's product launch. By mid-1930, it was clear this was not an economic condition that would change anytime soon. Lever had planned on introducing the product by then. There was tremendous pressure from within the company and the parent corporation to do so. The company had sunk a lot of money in Spry up to this point. Lever wanted to get on with it. However, Conway knew his strategy and the importance of timing. He made the decision to wait. Meanwhile, he did note that the sales of Crisco did not slow during the Depression, so vegetable shortening was still a winner. While Spry was shelved, the fine-tuning went on, and research into the best promotional approach was initiated.

**The Product Launch.** In late 1935, lard and butter prices rose. This created a situation whereby the higher-priced shortening would be more price competitive. Lever Brothers did not intend to compete with P&G on price, which would be a direct approach strategy. Instead, although it was competing with essentially an identical product, the approach was indirect in the sense that problems with Crisco, recognized by consumers but not by the manufacturer, were all corrected in the new product, Spry. Therefore, on the day it first appeared on the market, Spry was already free of the problems that Crisco still presented to the consumer.

Again, Conway economized elsewhere to concentrate and initiate a massive promotional campaign. Until this time, the conventional wisdom was to introduce advertising for a new product, then let it be assimilated gradually by the consumer. Conway eschewed this approach and gave it everything he had on day one. This included door-to-door salesmen distributing one-pound sample cans and free Spry cookbooks. Discount coupons and advertising were put in small-town newspapers. Conway also launched a mobile cooking school that went around the country doing two-hour demonstrations. P&G was stunned, and though it improved its product and manufacturing, it never recaptured the shares it had lost. Conway and Lever Brothers integrated the relevant variables with the principles, and using the resources available, developed and initiated a plan which made Spry a success, despite the seemingly overwhelming advantages enjoyed by P&G with Crisco.

| STRATEGIST'S LOG | APPLYING THE PRINCIPLES SCIENTIFICALLY |
| --- | --- |

Strategy is an art, but the ten essential principles are not meant to be applied haphazardly. They should be applied scientifically. The strategist analyzes his situation and identifies the relevant variables. He uses numbers where necessary, but he does not allow them to overrule his good judgment. Rather, he integrates the relevant variables with the principles. Using the resources he has available, he develops and then implements the plan that will help him lead his company to victory. ▪

## CHAPTER 14

# The Principles Are Not Only Essential . . . They're Universal

*"Win with ability, not with numbers."*
—FIELD MARSHAL PRINCE ALEKSANDR V. SUVOROV

*"Let us go down, and there confound their language, that they may not understand one another's speech."*
— GENESIS 11:7

I began this book with the insight that the ten essential principles of strategy lead to success not only in business and warfare, but in any competitive situation.

Having a well-defined objective is essential for life goals, too. When he was a teenager, General George S. Patton wrote in his diary that his life goal was to command an army in desperate battle. People who knew management guru Peter F. Drucker when he was a young newspaper writer said that even in those early days, Drucker set his sights on becoming a consultant and management writer. Both Patton and Drucker are men of considerable ability. However, others of equal ability did not rise to equal stature, or make equal contributions. Through the essential principles of strategy, both of these men succeeded in rising even beyond their early goals.

We've seen the ten essential principles work time and again in warfare and business. But if you really want to understand the power behind the concepts in this book, consider this "mission impossible." Assume our subject is a forty-year-old, once-divorced and now unhappily married, not particularly glamorous American matron. Can such an individual, with no royal blood and few prospects, somehow win the hand of royalty in matrimony? Using the principles we have discussed in this book, she can. In fact, on May 3, 1937, she did.

On that date, American commoner Wallis Simpson, by then twice divorced, married the former King of England, Edward VIII, to become the Duchess of Windsor. Edward had even abdicated his throne in order to marry her.

How did Wallis Simpson accomplish this? First, she clearly defined her objective. We know this from a good friend and schoolmate who explained that Wallis had set out from the start to win the prince. Quite simply, while still in America, she planned to meet him and get him to fall in love with her. Her plan was simple. Get to England. Meet the prince. Get him to fall in love with her. Divorce her husband. Marry the prince. Clearly, she was committed to her "impossible dream" from the start. And she used multiple, simultaneous alternatives to achieve it.

Either through luck, or with Wallis's encouragement, her husband moved to London. Simpson sought out and became a friend of Thelma, the Viscountess Furness, who was at that time Prince Edward's lover. Through Thelma, Wallis met the prince. Some months later, Thelma was called to America. By then, Wallis had seized the initiative and become Thelma's best friend. When Thelma expressed concern that other women might court the prince in her absence, her good friend Wallis volunteered to "look after" him. Wallis had again taken the initiative and seized the moment, as well as put herself in the right strategic position to accomplish her objective.

With Thelma's blessing, Wallis and the prince were together almost every evening. For all practical purposes, Wallis became mistress of Fort Belvedere, the prince's private retreat outside of London. She did everything, from redecorating his house to planning the daily menus and taking personal care of the prince's pet pug dogs. To do this, she economized her time elsewhere and concentrated it at the prince's estate. However, she didn't behave as did others who visited Fort Belvedere. She did the unexpected. For example, during one dinner party, she playfully slapped the prince's hand and scolded him for his poor table manners when he reached to take a lettuce leaf out of the salad with his fingers. None of Edward's girl friends, especially Thelma, had ever done anything like that. Others were scandalized that this commoner would treat the future king in so cavalier a fashion. The prince, however, was amused. It is important to understand that this happened before the two became lovers.

By the time Thelma returned to London two months later, Wallis had the situation well in hand. She had skillfully employed the principle of timing. Thelma was out; Wallis was in. "Wallis looked after the prince exceedingly well," Thelma wryly commented later.

However, Wallis was still married. She had to both get out of her marriage and convince the prince to marry her. She managed both. First, she deepened the prince's affections by supporting his love of all things American, from casual sportswear to jazz music. In other words, she exploited her initial success. At the same time, she continued to exhibit the principle of surprise. Refusing to play a subordinate role in the relationship, she dominated the prince (rather than the other way around, as in his previous affairs). At least one friend claimed that this hold became so strong that Edward became Wallis's "absolute slave."

On January 20, 1936, the King of England died, and Prince Edward became King Edward VIII. If anything, at this point it appeared a wedding was even less likely. The Church of England opposed divorce, and as king, Edward was charged with defending the faith. Moreover, the Royal Marriages Act of 1772 forbade a member of the royal family to marry without the consent of Parliament. Was Parliament likely to approve the marriage of the king to a married, once-divorced, American commoner? In her dreams!

Under these new conditions, Wallis demonstrated applications of the principles of doing the unexpected and taking the indirect approach. Wallis's husband, Ernest Simpson, was embarrassed by this affair, which had become public and was attracting increasing attention. Many women with similar designs might have asked for a divorce. Wallis did not. She did the unexpected once again. According to some sources, she actually told her husband that she would *not* divorce him . . . unless it was to marry the king. This was the indirect approach, and it was very clever. It meant that the only salvation for Simpson's honor (and ego) would be in Wallis's marriage to the monarch. So, Ernest Simpson actually asked for and received a private audience with the king. Advocating for Wallis, he told Edward that he would agree to divorce Wallis, but only on condition that the king marry and remain faithful to her. Wallis may have been stuck under English law, but by doing the unexpected and taking the indirect approach, she found a way to make it irrelevant.

The English Prime Minister, Stanley Baldwin, issued an ultimatum to Edward: Renounce Wallis, or abdicate. Otherwise, the government would resign, and the opposition party would refuse to serve.

On December 11, 1936, Edward abdicated to marry "the woman I love." He became the Duke of Windsor. He and Wallis were married a few months later. One of the great love stories of the century? Perhaps. However, the British government's secret files on Simpson and Edward were supposed to remain sealed for 100 years, that is, until 2067. In 1999 the law was changed, requiring the Public Records Office to open all files that did not affect national security. There was a shocking revelation. Simpson had a lover, a "charming adventurer" by the name of Guy Marcus Trundle, not only during her campaign to win Edward, but after Edward had resigned the kingship and married her as well.[1]

Her strategy may have been deceitful and without moral principles, but without a doubt, it was an amazing demonstration of the power of the ten essential principles of strategy in a situation that had nothing to do with either business or war.

You may well question the ethics of some of Wallis's tactics. Like "the Force" in *Star Wars*, the essential principles of strategy are phenomena that have a dark side. And like "the Force," the principles work no matter who uses them or for what purposes they are wielded. A skilled practitioner of the essential principles has a tremendous advantage, which can be employed for either good or evil. However, an evil practitioner loses these advantages if a practitioner with integrity understands them as well, or better.

---

**STRATEGIST'S LOG**

## UNDERSTANDING THE UNIVERSAL APPLICATION OF THE PRINCIPLES

During my research in developing the ten essential principles of strategy, I became convinced that they will lead to success in all competitive life situations, including warfare, politics, sports, games, finding a job, romance, and most important for our purposes, business. Over the centuries, they have worked time and again for those strategists who recognized their power. By mastering them and learning to apply them in all competitive situations you encounter, you'll find that they work for you, too. ■

# Notes

## CHAPTER 1

1. www.soapworks.com, December 24, 2002.
2. "How'd They Do That? The Mother of Invention," *Extra Daily News* (May 15, 2000); available at http://www.extratv.com/cmp/spotlight/2000/05_15c.htm.
3. Louis Baldwin, *Triumph over the Odds* (New York: Carol Publishing Group, 1994), pp. 172–176.
4. Peter F. Drucker, *Management: Tasks, Responsibilities, Practices* (New York: Harper & Row, 1973), p. 77.
5. Benjamin B. Tregoe and John W. Zimmerman, *Top Management Strategy* (New York: Simon & Schuster, 1980), p. 40.
6. Ibid., p. 146.
7. Eric Schine and Peter Elstrom, "Not Exactly an Overnight Success," *BusinessWeek* (June 2, 1997), p. 133.
8. Qualcomm 2003 annual report: http://www.qualcomm/IR/annualreport, p. 25.
9. Hoover's Online, December 24, 2002; available at http://www.hoovers.com/co/capsule/6/0,2163,11436,00.html.

## CHAPTER 2

1. Henri de Jomini, *The Art of War*, translated by G. H. Mendell and W. P. Craighill (Philadelphia: J.B. Lippincott & Co., 1862), p. 167.
2. Michael Liedtke, "VeriSign Spruces Up Domain Name Business," *Los Angeles Times* (January 13, 2003), p. C2.
3. Katrina Brooker, "Herb Kelleher: The Chairman of the Board Looks Back," *Fortune* (May 28, 2001); available at http://www.fortune.com/fortune/articles/0,15114,373551-1,00.html, and http://www.fortune.com/fortune/articles/0,15114,373551-6,00.html.

## CHAPTER 3

1. Brent Schlender, "Gates at Work," *Fortune* (July 8, 2002); available at http://www.fortune.com/fortune/ceo/articles/0,15114,371336,00.html.
2. Amanda C. Kooser et al., "Got ID?" *Entrepreneur Magazine* (November 2002), pp. 67–68.
3. Giovanni Giocomo Casanova, as quoted in Robert Greene, *The 48 Laws of Power* (New York: Penguin Books, 2000), p. 175.

## CHAPTER 4

1. "The History of Cigarette Advertising"; available at http://www.uchsc .edu/sm/cihl/history_of_cigarette_smoke.htm.
2. John A. Warden III, *The Air Campaign* (Washington, DC: National Defense University Press, 1988), p. 9.
3. Ibid., pp. 10–11.
4. Richard T. Reynolds, *Heart of the Storm: The Genesis of the Air Campaign Against Iraq* (Montgomery, AL: Air University Press, 1994), p. 17.
5. Rick Atkinson, *Crusade: The Untold Story of the Persian Gulf War* (New York: Houghton Mifflin, 1993), p. 59.
6. James Carney and John F. Dickerson, "W. and the 'Boy Genius,'" *Time* (November 18, 2002), p. 43.
7. Nick Anderson and Richard Simon, "Bush's Security Bill Foes Give Up," *Los Angeles Times* (November 13, 2002), p. 1.

## CHAPTER 5

1. Bridget McCrea, "Win the Funding Game," *Fortune* (December 11, 2002); available at http://www.fortune.com/fortune/smallbusiness/creative/0,15704, 398322,00.html.
2. Joe Mathews and Doug Smith, "Role Reversal: 'Predator's' Prey Stalks Statehouse," *Los Angeles Times* (August 7, 2003), p. A24.
3. Jerry Fisher, "Sushi Surprise," *Entrepreneur Magazine* (August 2001); available at http://www.entrepreneur.com/Magazines/Copy_of_MA_Seg Article/0,4453,29124 5----1-,00.html.
4. April Pennington, "Away Game," *Entrepreneur Magazine* (August 2001); available at http://www.entrepreneur.com/Magazines/MA_SegArticle/ 0,1539,291063----1-,00.html.
5. All Things Equal, Inc. Web site; http://www.loadedquestions.com/index .html.
6. George S. Yip, "Gateways to Entry," *Harvard Business Review*, Vol. 60 (September–October, 1982), p. 89.
7. Peter F. Drucker, *Innovation and Entrepreneurship* (New York: Harper & Row, 1985), p. 220.
8. Ibid., p. 225.

## CHAPTER 6

1. Tom Hansson, Jürgen Ringbeck, and Markus Franke, "Flight for Survival: A New Operating Model for Airlines," *Strategy + Business* (December 9, 2002); available at http://www.strategy-business.com/enewsarticle/?art= 19050189.

2. Kate O'Sullivan, "Duh-Sign of the Times," *INC.com* (November 1, 2001); available at http://www.inc.com/magazine/20011101/23624.html.

3. Jim Greeley, "Desert One," *Airman* (April 2001); available at http://www.af.mil/news/airman/0401/hostage.html.

4. Rudy Wright, "Calamity at Desert One," *Veterans of Foreign Wars* (November 2002); available at http://www.vfw.org/magazine/nov02/calamityat desertone.htm.

5. Peter Verburg, "Top Salesman: Bill Lamberton," *Canadian Business Magazine* (April 28, 2003); available at http://www.canadianbusiness.com/features/article.jsp?content=20030428_53464_53464.

6. Brian Milligan, "Harley-Davidson Wins by Getting Suppliers on Board," *Purchasing.com* (September 21, 2000); available at http://www.manufacturing.net/pur/index.asp?layout=article&articleId=CA139508&stt=001&text=harley%2Ddavidson.

7. Harley-Davidson Web site (May 14, 2003); http://investor.harley-david son.com/index.cfm?locale=en_US&bmLocale=en _US.

8. Christine Blank, "Preconstruction Communication Helps Reduce Resistance to Projects," *Hotel and Motel Management* (June 3, 2002).

9. "The Real Problem," *IndustryWeek.com* (June 8, 1998); available at http://www.industryweek.com/CurrentArticles/asp/articles.asp?ArticleId=321.

**CHAPTER 7**

1. William A. Cohen, *The Stuff of Heroes: The Eight Universal Laws of Leadership* (Atlanta: Longstreet Press, 1998), pp. 126–127.

2. Shelby Foote, *The Civil War: Secession to Fort Henry*, 40th Anniversary Edition (Alexandria, VA: Time-Life Books, 1998), p. 37.

3. Ibid., p. 51.

**CHAPTER 8**

1. Donna Fenn, "Leader of the Pack," *Inc. Magazine* (February 1, 1996); available at http://www.inc.com/magazine/19960201/1544.html.

2. Donna Fenn, "A Bigger Wheel," *Inc. Magazine* (November 1, 2000); available at http://www.inc.com/articles/marketing/market_research/market_ research_basics/20908.html.

3. Basil H. Liddell Hart, *Strategy, Revised Edition* (New York: Frederick A. Praeger Publisher, 1961), p. 18.

4. "Promotions for Pennies," *BusinessWeek Online* (October 30, 2002); available at http://www.businessweek.com/smallbiz/content/oct2002/sb2002 1030_4259.htm?c=bwinsidernov1&n=link13&t=email.

5. Olga Kharif, "Judy Estrin's Unfailing Eye for Opportunity," *BusinessWeek*

*Online* (May 29, 2003); available at http://www.businessweek.com/tech nology/content/may2003/tc20030529_8240_PG2 _tc111.htm.


## CHAPTER 9

1. Kathy J. Kobliski, "Timing Is Everything," *Entrepreneur.com* (February 1, 2001); available at http://www.entrepreneur.com/Your_Business/YB_Seg Article/0,4621,286610,00.html.
2. Kimberly McCall, "Crash and Learn," *Entrepreneur.com* (October 2000); available at http://www.entrepreneur.com/Your_Business/YB_SegArticle/ 0,4621,279211,00.html.
3. *Inc.* staff, "Instant Gratification," *Inc. Magazine* (January 1989); available at http://www.inc.com/magazine/19890101/5500.html.
4. Edward Tse, "Competing in China: An Integrated Approach," *Strategy + Business* (Fourth Quarter, 1998); available at http://www.strategy-business .com/press/article/?art=14788&pg=0.
5. Albert Aiello, Jr., "Timing Is Everything," *CIO* (September 1, 1997); available at http://www.cio.com/archive/090197/expert.html?printversion= yes.
6. Gregory S. Carpenter and Kent Nakamoto, "Consumer Preference Formation and Pioneering Advantage," *Journal of Marketing Research* (August 1989), p. 298.
7. "Creating and Implementing Effective IT and E-Business Strategy," *Microsoft bCentral for UK Small Business* (August 19, 2003); available at http://www.bcentral.co.uk/marketing/ebusiness/abcebusinessstrategy.asp.
8. "E-Business Strategy"; available at http://www.cbi.bc.ca/strategy.htm.
9. Colin Beveridge, "Making IT Strategy," *myITadviser* (October 18, 2002); available at http://www.ncc.co.uk/ncc/myitadviser/archive/issue18/gam bit.cfm.
10. "StrategyForum"; available at http://us.fujitsu.com/img_asset/FC/FC-corp_factsheet_StratForum.pdf.
11. American Society for Law Enforcement Training, "Richard Davis to Achieve Lifetime Achievement Award" (2002); available at http://www .aslet.org/i4a/pages/index.cfm?pageid=218.


## CHAPTER 10

1. Olaf Helmer-Hirschberg and Nicholas Rescher, "On the Epistemology of the Inexact Sciences," RAND Document P-1513 (Santa Monica, CA: RAND, 1958).
2. Murray Turoff, "Delphi Method"; available at http://pespmc1.vub.ac.be/ asc/Delphi_metho.html.

3. "The Delphi Method: Definition and Background"; available at http://www.iit.edu/~it/delphi.html.

## CHAPTER 11

1. Adolph von Schell, *Battle Leadership* (Ft. Benning Columbus, GA: The Benning Herald, 1933), p. 9.
2. Ibid., pp. 11–12.
3. Sun Tzu, *The Art of War*, translated by Samuel B. Griffith (New York: Oxford University Press, 1963), p. 129.
4. Sun Wu, *The Essentials of War*, translated by Zhong Qin (Beijing, China: New World Press, 1996), p. 41.
5. Hugo von Freytag-Loringhoven, *The Power of Personality in War*, translated by Oliver L. Spaulding, in *Roots of Strategy, Book 3* (Harrisburg, PA: Stackpole Books, 1991), p. 277.
6. Niccolo Machiavelli, *The Art of War*, translated by Ellis Farneworth (New York: Da Capo Press, 1965).
7. Quoted in Michael R. Solomon, *Consumer Behavior, Fifth Edition* (Upper Saddle River, NJ: Prentice Hall, 2002), p. 471.
8. Harry G. Summers, Jr., *On Strategy: A Critical Analysis of the Vietnam War* (Novato, CA: Presidio Press, 1982), p. 1.
9. Howard Johnson Web site; http://www.hojo.com/HowardJohnson/control/brand_history.

## CHAPTER 12

1. Montgomery of Alamein, *The Memoirs of Field Marshall Montgomery* (New York: The World Publishing Company, 1958), p. 94.
2. Adapted from William A. Cohen, *The New Art of the Leader* (Paramus, NJ: Prentice Hall Press, 2000), pp. 224–225.
3. "The Drive to Succeed: The Turnaround of Group Lotus" (London: Corven Partners); available at http://www.corven.co.uk/research/case-lotus.pdf (July 7, 2003), pp. 1–2.
4. Michael M. Kaiser, "American Ballet Theatre: A Classic Turnaround," *Lessons Learned: Case Studies* (National Endowment for the Arts Publications, 2002); available at http.//arts.endow.gov/pub/Lessons/Casestudies/Kaiser.html.
5. Alan Brookstone, "SARS Showed Value of Fast Communication," *Medical Post*, Vol. 39, No. 23 (July 10, 2003), p. 32.
6. Porter B. Williamson, *Patton's Principles* (New York: Simon & Schuster, 1979), p. 31.
7. Keith H. Hammonds, "Business Fights Back: Continental's Turnaround Pilot," *Fast Company* (December 2001), p. 96.

8. Insurance Conference Planner Staff, "Continental Turnaround: A J.D. Power First," *Insurance Meetings Planner* (December 1, 1997); available at http://icplanner.com/ar/insurance_continental_turnaround_jd/.

9. Stan Pace and Paul Rogers, "Making Change Stick," *CEO Forum*; available at http://www.ceoforum.com.au/200206_management.cfm#jump1.

## CHAPTER 13

1. This concept is based on an idea that originated with J.F.C. Fuller as developed in Anthony John Trythall, *"Boney" Fuller* (New Brunswick, NJ: Rutgers University Press, 1977), p. 108.

2. Robert F. Harley, *Marketing Successes*, 2nd ed. (New York: John Wiley & Sons, 1990), pp. 68–78.

## CHAPTER 14

1. Times Wire Services, "Mrs. Simpson Cheated on Edward, Papers Show," *Los Angeles Times* (January 30, 2003), p. A4.

# Index